CW00766120

INTERROGATING POLITICS AND SOCIETY: TWENTIETH-CENTURY INDIAN SUBCONTINENT

INTERROGATING POLITICS AND SOCIETY: TWENTIETH-CENTURY INDIAN SUBCONTINENT

SURANJAN DAS

PRIMUS
BOOKS

PRIMUS BOOKS
An imprint of Ratna Sagar P. Ltd.
Virat Bhavan
Mukherjee Nagar Commercial Complex
Delhi 110 009

Offices at CHENNAI LUCKNOW
AGRA AHMEDABAD BANGALORE COIMBATORE DEHRADUN GUWAHATI HYDERABAD
JAIPUR KANPUR KOCHI KOLKATA MADURAI MUMBAI PATNA RANCHI VARANASI

First published 2014

ISBN: 978–93–80607–77–1

Published by Primus Books

Laser typeset by Digigrafics
Gulmohar Park, New Delhi 110 049

Printed and bound in India by Replika Press Pvt. Ltd.

To
PROFESSOR TAPAN RAYCHAUDHURI
and
HASHIDI
for their constant
encouragement and support

CONTENTS

ACKNOWLEDGEMENTS

For permission to reproduce the material listed below, the author and publisher are grateful to:

Chapter 1: 'Communal Violence in Twentieth-Century Colonial Bengal: An Analytical Framework', *Social Scientist*, vol. 18, nos. 6–7, June-July 1990, pp. 21–37;

Chapter 2: 'Propaganda and the Legitimization of Communal Ideology: Patterns and Trends in Bengal, 1905-1947', in *Caste and Communal Politics in South Asia*, Sekhar Bandyopadhyay and Suranjan Das, eds., Calcutta, 1993, pp. 190–209;

Chapter 3: 'The Communal Challenge in Bengal Politics, 1900-1947', *The Calcutta Historical Journal*, vol. XVI, no. 1, January-June 1994, pp. 39–56;

Chapter 4: 'The 1992 Calcutta Riot in Historical Continuum: A Relapse into "Communal Fury"?', *Modern Asian Studies*, vol. 34, no. 2, 2000, pp. 281–306;

Chapter 5: 'Knowledge for Politics: Partisan Histories and Communal Mobilization in India and Pakistan' (co-authored with Subho Basu), in *The Past in Contemporary Global Politics: Partisan Histories*, Max Paul Friedman and Padraic Kenney, eds., New York, 2005, pp. 111–26;

Chapter 6: 'Calcutta in Turmoil: April 1919', *Bengal Past and Present*, vol. 112, nos. 214–15, pts. 1 and 2, 1993, pp. 1–16;

Chapter 7: 'The Politics of Agitation: Calcutta 1912-1947', in *Calcutta: The Living City*, vol. II, Sukanta Chaudhuri, ed., Calcutta, 1993, pp. 15–26;

Chapter 8: 'Nationalism and Popular Consciousness: Bengal 1942', *Social Scientist*, vol. 23, nos. 4–6, April-June 1995, pp. 58–68;

Chapter 9: 'The Indian National Congress and the Dynamics of Nation-Building: Aspects of Continuity and Change', in *State and Nation in the Context of Social Change*, vol. I, T.V. Sathyamurthy, ed., Delhi, 1994, pp. 274–97;

Chapter 10: 'The "Goondas": Towards a Reconstruction of the Calcutta Underworld through Police Records', *Economic and Political Weekly*, vol. XXIX, no. 44, 29 October 1994, pp. 2877–83;

Chapter 11: 'Behind the Blackened Faces: The Nineteenth-Century Bengali Dacoits', *Economic and Political Weekly*, vol. XLII, no. 35, 1 September 2007, pp. 3573–9.

Kolkata   SURANJAN DAS

INTRODUCTION

... historical explanation discloses not how history must have eventuated but why it eventuated in this way and not in other ways. ...

—E.P. THOMPSON, *The Poverty of Theory*, 1978, p. 50.

ALMOST IN THE SAME vein Eric Hobsbawm explicates the task of a historian: 'The past is ... a permanent dimension of the human consciousness, an inevitable component of the institutions, values and other patterns of human society. The problem for historians is to analyse the nature of this "sense of the past" in society and trace its changes and transformations'.[1]

Premised on this 'reason in history',[2] I have tried to ground the essays, written since the mid-1980s, within this methodological matrix.

Broadly speaking, the essays address three themes of South Asian history: nationalism, communalism and the social underworld. Except for two, they deal with these problems in the context of colonial and post-colonial Bengal. The first three articles are essentially based on my Oxford D.Phil. dissertation, subsequently published as *Communal Riots in Bengal 1905-1947*.[3] They highlight elements of continuity and change in communal violence of twentieth-century colonial Bengal, which have implications for understanding the pattern of communal riots in the colonial and post-colonial subcontinent itself. Eclecticism in Calcutta's cultural tradition received a rude jolt when, in the aftermath of the Babri Masjid demolition of December 1992, the city was rocked by organized communal rioting, the intensity of which recalled the carnage the city had experienced in August 1946. This prompted me to view this outbreak in the context of the earlier riots in the metropolis. The essay 'The 1992 Calcutta Riot in Historical Continuum: A Relapse into Communal Fury?' argues that the outbreak reflected multiple layers of contradictions arising from a not too perfect process of urbanization in post-independence Calcutta. The fifth article discusses, in a comparative context, the relationship between the practice of partisan history and communal mobilization in India and Pakistan.

At the time of India's independence, Bengal was certainly an important site of communal violence, a fact which paved the way for its 1947 Partition. But the province had also enthusiastically responded to nationalist politics. In fact, the political pendulum in colonial Bengal had constantly oscillated between nationalism, communalism and class-based politics. A characteristic feature of Bengal's participation in the freedom struggle was an intermingling of mainstream nationalism with agitational politics. This is explicated in chapters 6, 7 and 8. As in other developing countries, the post-colonial Indian state also faced the challenge of nation-building, necessitating the forging of a domestic political and social consensus for creating a nation, so that the state and nation became coterminous. The volume's ninth essay examines the role played in India's nation-building process by the Indian National Congress, the party which had the unique distinction of leading the freedom struggle and then assuming the mantle of governance after the Transfer of Power. This essay, along with the ones on the 1992 Calcutta riot and the comparative processes of communal mobilization in India and Pakistan, shares the common concern of the practitioners of contemporary history to foreground a contemporary issue in its historical roots, placing contemporary manifestations in historical contexts, and deciphering contemporary events for potential for change.[4]

The twentieth century witnessed a significant expansion of the scope of historical studies—an expansion of interest from the individual to the masses. It was a shift from historical reconstructions based on individual achievements or failures—to an understanding of structural transformations and fundamental transmutations of lives and conditions of ordinary men and women. An offshoot of such transformation was the increasing importance of social history, which now chose to address non-conventional themes, often based on non-archival sources. Consequently, 'social history became the history of society'.[5] Scholars working within the new paradigm of social history have made significant contributions to our understanding of crime and criminality, childhood, emotions, gender and identities. For instance, crime came to be viewed not in terms of paternalistic beliefs about authority but from a social, humanist perspective; the criminal, too, was not to be distinguished from the rest of the society as a person who was required to be controlled through prison and police. Instead, social scientists are today becoming more and more concerned with the context that makes a 'criminal', the forms of criminality and their links with the socio-economic structure, the geography of crime, and the contradictory perceptions of the police and the society in defining crime and a criminal. It is through using such new historical insights into crime and criminality, that I have tried to view the 'goondas', a part of Calcutta's underworld, and the nineteenth century dacoits of rural Bengal, in the last two essays in the book.

Most of the essays in this book fall within the realm of political history, which in current Indian historiography has been unfortunately relegated to the background of the historian's concerns in the wake of the avalanche of economic and social history and in the name of interdisciplinary historical exercises. But it would be simply absurd to deny politics its importance in history. Politics provides the field for public action and response to all issues: economic, social, cultural or environmental. Fortunately in Western historical literature, political history has experienced a revival in the form of 'new' political history, which developed from studies of popular politics, labour history, electoral sociology and women's history. There is an increasing stress on the 'autonomy' for politics and the need for a nuanced understanding of the evolution of 'political languages, representation and subjectivities'.[6] The new political history is seeking to move away from leadership, institutions and elites to the masses, from private papers to public records, from narration on the polity to the interrelationship between society, economy and politics. In so doing, it seeks to re-interpret 'the culture of representative politics' and its relationship to broader sections of society, so much so that some practitioners of this exercise are actually calling it 'social science history'.[7] There is an attempt to reconceptualize the relationship between politics and society by stressing the reciprocal interactions between institutions and social groups'.[8]

Indian historiography on the freedom struggle, agitational politics, and political developments that were crucial in the making of the Indian nation, too, can benefit from the perspectives developed by the scholars engaged in practising the new political history. In this context what becomes crucially important is the utilization of the hitherto untapped source-materials which are outside the archives—in the form of memoirs, organizational papers, local journals and newspapers, or oral evidence. Historians like Mushirul Hasan have already used cartoons to portray contemporary political and social anxieties and predicaments.[9] Such ventures will broaden the horizon of political history of modern India and enable historians to ask questions which have remained unasked and unanswered. For instance, the adoptions of both culture studies framework and post-modernist methodology to the study of history have certainly broadened our understanding of historical processes and drawn the attention of historians on India to themes and subjects hitherto considered 'marginal'. But perhaps we must also be careful when we do this. We need to maintain the rituals of the worship of Clio by restoring the centrality of the political narrative, thus lending due credence to empirical research, and not undermining overarching structures while discussing 'fragments'.[10] In other words, historians may rely on social science insights to analyse the past, but without compromising the methodological rigours of their own discipline so that the pursuit of history need not degenerate into a second-rank social science.

Our first Prime Minister Jawaharlal Nehru, although not a professional historian, correctly perceived: 'The individual human being or race or nation must necessarily have a certain depth and certain roots somewhere. . . . On the other hand, one cannot live in roots alone. Even roots wither unless they come out in the sun and free air. Only then can the roots give you sustenance. Only then can there be a branching out and a flowering. How, then, are you to balance these two essential factors.'[11]

What Nehru perhaps hinted at, was the historian's responsibility in striking this balance. I would be fulfilling in part, what I consider to be my social commitment, if the essays in the present volume contribute to meeting the challenge that Nehru envisaged for students of Indian history. A historian need not merely confine himself or herself to interpreting the past, but is required to use the knowledge gained from such interpretations in helping to change the present to ensure a better world to live in. At the same time, the pleasures and challenges of studying history require to be invoked to achieve such a better world, perhaps through seeing history, as A.L. Rowse saw it long ago, as 'a compound of fact and imagination, of the imagination picturing the facts, lapping round them, like the sea round the rocks upon the coast'.[12]

I have kept the essays in their original forms, except by way of making some minor editorial changes. Although the themes addressed in the essays are being constantly and fruitfully re-examined, the articles hopefully have relevance from colonial or post-colonial perspectives. Professor Hiren Chakrabarti, who initiated me to the joy of studying history at Presidency College, later introducing me to the world of research, as also Professor Mushirul Hasan, a source of inspiration and new ideas, both deserve my heartiest gratitude for helping me to plan the volume and write this introduction. Hari Vasudevan, as always, was forthcoming with editorial assistance. My colleagues in the History Department of University of Calcutta—especially Arun Bandopadhyay and Bhaskar Chakrabarti—were particularly instrumental in persuading me to bring together the essays. Mum, Suparna and Atluri, too, convinced me of the efficacy of this volume. For this and much, much more, I thank them all.

Notes

1. E.J. Hobsbawm, 'The Sense of the Past', in *On History*, E.J. Hobsbawm, ed., London, 1999, p. 13.
2. E.P. Thompson, *Making History*, New York, 1994, p. 363.
3. Suranjan Das, *Communal Riots in Bengal*, New Delhi, 1991.

4. See S. Gopal's General President's Address at the 39th Session of the Indian History Congress, 1978; Also see Ramachandra Guha, 'The Challenge of Contemporary History', *Economic and Political Weekly*, 28 June-11 July 2008, pp. 192–200.

5. E.J. Hobsbawm, 'From social history to the history of society', *Daedalus*, 1971.

6. David M. Craig, 'High Politics And the New Political History', *The Historical Journal*, vol. 53, no. 2, 2010, pp. 453-75; J. Vernon, *Politics and the People: A Study in English Political Culture c. 1815–1867*, Cambridge, 1993; D. Wahrman, 'The New Political History: A Review Essay', *Social History*, vol. 21, 1996, pp. 343-54; L. Black, 'Popular Politics in Modern British History', *Journal of British Studies*, vol. 40, 2001, pp. 431-45; Steven Fielding, 'Review Article: Looking for the New Political History', *Journal of Contemporary History*, vol. 42, no. 3, 2007, pp. 515-24; Kathryn Kish Skaler, 'The New Political History and Women's History: Comments on the Democratic Experiment', *The History Teacher*, vol. 39, no. 4, August 2006.

7. Gareth Stedman Jones and Raphael Samuel are generally credited for initiating this shift in the writing of political history. See Raphael Samuel and Gareth Stedman Jones, 'The Labour Party and Social Democracy', in *Culture, Ideology and Politics*, Raphael Samuel and Gareth Stedman Jones, London, 1982. Also see L. Black, 'What Kind of People are You? Labour, the People and the New Political History', in *Interpreting the Labour Party: Approaches to Labour Politics and History*, J. Callaghan et al., eds., Manchester, 2003; Kate Murphy, 'Feminism and Political History', *Australian Journal of Politics and History*, vol. 56, no. 1, 2010, pp. 21-37; Larrya A. Glassford, 'The Evolution of "New Political" in English-Canadian Historiography: From Cliometrics to Cliodiversity', *American Review of Canadian Studies*, vol. 32, no. 3, 2002, pp. 347–67.

8. Romain Huret and Pauline Peretz, 'Political History Today on Both Sides of the Atlantic', *The Journal of Policy History*, vol. 21, no. 3, 2009, pp. 300-7. This scholarship 'is not understood as a top-down model, but as a system of relations, which receives impulses from different directions according to each subject ...'. See Frank Bosch and Norman Domeier, 'Cultural history and politics: concepts and debates', *European Review of History*, vol. 15, no. 6, 2008, pp. 577-86. Issues relating to foreign policy are also being studied within this framework. Robert McMahen, 'Toward a Pluralist Vision: The Study of American Foreign Relations as International Relations and National History', in *Explaining the History of American Foreign Relations*, Michael J. Hogan and Thomas G. Paterson, eds., Cambridge, 2004. Also see Jussi Hanhimaki, 'Bernath Lecture: Global Visions and Parochial Politics: The Persistent Dilemma of the American Century', *Diplomatic History*, vol. 27, no. 4, September 2003, pp. 423-47; Mary Dudziak, *Cold War, Civil Rights: Race and the Image of American Democracy*, Princeton, 2000.

9. Mushirul Hasan, *The Awadh Punch: Wit And Humour In Colonial India*, New Delhi, 2007; Mushirul Hasan, *Wit And Wisdom: Pickings from the Parsee Punch*, New Delhi, 2012.

10. See Lawrence Stone, 'The Revival of Narrative: Reflections on a New Old History', *Past and Present*, vol. 85, 1979, pp. 3-24. Also see Kalle Pihlainen, 'The end of oppositional history?' *Rethinking History*, vol. 15, no. 4, December 2011, pp. 463-88.

12. See Jawaharlal Nehru: Selected Speeches, vol. 2, 1949–53, pp. 356–62, cited in Mushirul Hasan, ed., *Nehru's India: Selected Speeches*, New Delhi, 2007, p. 234.

13. A.L. Rowse, *The Use of History*, London, 1946.

CHAPTER 1

COMMUNAL VIOLENCE IN TWENTIETH-CENTURY COLONIAL BENGAL: AN ANALYTICAL FRAMEWORK

Understanding Communalism in Indian History

Communalism in the context of Hindu–Muslim antagonism in India is usually viewed in terms of the political experience. It was hoped both by the British and Indian ruling classes that the division of the subcontinent along religious lines would restore communal amity which had been badly shaken during the 'prelude to the partition'. But this was a fond hope. Continuing doses of communal violence in the post-independent period which reached climactic points with the anti-Sikh riots of 1984, the Babri Masjid demolition in 1992, and the organized carnage in Gujarat in 2002 have reinforced doubts in many quarters about the secular foundations of India's political structure. Similarly, East Pakistan (now Bangladesh) had witnessed spates of Hindu–Muslim riots in the post-1947 period which caused periodic influx of Hindu refugees across the borders to India and very few Hindus now inhabit that country. Communalism thus continues to be a live issue in the subcontinent. This has tended to make most of the studies on the topic highly subjective. The present essay seeks to highlight aspects of continuity and change in communal violence in twentieth-century colonial Bengal which have implications for understanding the pattern of contemporary rioting in the subcontinent.

Studies on communalism in India tend to fall into one of several competing stereotypes—ranging from the colonial to Muslim, Hindu and secular versions. Many of these works rely on one of two extreme positions—the 'pre-colonial golden age' of Hindu–Muslim relations, or a fundamental Hindu–Muslim rift as a fact of history. In such projections,

*This essay was published in *Social Scientist*, vol. 18, nos. 6–7, June-July 1990.

communal and religious conflicts are considered at the same level. But despite connections between religion and communalism, religious and communal identities are not identical.[1] The former concerns personal allegiance to a set of practices and dogmas, often in search of a reward from the transcendental reality. Communalism, on the other hand, entails individual commitment to special interests of a religious community for gaining worldly advantages at the expense of other communities. Religious violence is provoked by sectarian and doctrinaire differences; communal animosities are primarily motivated by conflicts over political power and economic resources.[2] What have usually been called 'pre-colonial communal riots'[3] were actually more religious than communal.

The concept of 'community' in the context of a confrontation between an essentially Hindu and an exclusively Muslim group in India, as I have tried to argue elsewhere,[4] thus needs to be re-examined. The notion of a community cannot be taken as an externally given fact, nor can it be conceived either as an organic unity or as a religious and political totality to which class interest and disunity are alien.[5] A community is formed when a group of people share something in common which distinguishes them from members of other groups and the shared element becomes the primary referent of identity. The nature of a community thus embodies a sense of discrimination—a feeling of what Barth has described as being encircled by a boundary within which members are supposed to act.[6] The consciousness of a community is encapsulated in the perception of its boundaries through the construction of symbols.[7]

Viewed in this perspective a distinction needs to be made in Indian history between, on the one hand, community consciousness, wherein religion was seen as a means of ordering the world, and communalism, a more recent concept. Community consciousness usually did not preclude the development of a strong syncretic tradition either at the popular level or in the world of high culture.[8] The world view of the people was ordered by local, largely inherited and socially enforced customs, some of which derived from, or were reinforced by awareness of the great traditions.[9] Communalism *per se,* though, was a product of the nineteenth and twentieth centuries which saw the gradual manifestation of a sense of community in overtly separatist forms involving a degree of intolerance for those outside the communal boundary.[10] While in pre-modern times the confessional faith was never the primary referent of identity, the nineteenth-century British conceptualization of Indian society as consisting of different religious communities, and attempts to use such categorization as a theoretical base for the pursuit of a policy to secure allies and 'shore up imperial power, helped to convert it into a social reality'.[11]

I also disagree with the view that there existed 'a well-defined set of ideas and ritualized behaviours underlying the religious conflict between Hindus and Muslims'.[12] On the other hand, the idiom, insignia and ritual of communal confrontation changed in accordance with historical specificities. For example, the question of 'music before mosques',[13] which had hardly bothered inhabitants in most areas for hundreds of years, was raised as a central point of communal dissension in large parts of Bengal by the 1930s. One thus needs to explain why certain targets and symbols were chosen during a riot and why various groups with conflicting interests so readily rallied round particular symbols and rituals such as 'idolatry', the 'cow' and 'playing music before mosques'. Sometimes traditions were invented to reinforce communal solidarity.[14] We have to identify popular perceptions of violence and their role in the moral order of the people, the development of new symbols and identities around which these perceptions were organized, and the construction of new cultural forms through which these gained public expression.[15]

It is perhaps imperative to comment on the relationship or difference between ethnicity and communalism. The two terms have been used in various contexts which are not always internally compatible. Ethnicity was originally used as a label for consciously shared racial characteristics. It is, however, nowadays used in contexts broader than just the idea of race to connote the conjunction of similar consciousness, flowing from language, permutations and combinations of common regional and cultural history, multi-class affinities on a broad front, and though, not necessarily so, religious. Racialism is bad ethnicity; ethnicity is supposed to be neutral, though one often shades into the other, as Sikh ethnicity in the Punjab or Gorkha ethnicity in Darjeeling. On the other hand, although communalism in its original meaning or etymological sense referred to excesses of sentiment of any feeling—localist; provincialist, tribalist or casteist—the term in the context of the colonial period of Indian history has assumed specific religious connotations in our ideological jargon. Many political scientists are also now arguing that in the background of the strong centralist tendency of the contemporary taken new overtones.[16] Indian states and its resulting alienation from individuals with diverse identities, the concept of communalism has today. But that is a different problematic issue from the concern of the present chapter which is restricted to the colonial period.

Changing Pattern of Communal Violence in Twentieth-Century Colonial Bengal

The evidence considered in my research suggests a definite shift in the nature of communal violence in Bengal between 1905 and 1947. While riots in the first three decades of the twentieth century demonstrated a complex coexistence of class and communal elements,[17] the fusion of communal with nationalist and class modes of consciousness in the 1940s culminated in relatively more organized and overtly communal riots. I propose to substantiate this hypothesis with an overview of some major Hindu-Muslim communal outbreaks in Bengal between 1905 and 1947.

Till the beginning of the 1940s whatever might have been the immediate trigger for an outbreak—music before mosques or a firing from a Marwari (a person from Marwar in Jodhpur, Rajasthan state) merchant house or an accidental killing of a Muslim boy—the collective violence, once it spread, came to be directed against symbols of class and colonial exploitation. In this connection the Mymensingh riot of 1906–7 experienced the first major Hindu-Muslim communal rioting. Troubles began on 21 April 1907 when Hindu volunteers advocating the cause of swadeshi (indigenous products) attacked Muslim shops selling *belati* (foreign) goods. For about the next three weeks the northern part of the Jamalpur subdivision—especially Dewanganj, Sherpur and Phulpur *thanas* (police stations)—was rocked by violence. The outbreak now assumed the form of the uprising of a Muslim peasantry against Hindu landlordism. Hindu zamindars (landlords) were deprived of their Muslim servants and prostitutes; Hindu *cutcheries* (offices of zamindars) and establishments of Hindu mahajans (moneylenders) were pillaged; temples raised with the hated *Iswar Britti* (the tax levied for the upkeep of temples and images) were desecrated. The Muslim rioters' high degree of conscious discrimination was demonstrated when they left untouched petty open-air traders and concentrated upon Hindu-owned flourishing shops. Contemporary Hindu newspapers reveal the extent to which the outbreak had 'completely shaken' the security of prosperity. The *Charumihir*[18] commented that wealthy Hindus could no longer live in villages 'with safety to life and property'.

Hindus from the lower social strata were not, however, totally unaffected by the riot. Attacks were recorded on huts of *dhobis* (washermen), *tantis* (weavers), *goalas* (milkmen), fishermen, carpenters, potters, cobblers and other low-caste Hindus. The pattern of violence against poorer Hindus was, nevertheless, different from that practised upon their richer co-religionists. The main purpose of assaults on the former appears to have been a simple desire to express a hatred for the community as a whole. There was neither arson nor idol breaking, whereas houses of Hindu notables were subjected to considerable damage.[19]

Both official and non-official sources cite instances of attacks on Hindu women. Rioters broke into houses and took away young widows, and women hid themselves in jungles for days to escape assaults.[20] The honour of women constituted one of the most sacrosanct features of Hindu social ideology, and violation thereof implied the total destruction of a Hindu's *izzat* (honour). Interestingly, most of the women who suffered during the riot belonged to respectable or established families. Offences against them can, therefore, be also seen as a part of the general Muslim assault against privileged Hindus.

The Mymensingh experience introduces us to complexities of communal rioting in twentieth-century Bengal which combined a generalized protest with communal hatred. The relative strength of these elements varied from one riot to another. But coexistence of 'community' and 'class' remained in all riots. This could be explicated with reference to major communal outbreaks of this period: Calcutta in 1918 and 1926, Dacca in 1926 and 1930, Pabna in 1926 and Kishoreganj in 1930.

The Calcutta riot of September 1918 began following an alleged 'unprovoked firing' from a Marwari house on an excited Muslim crowd protesting against the government's refusal to grant permission for a public meeting to register some political demands; in 1926 the immediate occasion of rioting was the playing of music by an Arya Samaj procession before a mosque and the violence continued in three phases from April to July. But both these outbreaks shared some common features. Main targets of the crowd were Europeans, the police, the transport system and the property of Marwari and Bhatia merchants.[21] Often Marwaris were killed in broad daylight. In 1926 a Muslim leader thus assured Bengali Hindus: 'We have no quarrel with you. We will not break temples which belong to you. We want to drive Marwaris to Bikaner and Jodhpur.'[22]

Shops were looted on a large scale, although there was a concentration on those dealing either with items of immediate consumption or goods whose price had registered a recent rise. Religious affinities with the crowd were no guarantee of protection from lootings. Muslims looted Peshwari (those hailing from Peshwar, then north-west India) fruit stalls; the Muslim crowd assailed those Muslim employees who sought to protect the establishments under siege. One can, however, doubt to what extent these were class conscious acts. The prospect of plunder at the disruption of normalcy could have been a sufficient motivation for marginalized sections of society to loot whatever was available at hand. The other important facet of riots was unrest among the upcountry Muslim millhands in the industrial suburb of Garden Reach, Howrah and Metiabruz, especially in 1918. Troubles in the mill areas manifested significant anti-European overtones. For instance, on the morning of 10 September the mill workers struck work, assaulted European foremen and then marched towards central Calcutta 'shouting and dancing to the beating of drums, carrying flags and brandishing *lathies* (sticks) and knives' until they clashed with the military.

Nevertheless, in two significant respects the 1926 riot differed from its predecessor. First, temples and mosques were now besieged on a scale hitherto unheard of in Calcutta. The other variation lay in an increased element of organization. Hindu rioters used the houses of their prominent co-religionists as bases of operation; leaflets were distributed urging Hindus not to use certain taxis which had Muslim drivers. The Muslim crowd did not display the same level of organization, although there were attempts at mobilization of Muslim subordinate social groups at local levels. Muslim inhabitants in Central Calcutta *bustees* (slums) were encouraged to rise up against Hindus by the beating of drums; sometimes Muslim rioters demonstrated a high degree of organization in perpetrating violence, as was seen during the attack on a Hindu boarding house in central Calcutta on 22 April 1926.

The September 1926 violence in Dacca was triggered off by the Muslim refusal to allow playing of music before mosques which lay on the traditional route of the age-old Hindu Janmastami (Hindu religious festival connected with the worship of Lord Krishna) procession.[23] Nearly four years later another outbreak resulted from an 'accidental injury' to a Muslim boy by some Hindu children playing with tops on Dacca town's main thoroughfare.[24] The characteristic feature on both occasions was Muslim attacks on their Hindu class-enemies and the police. The Hindu Basak and Saha merchants had their establishments pillaged in 1926; in 1930 Keyattuli with its strong concentration of Hindu merchants and *bhadralok* (a status group in Bengal who came from the upper castes, were economically dependent on landed rents and professional and clerical employment) was looted in quick succession; Muslim factory workers assailed their Hindu managers. Unlike in 1926, the riot in 1930 spread to neighbouring villages when imposing houses of zamindars and mahajans had 'their walls torn down, floors dug up and doors and windows hacked to bits'.[25] When a moneylender's house was raided the first aim of the rioters was not to commit physical violence on the owner but to search for his account books and burn them. This surely shows an emphasis on class than communal interests. Significantly enough, the violence in Dacca, especially in 1930, was not associated with a systematic destruction of temples. Only one or two temples were desecrated and that too, was a part of the general assault on Hindu wealth since these shrines were patronised by local zamindars and moneylenders.

The Dacca rioting crowd of 1930 also demonstrated 'an alternative concept of fair deal' which shows that they were aroused more by a sense of undoing economic injustice than by an unalloyed communal antipathy. For instance, the looters did not always appropriate the booty but sold it at 'ridiculously low prices'. In the wake of the riots the Muslims even imposed strict limits on the quality of goods that could be sold by shopkeepers to rich Hindus of the locality. There were also instances of Muslims being joined by low-caste Hindus such as *chamars* in looting upper caste Hindu shops.

The Pabna outbreak of 1926 was much wider in scope. It began in Pabna town on 1 July following the discovery of mutilated images. But once the violence spread to neighbouring villages it assumed an exclusively rural character. The grievances of a Muslim peasant community united by religion, found expression through this violence. Any Hindu with money and influence in villages—zamindars (holders of property in land who paid revenue to the government under the Permanent Settlement of 1793), *jotedars* (holders of cultivable land, often a substantial landholder), merchants, pleaders and owners of *hats* (open-air village markers, usually held once a week)—became targets of crowd fury. Well-to-do Hindu merchants were taken to Muslim houses and made to wear Muslim dresses (*tahaba* and *taj*), read *kalma* (Muslim attestation of faith in the unity of God and the prophethood of Muhammad) and utter *toba* (renouncing non-Islamic practices). Not surprisingly, such Hindus sent telegrams to the Viceroy and Governor of Bengal for immediate intervention and employed Gorkha and Sikh bodyguards for personal protection. Pabna did witness desecration of Hindu idols. But those were mostly worshipped in landlords' houses which provided such acts with a socio-economic dimension. Referring to these instances Partha Chatterjee thus remarks:

...in the world of religious symbols whose notions of authority and political ethics are coded and legitimised in religious terms, idol-breaking with all its overtones of mischievous criminality undoubtedly constituted a conscious act of defiance against feudal authority.[26]

While the validity of this statement cannot be perhaps denied, it is pertinent to note that there is no recorded instance of Hindu peasants breaking Hindu idols as a part of their anti-feudal acts. Rather, the *mehters* (sweepers) and *domes* (carriers of dead bodies)—usually considered untouchables in Hindu society—were instrumental in warding off Muslim attacks on temples to which they were normally denied entry.[27]

The Kishoreganj (Mymensingh district) riot of 1930 represented the last major communal violence in twentieth-century colonial Bengal which had strong class connotations. Troubles started on 11 July at Pakundia thana when Muslim peasants attacked the establishments of Surendra Nath, one of the richest Hindus of the locality. Hostilities then spread to hundred adjacent villages, the violence in its 'worst form' continuing till the 15th. About 1,033 Hindu houses and shops were looted, the total value of Hindu property destroyed was no less than Rs. 4,01,666, excluding the value of stolen documents. The primary concern of the 1930 rioters was to attack the physical manifestations of the power of Hindu landlords and moneylenders. The crowd behaviour represented in many respects, what Hobsbawm has called 'social banditry'.[28] The usual *modus operandi* of the crowd—numbering from 100 to 1000—was to gather at the house of a moneylender and demand from him all credit documents and tear them to pieces. If a mahajan (moneylender) pleaded non-possession of documents he would be given a specific time to produce them; attempts of mahajans to ward off attacks on their establishments by offering sums of money usually failed. Only when mahajans and landlords offered resistance were their houses looted and in some cases burnt. From one house in Kumarpur alone debt-bonds of Rs. 3,00,000, furniture worth Rs. 30,000 to Rs. 40,000 and 1,500 maunds of rice were taken away. There were instances of Muslim crowd forcing Hindu notables to eat beef with them. Such actions were in the nature of violent protest against Hindu ritual taboos on social intercourse with non-Hindus and lower-castes.

Further evidence of the economic content of the 1930 outbreak was provided by the fact that the Muslim crowd did not spare the richer sections of its own community. At least one Muslim talukdar (holder of an estate) and eight moneylenders had their houses looted and money-bonds taken away. Some police stations received continuous requests from Muslim notables for protection against their co-religionists.

By the 1940s, however, the communal outbursts relatively lost their initial class basis, became more organized, and were directly connected with developments in institutional politics and consequently exclusively related to communal politics rather than class interests. This trend is apparent in the Dacca riot of 1941.[29] Crowd violence no longer focused primarily on the richer and more influential sections of the two communities but was instead directed at any manifestation of the rival community, such as religious centres, clubs and schools. In 1930 Kishoreganj was the site of the last major outbreak to display a strong class motivation on the part of the Muslim crowd. Twelve years later in October 1942, when an immersion ceremony provoked a communal outbreak in the same region, the Muslim crowd no longer chose Hindu zamindars and mahajans as prime targets of their attacks but proclaimed their determination to sacrifice lives for the cause of 'Islam' and 'Pakistan'.[30] This clearly illustrates the changing nature of communal violence.

Certain features in the riots of the 1940s indicated considerable planning before and during each outbreak: attacking Hindu shops and houses in a number of villages in a similar manner at a particular time (Dacca, 1941), marking Muslim shops to prevent their looting by the Muslim crowd (Calcutta, 1946), using Red Cross flags in vehicles to avoid interception by police and members of the rival community (Calcutta, 1946) and carrying out uniform methods of arson and conversion (Noakhali, 1946).[31] The crowds no longer overwhelmingly consisted of subordinate social groups but became a mixture of the upper and lower social strata. For the first time, Bengali Hindus and Muslims joined their co-religionists of upcountry origin on a large scale in the Great Calcutta Killing of 1946. Unlike the earlier pattern of lootings and other forms of violence by a large crowd, the riots of the 1940s witnessed the killing of individuals by small groups. The emphasis now was not on economic gain but on revenge and humiliation of members of the rival community. This rite of violence displayed communal animosity at its peak, thereby completing the process of dehumanization.[32] During the 1946 Calcutta carnage, for example, a man was tied to a tramway electric junction box, and left to bleed to death through a hole in his forehead.[33] Such brutalities and sadism with their emphasis on torture and revenge are reminiscent of the sixteenth century French religious riots when, for example, a priest in the Fouquebrune parish was yoked with oxen to a plough and driven along until he died from Protestant blows.[34]

Communal Riots and Politics in Colonial Bengal

An important feature of the communal violence surveyed above was the process of legitimization. As in European popular outbreaks, the acts of Bengal rioters derived legitimacy from a whole range of sources: economic, political, religious and a sense of group identity. At one level the Muslim subordinate social groups were motivated by—howsoever temporary—an aim to turn upside down the social configuration of colonial Bengal which contained an inherent communal contradiction: Hindus monopolizing landholdings and moneylending in villages and education and professional jobs in towns. This becomes explicit from the nature of Muslim collective violence.

In this realm there were significant instances of self-mobilization. In 1918 the Calcutta Muslim crowd started committing acts of violence when their community leaders were repenting 'for having raised a Frankenstein'.[35] Similarly, the Muslim outburst in 1926 Pabna revealed a high degree of spontaneity. The rioters looted Hindu establishments, moved on to neighbouring villages for food and shelter from their co-religionists, gained new support by narrating stories of Hindu oppressions and then carried out further attacks in other villages with added strength. All these suggest features of 'a jacquerie—an entire rural community combined for violent action'.

A striking feature of such outbreaks with considerable spontaneous protest element was the widespread circulation of popular rumours that higher authorities had sanctioned the violence. This was particularly apparent with the Muslim crowd. The Muslim peasantry, especially prior to the 1940s, believed that the British officials approved of their uprising against Hindu zamindars and moneylenders, many of whom had antagonized the Raj with their nationalist connections. On some occasions the Muslim crowd was encouraged to think that the British administration was in the process of being substituted by a Muslim rule. Involvement of the mullahs (Muslim preachers), especially in the first phase of communal violence, provided the rioters with religious approbation for their conduct. This process of self-legitimization has also its parallel in the Catholic-Protestant riots in sixteenth-century France. The French crowd on both sides believed they were defending their faith and the 'true church'; the presence of clerics and political members among each crowd fuelled the belief that participation in the violence was legitimate.[36]

We need not, however overstress the element of self-mobilization. For, the political world of twentieth-century Bengal witnessed two important developments. On the one hand, the instruments of colonial rule had penetrated deep down into indigenous society through various constitutional Acts and the widening of local self-governments.[37] On the other hand, the mainstream nationalism had succeeded to a large extent in incorporating various strands of protest politics. The consequence was that organized or institutional politics made significant inroads into the unorganized political realm so much so that even scholars such as Partha Chatterjee have admitted that it would be difficult to speak of an unalloyed unorganized political realm in Bengal from the 1920s.

An inevitable outcome was that the rioting crowd in twentieth-century Bengal came to increasingly seek legitimacy from developments in institutional politics. The constitutional reform of 1909 introduced and the Act of 1919 expanded separate electorates which encouraged politicians to work along communal lines. As David Page has shown, Muslim politicians in particular now developed a vested interest in the operation of separate electorates.[38] These tendencies were strengthened by another contemporaneous development, the expansion of a corresponding rise in employment opportunities which produced a scramble for scarce jobs along communal lines. All these strengthened communal solidarities in the realm of organized politics. This was a source of great satisfaction for the Raj, a fact aptly revealed when the Chief Secretary to Government of India remarked: 'The prevalence of communal rancour inevitably tends to mitigate the area and intensity of racial hatred.'[39]

At the same time the Khilafat movement marked an important landmark in the evolution of a separate Muslim identity. It forged an alliance between Hindus and Muslims on a religious issue which, once broken, generated a communal backlash. The Khilafat agitation led to the emergence of new Muslim leaders possessing strong connections with peasantry. They had made the Muslim masses more conscious of their interests and the potency of their actions and organization. In the specific context of Bengal the revocation of Chittaranjan Das' Bengal Pact was the last straw for the uneasy peace between the two communities attained through unity from the top.[40]

In such circumstances Bengal's Muslim leaders 'cast around for a viable alternative to the Swaraj Party'. The period witnessed a gradual emergence of a more nebulous focus of Muslim attention, evident in the rise of a number of regional and cultural organizations. Activities of itinerant maulvis (Muslim learned men/gentlemen) increased significantly in the Bengal villages during the 1920s, as they openly encouraged their co-religionists to take revenge for Hindu misdeeds. Almost simultaneously the hitherto non-functional local organizations such as the *Anjuman Islamia* in Pabna became active and assisted mobilization along communal lines.[41] Issues such as music before mosques which hardly worried Muslims in the past, now emerged as an important nucleus around which Muslim communal solidarities developed.[42] Similarly such syncretic traditions as the participation of Muslim musicians and labourers in Janmastami processions in Dacca were now questioned.

The strengthening of Muslim identity was matched by a rapid rise of Hindu revivalism. In districts such as Pabna and Dacca local Hari Sabhas and Arya Dharma Pracharani Sabhas organized *yajnas* (public worship) and kirtans (devotional music) to generate solidarity amongst the Hindus; the Marwaris in Calcutta formed defence parties to forestall attacks on Hindu property; newspapers such as the *Amrita Bazar Patrika* (30 June 1926) wrote of establishing Hindu organizations in every part of Bengal. Organizations as the Hindu Sabha in Pabna, which since its establishment in 1921/22 had not been particularly anti-Muslim, now became active in educating its followers on important communal rights such as playing music in religious processions without any obstructions.[43] Madan Mohan Malaviya and other Hindu political personalities now openly raised the cry of Hind-Hindi-Hindu; even Motilal Nehru appealed to communal feelings in the pre-election days of 1926 in desperate attempts to counter the propaganda branding him a pro-Muslim and beef-eater.

Results of the November 1926 elections to the Bengal Legislative Council and the Calcutta Corporation elections of April 1927 reflected the growing communalization in institutional politics. Hindu and Muslim blocs developed within both these bodies and Muslim politicians in Bengal of the 1920s were definitely seizing the initiative in legislative politics. Yet the growing communal alignment of political forces was still largely reflected in economic terms, as evidenced from the legislative debates centring round the Bengal Tenancy Amendment Act of 1928. Even the immediate issues inciting communal violence were coloured by short-term economic developments. The rising price curve of food and a malaria-cholera epidemic added further to the distress of the Muslim peasantry of Mymensingh in 1907 and subordinate Muslim social groups in 1918 Calcutta; in 1926 the social disaffection of the Muslim labouring class was accentuated by a general economic boycott by Marwari shopkeepers and traders; in the popular perception of the Dacca Muslims the local Hindu leaders, by 1930, had lost their credibility as protectors of peasant interests which certainly contributed to the fuelling of communal tensions; finally, the 1930 communal tensions in Mymensingh were accelerated by economic difficulties of the predominant Muslim peasantry, resulting from a slump in the jute trade.

When, by the 1940s, the riots in Bengal assumed an overtly communal and political character, the crowd—Hindu as well as Muslim—came to be primarily motivated by a kind of political legitimization. The enforcement of the 1935 Act, which provided provincial autonomy based on separate Hindu and Muslim electorates, was a turning point in the development of communal politics in Bengal. Fazlul Huq's Krishak Praja Party–Muslim League coalition ministry in 1937 gave the Muslim political elite of the province their first taste of political power. The League's separatist politics had already attracted considerable support from Muslim business and intellectual circles. When Huq subsequently joined the League, the party was greatly assisted in acquiring the agrarian base which it had lacked for so long.

In this context, the launching of the Pakistan movement presented the Muslim mass with an ideology which promised them a 'bright future'. Until the 1930s, the Muslim leadership coded its message in religious and economic terms. The mullahs, for example, urged their audience to purify Islamic practices, convert as many Hindus as possible and discontinue economic transactions with Hindus. Past glories were resurrected to enthuse co-religionists; solemn warnings and fierce threats were directed against the opposing community. But in the 1940s, as Jinnah emerged as the 'sole spokesman'[44] for Indian Muslims, the Muslim leadership no longer relied only on religious and economic categories but sought to rally public opinion around a distinct notion—the concept of a separate Muslim state. In propagating the idea of consolidating Muslim strength under an all-powerful Muslim state free from Hindu interference, the League in Bengal utilized its control over the government machinery. Thus in the months preceding the 1941 Dacca outbreak, the League ministers extensively toured Dacca town and its suburbs, organizing conferences to propagate the idea of Pakistan. Similarly, shortly before the riot of 1946, the Muslim press and leadership urged their co-religionists to fight for their political rights even at the cost of their lives. Through such propaganda, the Muslim masses were led to associate the concept of Pakistan with the establishment of an Islamic rule bereft of Hindu economic domination, where Hindus would be required to become Muslims if they wished to stay.

The Pakistan ideology was diametrically opposed to the idea of *Akhand Hindustan* (United India), increasingly propagated by Hindu political forces and the Congress. The Hindu Mahasabha formally gave a call in December 1939 for the overthrow of the Bengal Muslim League ministry; India was proclaimed a Hindu *rashtra* (nation) where Muslims could live only by adopting a Hindu way of life. Hindu leaders visited different districts to raise volunteers and to initiate training in martial arts for Hindu youth. It is significant that the 1941 riot at Dacca broke out shortly after a visit by the Mahasabha leader, Shyama Prasad Mukherjee. The Calcutta outbreak of 1946 was also preceded by a propaganda campaign by such Hindu revivalist organizations as the Arya Samaj, Hindu Mahasabha and Hindu Shakti Sabha. The common theme of this Hindu propaganda was depiction of the 'Muslim threat' not merely in religious but also in political terms. Inside the Bengal Congress, too, the influence of the Mahasabha had increased substantially during this period and its criticism of the League broadened from complaints against the League's narrowly sectarian base of support to its denouncement as a threat to the political and civil liberties of non-Muslim communities.

The political impact of this new propaganda campaign was reflected in the slogans voiced by the riotous crowd. In 1926 the Muslim rioters had raised religious and communal cries such as *Alla Ho Akbar* or *Hindu sala log ko maro* (kill the Hindus) but in 1941 and 1946 they were raising political slogans like *Pakistan ki jai* (victory to Pakistan), *Huq sahib ki jai* (victory to Huq, the Chief Minister). Similarly, the Hindu crowd now called for *Pakistan Murdabad* (death to Pakistan), *Akhand Hindustan ki Jai* (victory for undivided India).

This period of propaganda warfare was matched by a transformation in the character of the Hindu–Muslim leadership. Initiatives for the mobilization and direction of violence no longer came chiefly from local religious and other influential figures, but from such political personalities as members of the District Boards and leaders of the Muslim League, Hindu Mahasabha and Congress.

Thanks to the propaganda drive, what occurred in the late 1940s in Bengal was, to borrow a term from Ellul, a 'psychological crystallization' of communal identity among Hindus and Muslims.[45] Polarized stereotypes were evoked and fears and apprehensions were channelled against specific individuals, objects and symbols. Perhaps Bengal witnessed in the 1940s what Scribner has called, in the context of the German Reformation movement, the process of 'negative assimilation'[46] wherein the common person became convinced of the Tightness of the 'evangelical cause' and therefore felt compelled to support the movement. In similar fashion, the Bengal riots of the 1940s seemed to display a conjunction or symbiosis between elite and popular communalism. Evidently, this benefited the colonial state by allowing exploitation of the communal division to counteract the developing national movement.[47]

It has been suggested that the Partition of India was not merely the result of 'tortuous negotiations' between the British, Congress and the League but also a reaction to 'pressures from below'.[48] Fears of 'popular excesses' resulting from successive militant outbreaks in 1945–6 made the Raj, the Congress and the League equally apprehensive of a 'left-wing alternative' and this drove them to cling to the path of negotiations and compromise. The subsequent chain of communal disturbances in Bengal, Bihar and UP in 1946–7, precipitated an 'administrative breakdown' which made Viceory Wavell suggest an early termination of the Raj.[49] At the same time the riots in Bengal during the 1940s reconciled a large section of subordinate social groups amongst both Hindus and Muslims to the idea of the Partition. This was reflected in the changed attitude of nationalist Muslims and the Congress leadership (except Gandhi) whose secular stance gave way to an acceptance of Pakistan as 'the only real alternative'. Muslim and Hindu community consciousness had assumed a distinct political identity, nourished by propaganda and hardened by the riots of the 1940s.

Riots are transformatory as well as historical events. They shape and alter perceptions and aspirations. People are changed: their attitudes to each other and their ways of thinking about themselves are transformed. The violent and intense nature of a riot is not easily forgotten by individuals involved or threatened, and tends to overshadow their other personal and historical experiences,[50] thus affecting class forces.[51] The transfer of power to a truncated India in 1947 resulted in what has been called a 'passive revolution'[52]—not passive in the sense that popular forces were inactive but because the privileged groups in town and country were able to successfully detach the attainment of political independence and unity from radical social change. To describe these subsequent events as the outcome of developments within a wholly autonomous realm of ideology and politics would perhaps be a mistake. However, during those crucial days in 1946–7 communalism in Bengal had established its temporary hegemony over the realms of ideology and polity and one possible contribution towards an assessment of this phenomenon can be made by examining the changing form of communal outbursts and some of its consequences which have hitherto been unexplored.

The organized and political shape that communalism assumed in the 1940s still survives in independent India. In the aftermath of the Partition the average Hindu in India viewed a Muslim with suspicion, as if he/she was responsible for the Partition of the motherland—little appreciating the risk of political uncertainty that the Muslim had undertaken by staying back in his native soil. On the other hand, the average Muslim, faced with an abnormally tense atmosphere, fell back—perhaps unconsciously—on the idea of Pakistan as 'the safe haven'. Even in 1971–2 in the midst of a national euphoria over the liberation of Bangladesh, a large section amongst the Indian Muslims remained for a considerable period of time in a state of confusion at the bifurcation of Pakistan itself. A fragmentation of the 'national ethos' which followed the truncated settlement of August 1947 continues to plague India's polity.

We in West Bengal have been fortunately relatively free of communal violence. Why this has been so requires a separate explanation. Yet, it would be wrong to deny the existence of communal tensions in Bengal. Potential as communal violence is not totally absent, is amply testified by what happened in Kolkata after the demolition of Babri Masjid in December 1992. Religious identities remain strong; people voting the Left in elections remain astute Hindus and Muslims; continuous infiltration across the borders is providing fertile ground to the Vishva Hindu Parishad; despite strong leftist and democratic traditions the dangers of communal solidarities haunt secular forces. In such a situation social scientists in general, and historians in particular, need to be active in making the people aware of the distortions of history which is one of the most handy weapons for the communalists.

Yet, it will be wrong to assume that communalism in Bengal has been a static phenomenon. The expression of Hindu revivalism and Pan-Islamism alternated between expressions of lower-class discontent, communal hostility and anti-imperialism. Hindus and Muslims, who fought on the streets of Calcutta in September 1918, joined hands during the Rowlatt Satyagraha of April 1919; the three bouts of rioting in Calcutta in 1926 were followed by demonstrations of communal solidarity during the anti-Simon Commission upsurge; communal violence in 1930 could not deter the demonstration of Hindu-Muslim unity during the Civil Disobedience movement; the Great Calcutta Killing of August 1946 was followed by the historic Tebhaga Movement which saw peasants joining the struggle across religious lines; despite continuing communal skirmishes throughout the early months of 1947 the people of the two communities celebrated the independence day in Calcutta on 15 August 1947 in an unprecedented show of communal solidarity. Communalism in Bengal thus requires to be seen as a developing process which culminated in an individual's perception of himself or herself as primarily Hindu or Muslim, often either prior to or during a riot, whilst at other junctures the loyalties of class or locality may intervene to obscure this overt communal self-perception. It is doubtful if the Bengali peasant or his/her urban counterpart was ever solely or even largely motivated by hostility towards Hindu or Muslim brethren except at brief moments of violence. Even at the height of a riot, instances of solidarity and compassion across communities were manifold. Momentous experiences as they were, the riots were closely related to alternative or opposing forms of antagonism of a class or regional nature. People in the subcontinent—and Bengal is no exception—have multiple identities and historians need to unfold why and how at particular conjunctures one form of identity gains precedence over others. Only then the historical contexts of communal riots in Bengal can be properly explicated.

Notes

1. S. Das, *Communal Riots in Bengal 1905–1947*, Delhi, 1991. See the Introduction.
2. A.A. Engineer, *On Developing Theory of Communal Riots*, Bombay, 1964.
3. C. Bayly, 'The pre-history of Communalism? Religious Conflict in India 1700–1860', *Modern Asian Studies* (hereafter *MAS*), vol. 19, no. 2, 1985.
4. S. Das, *Communal Riots*, op. cit.
5. D. Sabean, *Power in the Blood: Popular Culture and Village Discourse in Early Modern Germany*, Cambridge, 1984.
6. F. Barth, ed., *Ethnic Groups and Boundaries: The Social Organisation of Cultural Difference*, London, 1969, pp. 9–38.
7. A.P. Cohen thus entitles his book *The Symbolic Construction of Community*, London, 1985.
8. A. Roy, *The Islamic Syncretistic Tradition in Bengal*, Princeton, 1983; A.A. Engineer, 'Islamic Fundamentalism and Communalism in India', in *Islam in Asia: Pakistan, India, Bangladesh, Sri Lanka, Indonesia, Philippines, Malayasia*, A.A. Engineer, ed., Lahore, 1986; E.C. Dinock Jr. has used literary evidence from the Muslim Vaishnava poets of Bengal to show that Hindus and Muslims shared pastoral and other festivals and that the similarities of devotional Sufi doctrines to those of Hindu *bhakti* made it but a short step from one religion to another, see his 'Muslim Vaishnava poets of Bengal' in *Languages and Areas: Studies Presented to George V. Bobrinskoy*, Chicago, 1967.
9. Recalling his experiences in India, the Earl of Lytton remarked that 'the rank and file of these two communities are not nearly so instransigent as their leaders'. The Earl of Lytton, *Pundits and Elephants*, London, 1942, p. 172.
10. For a general discussion on how 'Communal identities existed in the pre-colonial period, but communalism and communal politics took shape and acquired divisive proportions in the colonial period', see Z.K. Hasan, 'Communalism and Communal Violence in India', *Social Scientist*, February. 1982.
11. Tapan Raychaudhuri, 'A Poison Tree and its Fruits', *The Statesman Miscellany*, 15 August 1987. He demonstrates that ethnic rather than religious identities were important during the pre-colonial times. This view goes against the contention of anthropologists such as Gaborieau who contend 'the deepest sentiments of opposition, on which both the Hindu and Muslim communities found their identity, are traceble throughout the nine centuries of Indo-Muslim

history'; see M. Gaborieau, 'From Al-Beruni to Jinnah: Idiom, ritual and ideology of the Hindu-Muslim confrontation in South Asia', *Anthropology Today,* vol. 1, no. 3, 1985.

12. M. Gaborieau, 'From Al-Beruni to Jinnah', op. cit.

13. The question related to a Hindu claim to the right of playing music uninterruptedly during religious processions on thoroughfares, while Muslims refused to allow the passage of such processions in front of mosques on the grounds that it disturbed their prayers. In Europe also religious processions provoked Catholic-Protestant riots. See Davis, *Society and Culture in Early Modern France,* Duckworth, 1975.

14. For a comparative discussion of the invention of tradition in history, see E.J. Hobsbawm and T. Ranger, eds., *The Invention of Tradition,* Cambridge, 1973.

15. Gyanendra Pandey thus emphasizes the need to go beyond the traditional approach of merely viewing communalism as a 'negative' phenomenon, opposed to the superior force of nationalism, as something 'worth noticing in the making (or unmaking) of some other history—whether that of nationalism, Indian or Pakistani, of working-class struggle and the advance towards socialism or the development of a representative/democratic form of government and polities'. See his 'Liberalism and the Study of Indian History: A Review of Writings on Communalism', *Economic and Political Weekly,* 15 October 1983; *Rallying Round The Cow: Sectarian Strife in the Bhojpuri Region c. 1885–1917,* Calcutta, 1981, *The Construction of Communalism in Colonial North India,* Delhi, 2006. See C. Ginzberg (tr. J. & A. Tedeschi), *The Cheese and The Worms: the Cosmos of a Sixteenth Century Miller,* London, 1980, for a fascinating study of popular perceptions of religion in sixteenth century Italy in the context of a 'compelling . . . conflict between learned culture and popular culture'.

16. See for example, the inaugural address by M. Mohanty at the seminar on Communalism organized by the Institute for Jammu and Kashmir Affairs, February 1987.

17. It should, however, be noted that 'class' and 'communal' are not simple analytical categories. For the present purpose the term 'class' has been broadly used to describe strong economic motivations, e.g. the contradictions between Hindu *zamindars*/moneylenders and a predominantly Muslim peasantry. On the other hand, the term 'community' has been employed to indicate principally non-economic motivations and categories.

18. *Report on Native Newspapers in Bengal* (hereafter *NNR*), No. 22 of 1906, para-2, p. 485.

19. L/P & J/3081/07, India Office Library, LeMesurier to Secy, Home, India, October 14, see the judgement in Case No. 9 of May 1907, Phulpur station.

20. S. Das, *Communal Riots,* op. cit., see Chapter Two.

21. The discussion on the Calcutta riots of 1918 and 1926 is based on ibid., Chapter Three.

22. *Amrita Bazar Patrika* (hereafter *ABP*), 30 April 1926; *Matwala,* 1 May 1926.

23. For details of this outbreak see S. Das, *Communal Riots,* op. cit.

24. See ibid., for details on 1930 Dacca riot.

25. *The Modern Review,* Calcutta, July 1930.

26. P. Chatterjee, *Bengal 1920–1947: The Land Question,* Calcutta, 1984, op. cit., pp. 134–5.

27. *The Statesman,* Calcutta (hereafter *ST*), 18 April 1926.

28. E.J. Hobsbawm, *Bandits,* London, 1969.

29. S. Das, *Communal Riots,* op. cit., Chapter Five.

30. File-P5R/27/42, Dacca Secretariat Record Room.

31. Conversion here implies converting Hindus to Islam.

32. S. Das, *Communal Riots,* op. cit., Chapter Six.

33. Sir F. Tuker, *White Memory Serves,* London, 1950, p. 163.

34. N.Z. Davis, 'The Rites of Violence: Religious Riot in Sixteenth Century France', *Past and Present,* no. 59, 1973.

35. S. Das, *Communal Riots,* op. cit., Chapter Three.

36. N.Z. Davis, *Society and Culture in Early Modern France,* op. cit.; *George Rude,* The Crowd in History: A Study of Popular Disturbances in France and England, 1730–1848, New York, 1964.

37. See D. Washbrook, 'Law, State and Agrarian Society in Colonial India', *MAS,* vol. 15, no. 3, 1981.

38. D. Page, *Prelude to Partition: The Indian Muslims and the Imperial System of Control 1920–32,* Delhi, 1982.

39. T. Sarkar, *Bengal 1928–1934: The Politics of Protest,* Delhi, 1988, p. 77.

40. See B. Chandra, 'Secularisation—Retrospect and Prospect' in *Secular Democracy,* Annual Number, 1973, for an analysis of the attempts by the Congress leaders to secure Hindu-Muslim understanding through 'unity from top'.

41. *Indian Annual Register* (hereafter *IAR*), July-September 1926, pp. 79–81.

42. *ST,* 15–18 May, July 1926.

43. *IAR,* pp. 79–81.

44. A. Jalal, *The Sole Spokesman: Jinnah, the Muslim League and the Demand for Pakistan,* Cambridge, 1985.

45. J. Ellul (tr. K. Kellen and J. Lerner), *Propaganda, The Formation of Men's Attitudes,* New York, 1969, p. 162. Ellul shows that under the influence of propaganda, certain latent drives that are vague, unclear and often without any particular objective become powerful, direct and precise. See also A.P. Foulkes, *Literature and Propaganda,* London, 1983.

46. R.W. Scribner, *For the Sake of Simple Folk Popular Propaganda for the German Reformation,* Cambridge, 1981, pp. 245–6.

47. The police, as the foregoing chapters show, were deliberately rendered inactive or made to act in a partisan manner on behalf of one community or another in accordance with the interests of the state.

48. S. Sarkar, 'Popular Movements, National Leadership and the Coming of Freedom with Partition, 1945–47' in *Economic and Political Weekly,* Annual Number, 1982.

49. I have analysed the adverse impact of the 1946–7 communal riots on the Bengal administration in *Communal Riots,* Chapter Six. The role of communal violence in causing an administrative breakdown on a general all-India level has also been emphasized in Anita I. Singh, 'Decolonisation in India: The Statement of 20 February 1947' in *The International History Review,* vol. VI, no. 2, May 1984; see also A.I. Singh, *The Origins of the Partition of India,* Delhi, 1987.

50. The survivors of the Great Calcutta Killing, for example, still talk about their experiences in the same way the Second World War provides a framework for Europeans who lived through it.

51. Althusser would argue that ideological contradiction in the last resort is connected to class struggle, see his 'Ideology and Ideological State Apparatus (Notes towards an Investigation)' in L. Althusser (tr. Ben Brewater), *Lenin and Philosophy and Other Essays,* London, 1970.

52. This concept is borrowed from A. Gramsci, see his *Selections from the Prison Notebooks* (tr. Hoare and Nowell Smith), New York, 1971. This concept has been used by S. Sarkar in 'Popular Movements', op. cit., and D. Arnold, 'Gramsci and Peasant Subalternity in India,' in *The Journal of Peasant Studies,* vol. II, no. 4, July 1984.

CHAPTER 2

PROPAGANDA AND THE LEGITIMIZATION OF COMMUNAL IDEOLOGY: PATTERNS AND TRENDS IN BENGAL, 1905-1947

PROPAGANDA HAS GENERALLY been a determining factor in the mobilization of popular forces in society. This role of propaganda increased with the spread of literacy and an expansion of information network and communication system. Modem researches have demonstrated how an effective propaganda based on appropriate collective sociological presuppositions and broad 'ideological moorings' can work 'miracles'. To quote one such commentator: 'Starting from apparently fixed and immovable positions, we can lead a man where he does not want to go, without his being aware of it, over paths that he will not notice.'[1]

Four types of propaganda have thus been identified in modern political process—political and sociological propaganda; vertical and horizontal propaganda; rational and irrational propaganda; propaganda of agitation and integration.[2] They are not necessarily exclusive but intersect with each other to create 'forms of communication' and 'structures of meanings' through which individuals may relate to one another. Scribner thus recounts how during the German Reformation such 'structures of meanings' were constructed by 'appropriating' the experience of the past and 'supplying' it with a new context.[3] At the other end of the spectrum scholars have been sceptical of the role of propaganda in motivating popular actions. They emphasize the relative 'autonomy' of 'subaltern political movements', with popular consciousness, more than anything else, providing the main stimulus behind mass upsurges.[4] This school of opinion does not necessarily deny

*This essay was published in *Caste and Communal Politics in South Asia*, Suranjan Das and Sekhar Bandyopadhyay, eds., Calcutta, 1993.

the impact of propaganda on the 'unorganized' political world. What is emphasized is that the subordinated social groups are not passive recipients of ideas/ideologies emanating from the elites or the world of organized politics, but constantly reinterpret such ideas in terms of their own perceptions and consciousness. A certain idea could thus be used by 'subaltern groups' to sanctify their moves, although its original proponent would have hardly thought in such terms. For example, in the case of South Asia it has been shown that very often the Mahatma's message was used to justify some radical demands which Gandhi himself would not have approved of.[5]

The relationship between ideology, formalized and shaped by propaganda, and that of unstructured inherent consciousness is, however, problematic. Discourses in our daily lives are shaped by structures of power in society; our society is defined by 'the dialectics of conflict', and discourses reflect and often create conflicts. This may lead one to draw a deductive link between discrepant categories or ideas in the mind and technical aspects of the economy. Such an approach presupposes the shaping of ideology by consciousness, true or false. But Althusser[6] has demonstrated how consciousness is constructed through ideology. In this context ideology is a system of meanings which through propaganda seeks to 'install everybody in imaginary relations in which they live'. Ideologies exist in apparatuses—religion, education, family, law, system of party politics, trade unions, communication and culture—where they are shaped by social, and ultimately, class conflicts. Althusser does not consider differing ideologies as necessarily expressing the subjective consciousness of the different classes, although ideologies may be set up in antagonistic relations. No system or action, meanings and beliefs exist by themselves, but assume shapes in relation to opposing ideologies.

In this Althusserian context a linkage can be established between ideological propaganda and communal violence in colonial Bengal. Hindu-Muslim riots in India have been seen either as a result of 'manipulative politics'[7] or as self-assertion moves by subordinate social groups through the use of symbols and rituals that had been the traditional preserves of the upper caste.[8] What has been unfortunately underestimated is the role of propaganda in generating communal tensions and provoking riots. The present paper seeks to redress the imbalance by explicating aspects of this relationship between propaganda and nature of communal violence in twentieth-century colonial Bengal.

I have elsewhere sought to make a distinction between community consciousness in which religion is seen as a means of ordering the world, and communalism, a more recent concept.[9] Community consciousness usually did not preclude the development of strong syncretist traditions either at the popular level or in the world of high culture.[10] The world view of the people was ordered by local or inherited and socially enforced customs, some of which were derived from or reinforced by awareness of the great traditions. Communalism, *per se* though, was a product of nineteenth and twentieth centuries which saw the gradual manifestation of a sense of community in forms overtly separatist from broader societies within which they were constituted and involved a degree of intolerance for those outside the communal boundary. In pre-modern times the confessional faith was never the primary referent of identity. But the nineteenth-century British conceptualization of Indian society as consisting of different religious communities and attempts to use such categorization as a theoretical base for the pursuit of a policy to secure allies and 'shore up imperial power helped to convert it into a social reality'.[11] The transition from community consciousness to communalism in the late nineteenth and early twentieth centuries was certainly conditioned by socio-economic and political changes introduced by the British rule.[12] But what was also important in this process was the attempt by communal discourses to provide ideological legitimization for both Hindu and Muslim solidarities. Significantly, the nature of communal propaganda underwent changes in response to transmutation of interactions between organized and unorganized politics.

II

The nature of communal riots in Bengal registered a definite shift during the period under review.[13] While the pre-1941 outbreaks tended to be relatively less organized and more related to the expression of class or economic grievances, the post-1941 riots were organized, directly connected with developments in the organized political world, and consequently became overtly communal. But an important feature of communal violence in both periods was a process of legitimization wherein the Bengal rioters derived legitimacy for their group action. In this chapter I would argue that the propaganda literature not only reflected but contributed to the transformation in the nature of communal violence.

During the first three decades of the present century the riots mostly originated from incidents unrelated to institutional politics. Leadership for both Hindu and Muslim rioters came from local religious or influential personalities; the messages from leaders to the crowd were coded in religious or economic terms. Past glories were recreated to enthuse the co-religionists; solemn warnings and fierce threats were directed against the opposing community. On the eve of the 1906–7 Mymensingh riot—the first major riot in twentieth-century colonial Bengal—the mullahs had thus urged their audience to purify Islamic practices, convert as many Hindus as possible, and discontinue economic transactions with Hindu neighbours. The Muslim peasantry was exhorted to pray five times a day, refuse food from Hindus, refrain from performing customary menial jobs for the idolaters, stop subscriptions to pujas and prevent indiscriminate prostitution of their women for sexual desires of men of another faith.[14] Muslim newspapers such as the *Islam Darpan* emphasized the essential differences between the two communities and warned the Hindus: 'the Moslems will give battle and destroy their *religious* enemies. . . . For one Moslem killed . . . the taking of the lives of thousands upon thousands will be the retaliation'.[15] Again, the *Nawab Saheber Subichar* and other pamphlets preached apocalyptic messages with the Nawab Salimulla as the 'messiah . . . who will conquer Assam, Sylhet and Chittagong and save the Muslims from Hindu atrocities'.[16] Other pamphlets like the *Red Pamphlet* stressed the economic importance of the Muslim community and urged its readers to rise up against Hindu economic domination. To quote the *Red Pamphlet*: 'You (the Muslims) form the majority; you are the peasants, and from agriculture comes all wealth'. The Muslims were encouraged to develop a *Swajati* movement which would 'send all Hindus to hell'. Yet another leaflet in popular vernacular urged: 'Dewanganj Hindus, you have lived through the favour of the Musalmans. Within five days from today we shall loot shops of Shapara Sthah and Mahajans . . . . He who will be a true Musalman will not side with you.'[17]

The Muslim press in the 1920s and 1930s likewise reminded its readers of their domination over Hindus 'for thousands of years' and exhorted them to face the current 'challenge that has been thrown to the living Islam paganism'.[18] The *Asr-e-Jadid* induced the Muslims 'not to surrender . . . to the mercy or whims of Hindus'[19] and appealed: 'O! Lord Medina send your Omar and Khalid for some days so that they may infuse a new spirit in us, make us true Muslims, and show to us what a Moslem is like and for what purpose he has been sent into the world.'[20]

Again, the *Mohammadi* of 29 January 1926 called for a re-organization of the one lakh mosques in Bengal, Assam and Burma to impart religious fervour amongst the four crore of Muslims in this region. Other newspapers such as the *Dainik Soltan* warned: 'Muhammadans have proved that however inferior they may numerically be they can fight against people ten or eleven times as numerous.'[21]

The *Forward* of 28 September 1926 referred to an Urdu leaflet 'advising the Calcutta Muslims': 'For one Mahomedan life hundreds of Kafer (Hindu) lives should be taken. Whenever a Marwari, a Bengali or an upcountry Hindu is found, he is to be butchered. Slay as many of them as in your power lies.'[22]

District Muslim newspapers of the period also utilized local events for provoking communal animoisties. In Pabna, for instance, the *Sultan* indulged in a personal vilification campaign against some elected members of the District Board, recalling the proverb: 'The more indulgence you show to a monkey the greater becomes his impertinence'. The *Raushan Hedayat* assured the Muslims that sovereignty 'of the earth as well as of the heaven belongs to you'.[23]

The Hindu press matched its Muslim counterpart. 'The behaviour of Mussalmans' was characterized in general terms as 'intolerable'. Newspapers such as the *Matwala* deplored the fact that the Muslim 'considers his stubbornness to be his love of religion, stupidity to be the devotion to God, and madness to be religious'.[24] During the Mymensingh riot of 1906–7 the Hindu newspapers published provocative accounts of mutilated images and urged their readers to rise up 'in defence of religion'. The *Sandhya* of 30 April carried the picture of the desecrated goddess Basanti with the following remark: 'Brother what is there more to do? They (Muslims) have put indignity on the Mother. You do not know them for what they are. When their interests are jeopardized they are ready to become demons.'

Likewise the *Ananda Bazar Patrika* in a leading article of 5 May 1926 asked the Hindus: 'Will you receive the news of the desecration of temples hanging your heads in shame and disgrace and remain silent? Let the eternal youth of Bengal come forward. Let the wild dance put fury and seize the soft feet of the youth and hoods of viciousness break and fall to the ground at every stroke of their feet.'

In an issue of 1930 the *Matwala* cautioned the Muslims: 'Hindus can tear every hair on the beard of . . . Moslem *goondas* if their religion continued to be attacked.'[25]

The 1920s coincided with a resurgence of Hindu revivalist activity in a more organized form. Hari Sabhas and Arya Dharma Pracharani Sabhas in Pabna, Dacca and other neighbouring districts performed *yajnas* and kirtans to promote Hindu solidarity; the Marwaris in Calcutta formed defence parties to safeguard Hindu property; a call was given to establish Hindu organizations in every part of Bengal.[26] Such local bodies as the Hindu Sabha in Pabna which had not been particularly involved in overt anti-Muslim activities, now became preoccupied with a campaign to impress upon its followers the need to 'safeguard' traditional communal rights like the playing of 'uninterrupted music in religious processions'. The Hindus were even directly encouraged to take recourse to arms if a safe passage of their religious procession faced obstructions. The *Arya Samaj*, too, published such Hindi and Urdu pamphlets as *Islam Tur* (destruction of Islam), *Gostkhur Mussalman* (beef-eating Muslims) which contained 'indelicate abuse of Islam'.

The Hindu propaganda literature was not deprived of an economic content. But there was a qualitative difference with its Muslim counterpart in this aspect. While the Muslim discourse sought to expose Hindu economic exploitation, the Hindu literature highlighted the depredations caused to Hindu notables by 'Muslim vandalism' in a bid to arouse Hindu fraternity across class and caste lines. The *Bangabasi* of 11 May 1907 thus published photos of the plundered Gouripore *cutchery* (zamindar's office) and the ransacked house of the naib Biswesar Roy of Ramgopalpur estate with the note: 'When we saw this sight, we felt as if in Bengal the frightful Bargi anarchy was being re-enacted: the sinews of our hearts were as if broken by the sight.'[27]

Referring to the lootings at Dewanganj the *Sandhya* of 8 May 1907 wrote: 'All is about to be lost. Heard you ever of 16 well-to-do females having been violated? The bazars have been looted and inhuman murders done.'[28]

Interestingly, another favourite theme of the Hindu vernacular press in 1907 was the reported complicity between Muslim rioters and the British government. To quote the *Amrita Bazar Patrika* of 24 April 1907: 'local authorities are not only apathetic in respect of the troubles of the Hindus but have not even the decency to conceal the secret pleasure at the misfortunes of the Hindus.'

III

In the 1940s the rioting crowd, however, became primarily motivated by a kind of political legitimization. Bengal witnessed in this period not only communal solidarities in the realm of institutional politics but also an increasing interaction between this face of communalized organized politics and the unorganized political realm. The implementations of the 1935 Act for provincial autonomy based on separate electorates was a turning point in this direction. Fazlul Huq's Krishak Praja Party-Muslim League coalition government gave the Muslim political elite the first real taste of provincial power in Bengal. The League's separatist politics had already won the support of Muslim business and intellectual circles, and once Fazlul Huq joined the League it acquired an agrarian base which it so long lacked. In this context when the Pakistan movement was launched, the Muslim popular mind in Bengal was presented with an ideology that promised a bright political future. The Muslim leadership no longer merely coded its message with religious or economic idioms, but sought to rally the Muslim public opinion around a distinct political notion—the idea of a separate Muslim state of Pakistan. This change was clearly reflected in the Muslim propaganda literature of the 1940s.

A general aim of the Muslim press now was to convince its readers that the Muslims did not merely have a religious identity to self-determine their social affairs but had a political right to rule the province because of their demographic superiority.[29] 'Today it has become *farz* for all Muslims to strengthen the Muslim League. . . . This is the command of the Quoran'— such was the spirit of the ulema message.[30] The following ulema exhortation from a public platform was typical:

Islamic Tamaddun cannot exist without Islamic Hukumat. So this demand for Pakistan is based on the claim of justice. In the name of independence the Muslims cannot tolerate slavery of the Hindu Congress. There are differences between the Hindus and Muslims in religion and Tamaddun. India should be partitioned into Pakistan and Hindusthan for the development of the two nations.[31]

The Muslim peasantry was encouraged to be defiant towards their Hindu zamindars and urged to join a political struggle to establish a *Muslim Raj*. One month before the 1941 Dacca outbreak the *Star of India* of 4 March 1941 thus warned the Hindus:

The time has come to teach the little rats (Hindus) that the lion (Muslims) is not dead, only sleeping; the challenge is to be accepted; the enmity is to be met on its own ground; Mussalmans cannot resort to meanness and trickeries which characterize their political enemies; the Hindus will see to whom Bengal politically belongs; they shall be taught the lesson they need.

A poem published in the *Azad* of 23 March 1941 represented a similar political mood of the Muslim press: 'If you want political freedom, Burn, Burn, Burn the Jatu Griha (Hindu houses) and let all troubles end.'

An Urdu circular issued by the Calcutta District Muslim League on the eve of the Direct Action Day of 16 August 1946, also expressed in no uncertain terms the political aim of the Muslim League when it emphasized the need to:

proclaim to the world at large that the Muslims are awake, that they are brave people and that they are determined to secure their freedom. Let the blind see, the deaf hear and the dumb speak out that the Muslims are a living nation and will not rest till freedom is achieved. . . . Let them exhibit their action that they are ready to sacrifice themselves like . . . Serajuddoulla, Syed Ahmed Baralvi, Tipu Sultan and that they are prepared to be annihilated rather than be slaves of the British and the Hindus and that they will not rest until India is freed from British domination and the Brahmin-Baniya grip. . . . The time has now come when you are called upon to lay down your lives in the final battle for freedom, and God willing this will lead to the establishment of the Great Muslim State of which Pakistan will be the corner stone.[32]

The *Asr-e-Jadid* in its editorial of 1 August 1946 did not accordingly hesitate to admit that the Direct Action meant for the Muslims a political fight which 'implied violence'. The Bengali pamphlet *Mugur* issued by the Calcutta Muslim League went a step further to explicate the 'political task' for the Indian Muslims:

The day for an open fight which is the greatest desire of the Muslim nation has arrived. Come, those who want to rise to heaven. Come those who are simple, wanting in peace of mind and who are in distress. Those who are thieves, goondas, those without the strength of character and those who do not say their prayers—all come. The shining gates of heaven have been opened for you. Let us enter by thousands. Let us all cry out victory to Pakistan, victory to the Muslim nation and victory to the army which has declared a Jehad.[33]

The Muslim propaganda certainly continued to use religious idioms and symbols, but to reinforce political notions and messages. Take for instance the following exhortation from a Muslim League manifesto:

BRETHREN OF ISLAM:
Let it be remembered that in this holy month of *Ramzan,* the Holy *Koran* revealed itself, and Ummat Mohammad appeared as the prophet. In this month the *Kafirs* (non-believers) were annihilated in the great battle of Badr, and Mecca . . . [was] wrested from their hands. The Holy *Kaaba* was freed from the hands of infidels and the foundation of Islam was laid. It is by the grace of God that the All-India Muslim League has selected this very month . . . for Crusade for the establishment of Pakistan and has resolved that the 16th of August should be observed as an All-India Hartal day.[34]

The Muslim League also sought to impart an international flavour to its propaganda discourse by presenting the Pakistan movement as a part of the general struggle of the Muslim community all round the world for justice and equity. The Indian Muslims were thus reminded of their unique position in the Islamic world:

India is the only country where 10 crores of Muslims live together. Neither Arabia nor Turkey, Iran, Afghanistan nor any other country is inhabited by such large numbers of Muslims. The geographically central position of India in the Muslim-inhabited countries in the world gives a new importance to the 10 crores of Indian Muslims. The Indian Muslims are flanked on the east by Indonesia, Malaya, Java, Sumatra, China, Manchuria, Mongolia, Turkistan; on the west by Arabia, Turkey, Iraq, Palestine, Egypt, . . . Sudan and Tripoli and also by the Muslim-inhabited countries of Africa, Somaliland, Nigeria, Tunis, Algiers, Riff and Morocco. The Muslims of India occupy a central position.[35]

In this context the Indian Muslims were exhorted to appreciate that an independent state of their own held the key to a general liberation of all the enslaved Muslim countries:

The establishment of Pakistan would inevitably bring independence to all the enslaved Muslim countries of the world, whereas the foundation of Ram Raj in united India would not only enslave the Muslims in India but would also bring the Muslims of Indonesia, Malaya, Iran and West Africa under the Hindu-cum-Baniya Raj.[36]

The Muslim propaganda literature of the 1940s even advised its readers not to trust the British who had become the enemy of the 'Muslims all over the world'. To quote from a Muslim League manifesto:

The British are over suspicious of the Muslims. Britain is not only playing the traitor in India and trying to make them slaves of the Hindus, but has now become the arch-enemy of the Muslims all over the world. In the East, Britain is determined to ruin the crores of Muslims, inhabiting Indonesia, Java, Sumatra, Malaya and China and is conspiring to make them slaves of the Dutch and the Chinese imperialists. In the West, Britain is likewise determined to crush the spirit of independence which burns in the hearts of Muslims inhabiting Arabia, Egypt, Sudan, Palestine, Iraq, Iran and Turkey. She is trying to oust the Palestinian Arabs from their home by planting the Jews in the place for the sake of creating a sphere of Anglo-American influence in that part of the Muslim world. The real motive behind this is to safeguard the Anglo-American interests in oil and minerals in Persia. They went to install the infidel Jews in the Holy Land of the Great Prophet. . . . The same British are trying to uproot the Muslims from the Indian soil and invest the Hindus with powers in the same manner as they have been endeavouring to plant the Jews in Palestine.[37]

This anti-British ingredient in the Muslim League propaganda was ironical since it came at a time when the Raj was successfully playing the Muslim card to weaken the resurgent anti-imperialist secular force.

The Pakistan ideology existed in opposition to the ideal of *Akhand Hindusthan* with which the Hindu political forces and certain sections of the Congress became identified. The Hindu press gave a formal call to oust the Muslim League government in Bengal, raise Hindu volunteers trained in martial arts, and protect Hindu rights and interests. Leaders such as S.P. Mukherjee plainly told the Muslims that if they wanted to live in Pakistan they should 'pack their bag and baggage and leave India. . .'.[38] The Hindu leadership no longer perceived the Muslim challenge in religious terms but viewed it as a threat to their hitherto political authority. This becomes clear when one goes through the *Amrita Bazar Patrika, Ananda Bazar Patrika, Hindusthan Standard* and *Basumati*. In its editorial of 16 August 1946 the *Hindusthan Standard* thus observed:

Nationalists of Bengal . . . are opposed on principle to the mandate of the League. With them [the Hindus] the issue is a vital one. They cannot and will not participate in a demonstration the object of which is the repudiation of all their cherished political principles. Millions of such Nationalists all over Bengal claim protection from the Government against coercion to which they are likely to be subjected by the overzealous followers of the League.

A series of pamphlets published on the eve of the 1946 Calcutta riot revealed this dominant political tone of the Hindu propaganda literature. For instance, the pamphlet *16th August Beware* remarked: 'Hindus should give a clear answer to this act of effrontery. It is the duty of every Hindu to carry on organized efforts to frustrate the Direct Action Day. Remember, to join the Direct Action is to support the political demand of Pakistan.'[39]

Inside the Bengal Congress, too, the Hindu influence had increased substantially and its critique of the League went beyond the traditional sectarian/secular dichotomy. The League was now sought to be presented as an organization violating the civil liberty of non-Muslim communities. Pointing to the Bengal Chief Minister Suhrawardy's declaration of a public holiday on 16 August to allegedly ensure the success of the Direct Action Day, the Bengal Pradesh Congress Committee President Surendra Mohan Ghosh thus remarked in a statement of 15 August 1946: 'But what is most amazing is that the Muslim League Government in Bengal have come forward to implement the decision of the League and to impose that decision on the entire people of Bengal with all the authority and sanction of Government behind them.'[40]

The Bengal Congress made a mockery of the Muslim League's claim to have become 'revolutionary' when its role in the country's freedom struggle had been 'historically inglorious'. In his circular of 7 August 1946 to all District Congress Committees the Bengal Pradesh Congress Committee Secretary, Kalipada Mukherjee, accordingly characterized the Direct Action programme 'not (meant) for the freedom of the country . . . but . . . to strengthen and consolidate the reactionary forces of the country which in ultimate reality will retard our achievement of national freedom'.[41] The League's call for the general strike on 16 August was in the Congress opinion 'communal and anti-national', although the Hindus were apparently implored to 'remain calm' and 'not to be provoked'.[42]

Interestingly, the impact of this new political propaganda campaign was reflected in slogans voiced by the riotous crowd. In 1926 the Muslim rioters essentially raised such economic and religious slogans as *Alla Ho Akbar, Hindu sala log to maro* (death to Hindus), *Hindu zamindar murdabad* (down with the Hindu zamindars). But in the 1940s the same crowd shouted: *Pakistan ki jai* (victory to Pakistan), *Haq sahab ki jai* (victory to Haq), *Hindusthan dhansa hauk* (death to Hindusthan), *Jinnah zindabad* (victory to Jinnah), *Hindu Mahasabha murdabad* (down with Hindu Mahasabha). Similarly, the Hindu rioters cried: *Akhand Hindusthan* (united India) in clear political counterdependence.

IV

The propoganda 'warfare' of the 1940s just referred to, was matched by a significant change in the nature of both Hindu and Muslim leaderships. Initiatives for mobilization passed from the hands of local religious and influential notables to political leaders. Members of District Boards, leaders of the Muslim League and Hindu Mahasabha and even Congressmen of local and provincial standing became directly involved in riotings.

Evidently, this propaganda warfare first affected the educated section of both communities. But there is evidence to show that before every major outbreak the ideas imparted to the original credulous readers were disseminated amongst the subordinate social groups, categorized in official and elite discourses as 'the illiterate population'. Pamphlets and notices were read aloud before gatherings and religious congregations; leaflets were distributed on street corners; notices were displayed at strategic places. Sometimes the original message got more distorted and violent in the process of this transmission. It is not a mere coincidence that the most disturbed areas during a riot were those which had the highest circulation of such propaganda literature.

The process of communal mobilization from above need not, however, be overemphasized. There could be significant gaps between expectation, methods and frames of reference of the established leaders, and that of the crowd. My own research has shown how once a particular riot gained a momentum, the conventional leaders usually withdrew from the scene and collaborated with the authorities in restoring order.[43] We had then the emergence of leaders from men on the spot in whose hands the rioting tended to become unrestrained. At many such conjunctures a central factor motivating the collective violence was a popular conviction about a breakdown of the existing order. Sometimes the rumours of an anticipated change contributed to the creation of a popular mentality favouring an outbreak. For instance, the Muslim rioters were encouraged by rumours of the substitution of the British Raj by an Islamic rule. They were also sometimes enthused by the rumour of an official sanction for any rising against the Hindus who had fallen out of British favour because of their nationalist aspirations.[44]

Nevertheless, the fact remains that in the post-1940 period in the background of increasing inroads of organized politics into the unorganized realm on the one hand, and growing communal orientation of organized politics on the other, the communal propaganda assumed an organized political form. Throughout the 1940s Hindu and Muslim leaders undertook district tours, addressing large public rallies and recruiting cadres from the lowest strata of the society. Competing ideologies of the League and Hindu Mahasabha were propagated in the most organized manner. What occurred in Bengal during the 1940s was, to borrow Ellul's terminology, a 'psychological crystallization'[45] of communal identity among Hindus and Muslims. Muslim and Hindu community consciousness assumed a distinct political identity, nourished by propaganda and hardened by riots. The subsequent partition of the country along religious lines and the 'refugee problem' resulted in a permanent fragmentation of the national ethos, the impact of which we feel still today.

V

It is in this contextual framework that contemporary communal politics operates in India. Despite increased class polarizations, the articulation of class politics has not considerably advanced on the all-India plane. At the regional level, as for example in West Bengal, a significant strengthening of leftist forces has occurred. But at the macro level we are still faced with a semi-capitalist and semi-feudal setup where casteist and communalist votebanks have been created and most of the organized national political parties compete with each other in the use of religious symbols and rituals. The Babri Masjid-Ramjanmabhumi episode[46] proved that we can no longer speak of any sort of autonomy of communalism from institutional politics. The trend of organized and overt communal rioting which had started in the post-1940s assumed serious heights in such massacres as the Bhagalpur carnage of 1990 and the violence which followed the demolition of the Babri Masjid. In the face of this organized communalism—which I consider to be a potent source of totalitarianism in India—the riots have become today the handiwork of organized politics. The contemporary communal discourse has not developed in vacuum, but has a history of its own which I have sought to delineate in the case of twentieth-century colonial Bengal. If we have to counter communalism today we need to develop an effective anti-communal propaganda, highlighting the essential cultural unity of India, not in terms of the traditional dictum of 'unity in diversity' but on the basis of 'diversity in unity'.[47]

The growing contemporary political importance of propaganda may be illustrated with reference to an incident during the 1988–9 session of the Indian History Congress at Gorakhpur which I had attended. Here, on the last but one day of the Congress, the local Member of Parliament—Mahant Avaidyanath of the Visva Hindu Parishad—with the connivance of the authorities of Gorakhpur University insisted on making his views vocal on, what may be called, the Hindu view of Ramjanmabhumi-Babri Masjid issue. He had neither the membership nor an invitation from the Congress which could justify such platform-capture. The violence on the part of his holy henchmen which followed is a different story. But this direct attempt by organized Hindu communalism to intervene in the Indian History Congress should lead to a fresh thinking among those who believe that communal historiography is either unimportant, or that it has to be pandered to by the opposition of a term like 'community consciousness' to 'class consciousness', or by merely speaking of the exclusion of the peasantry from bourgeois ideology as 'autonomy'. It is, however, significant that not all historians of the History Congress left the Hall in protest against the Mahant's platform capture. This is the confusion that Indian historical thought will also have to grapple with.

Why have ideals of majoritarianism and contempt for minorities entered the minds of a sizeable section of the Indian populace? Has the emphasis on elements of 'sacred space' and 'spiritual integrity', as distinct from the secular and material values of democracy and fair play, obscured the secular thinking of a cognizable number of Indian citizens?—such questions can no longer evade the attention of socially conscious historians in India today. Thanks to a concerted propaganda drive by the Bharatiya Janata Party, Viswa Hindu Parishad and Shiv Sena, crude anti-Muslim rhetoric is becoming 'household' saying and 'threatens to reinforce the traditional vocabulary of communal prejudices with new abusive catch-words'.[48] This propaganda warfare of the Bharatiya Janata Party is based on two ideological premises: the synonimity of Indian with Hindu tradition and a redefinition of Indian nationalism to justify the authority of Hindu majority over other communities in the country. The Golwalkar dream of a Hindu India is being resurrected where the minorities would have to 'merge' themselves in the national (Hindu) race and adopt its culture, or to live at its mercy so long as the national race may allow them to do so and to quit the country at the sweet will of the national race.[49] In this context the Viswa Hindu Parisad leader Ashok Singhal's following warning does not come as a surprise: 'If the Hindu sentiments sweep the whole country, the Muslims would realize that neither the police nor the government nor political parties would be able to save them from the wrath.'[50]

Such slogans raised by the Ayodhya *karsevaks*[51] as: *Jab jab Hindu jaga hai, desh me molla bhaga hai* (When Hindus had woken the Muslims had fled) or *Mussalmano ko dono sthan Pakistan aur Kabarasthan* (Muslims have two places—Pakistan and graveyard)[52] amply indicate the popular absorption of Hindu revivalist propaganda.

The 'prelude to the Partition' was associated with a hegemony of communal ideology which caused a structural disarticulation between politics and class, resulting in, what has been called, a 'passive revolution' of 15 August 1947.[53] The element of class, certainly came to be reflected in politics once India and Pakistan settled down as independent entities. Unfortunately, the spate of post-independent communal riots has threatened the secularist foundations of Indian polity and we are threatened with some other gory version of the 1946–7 situation. The sources of legitimization of this contemporary communal backlash are many. Propaganda, however, has been crucial in creating the psyche for communal distemper. But this is not a novel role that propaganda has played in South Asian history. What we see today is the continuation of a historical trend.

Notes

1. J. Ellul (tr. K. Kellen and J. Lermer), *Propaganda: The Formation of Men's Attitudes,* New York, 1969, p. 35.
2. Ibid.; A. P. Foulkes, *Literature and Propaganda*, London, 1983, pp. 10–11.
3. R. W. Scribner, *For the Sake of Simple Folk—Popular Propaganda for the German Reformation*, Cambridge, 1981.
4. See the contributions to R. Guha, ed., *Subaltern Studies,* vols. I–IV, Delhi.
5. S. Amin, 'Gandhi as Mahatma: Gorakhpur District, Eastern UP, 1921–2', in R. Guha, ed., *Subaltern Studies III: Writings on South Asian History and Society*, Delhi, 1984.
6. L. Althusser, *Ideology and Ideological State Apparatus* (Notes towards an Investigation) in *Lenin and Philosophy and Other Essays*, L. Althusser, New York and London, 1971.
7. J. R. Mclane, *Indian Nationalism and the Early Congress*, Princeton, 1977; P. Robb, 'The Challenge of Gau Mata: British Policy and Religious Change in India', *Modern Asian Studies,* vol. 20, no. 2, 1986.
8. G. Pandey, 'Rallying Round the Cow: Sectarian Strife in the Bhojpuri Region *c.* 1885–1947', Occasional Paper No. 39, Centre for Studies in Social Sciences, Calcutta.
9. S. Das, *Communal Riots in Bengal 1905–1947,* Delhi, 1991.
10. A. Roy, *The Islamic Syncretic Tradition in Bengal,* Princeton, 1983, A. A. Engineer, 'Islamic Fundamentalism and Communalism in India', in *Islam in Asia: Pakistan, India, Bangladesh, Sri Lanka, Indonesia, Philippines, Malaysia,* A. A. Engineer, ed., Lahore, 1986.
11. T. Raychauddhuri, 'A Poison Tree and its Fruits', *The Statesman Miscellany,* 15 August 1987.
12. S. Das, *Communal Riots,* op. cit.
13. Ibid.
14. S. Das, 'The Complexities of Communal Violence in Twentieth Century Bengal: The Mymensingh Experience 1906–1907', *The Calcutta Historical Journal,* July 1987–June 1988.
15. *Report on Native Newspapers in Bengal* (hereafter NNR) No. 22 of 1907, para 8, p. 475.
16. S. Das, 'The Complexities', op. cit.
17. *NNR* No. 21 of 1907, p. 439, para 3.
18. *NNR* No. 19 of 1926.
19. *Report on the Administration of Bengal* BAR 1926–7, pp. 24–5.
20. *NNR* No. 19 of 1926.
21. File—Home (Confidential) 224/26, West Bengal State Archives (hereafter WBSA).

22. File—228/26, Home (Confidential), WBSA.
23. BAR, 1926 p. 25.
24. Ibid., pp. 24–5.
25. S. Das, *Communal Riots,* op. cit.
26. Ibid.
27. *NNR* No. 20 of 1907, para 70, p. 424.
28. *NNR* No. 19 of 1907, para 16, p. 385.
29. *Dhaka Prakash,* 14 Bhadra 1348.
30. See Md. E. H. Khan, 'Role of the Ulema in Bengal Muslim Politics 1937–47' in *Clio,* vol. 1, 1983.
31. Cited in ibid., p. 53.
32. *Notes on the Causes of the Calcutta Disturbances, August 1946,* Government of Bengal, Home Department, Political, Calcutta 1946, see Appendix C.
33. Ibid., Appendix C, Item 6.
34. Ibid.
35. Ibid.
36. Ibid.
37. Ibid.
38. See speech by Haq, *Proceedings of the Bengal Legislative Council* (hereafter *BLCP*), 1941, vol. lix, no. 6, p. 216.
39. *Notes on the Causes,* op. cit., Appendix D, Item 3.
40. Ibid., Annexure D, Item 2.
41. Ibid., Item 1.
42. Ibid., Item 2.
43. S. Das, *Communal Riots,* op. cit.
44. Ibid.
45. J. Ellul, *Propaganda,* op. cit.
46. The dispute centres around the question whether the present site of Babri Masjid—claimed to be the birthplace of the epic hero Rama—had been constructed on the ruins of a temple.
47. For an elucidation of this alternative notion of 'diversity in unity', see B. De, 'Political Aspects In The Evolution On India's Composite Culture', paper presented at the *Festival of India Symposium on Indian Culture: Diversity in Unity,* Moscow, May 1988.
48. S. Banerjee, 'Hindutva—Ideology and Social Psychology', *Economic and Political Weekly,* 19 January 1991.
49. Quoted in Ibid.
50. *The Indian Express* (Delhi), 15 November 1990, cited in Ibid.
51. The people who responded to the Viswa Hindu Parishad's call to offer their free manual labour for building a temple in Ayodhya, the supposed birthplace of Rama.
52. See S. Banerjee, *Hindutva,* op. cit.
53. For the use of the concept of 'passive revolution' in the context of the Transfer of Power in India in August 1947 see S. Sarkar, 'Popular Movements, National Leadership and the Coming of Freedom with Partition 1945–47', *Economic and Political Weekly,* Annual Number, 1982.

CHAPTER 3

THE COMMUNAL CHALLENGE IN BENGAL POLITICS, 1940–1947

Rᴇᴠɪᴇᴡɪɴɢ ɪɴ ᴀɴ article 'The Structure of Politics in India on the Eve of Independence' Ravinder Kumar had perceptively remarked:

In reinforcing the vested interest of the propertied classes, the communal world view had an edge over the liberal and capitalist world view, in that it would draw upon a wide range of symbols and associations dear to the popular classes in the country. Small wonder, then, that communalism exercised a powerful appeal . . . and even when it did not achieve a clear triumph, it was successful in constricting the arenas of liberal or socialist action open to those leaders who were located within the Congress.[1]

The present essay seeks to recapture this communal challenge experienced in Bengal during the 'prelude to Partition'. Initially I had thought of concentrating on the Hindu aspect of this challenge primarily on the basis of a series of hitherto unutilized Special Branch and Intelligence Branch Files of Calcutta and Bengal Police. This would have rectified an imbalance in my earlier work on *Communal Riots in Bengal, 1905–1947*[2] caused by an inadequate discussion on Hindu communal activity and organization. But unfortunately I have not been able to accomplish that project within the given time. I have accordingly taken the opportunity to present a broad overview of communal identities in Bengal politics in the 1940s from which national consciousness still needs to free itself.

*This paper was presented at the Nehru Memorial Library-Cambridge workshop on 'Northern India and Indian Independence' at Nehru Memorial Library, New Delhi, 6–8 December 1993. I am indebted to Professor Ravinder Kumar, Director of Nehru Memorial Library, for giving me permission to publish it now.

The Analytical Framework

The notion of communalism has evoked diverse responses from social scientists. It has been used to explain the 'political assertiveness' of a community trying to maintain its identity in a plural society undergoing a process of modernization.[3] Others have used the term to analyse the 'discrimination' or 'protection' of interests on religious grounds.[4] Communalism in India has been also seen as 'false consciousness' or distorted reflection of aspirations, fears and sentiments of the people.[5] In this connection a distinction has been made between communal politics and communal tension: the former being 'long-term, persistent and continuous' involving 'the middle-class', landlords and bureaucratic elements and the latter 'spasmodic' directly involving 'the lower classes only'.[6] Again, some recent scholars tend to consider communalism as a product of nationalist discourse. Communalism and nationalism are both viewed as a 'feeling of community' and hence communalism is seen as a form of nationalism. Such commentators argue that when religion provides the bond of national unity, secular nationalists call it communalism. To quote one of them: 'What is communalism in India is Nationalism in Pakistan.'[7] Another variation of this school of thought opines that as categories of thought both nationalism and communalism are constructed out of shared as well as contested experiences, our common as well as mutually contradictory visions and struggles.[8] We have, however, been cautioned against the adoption of a homogeneous view on Muslim political particiaption in India. Various segments amongst Indian Muslims were related to and defined their relationship differently with mainstream nationalism.[9] Attempts have been undertaken too to analyse the role of religion in the context of 'the actual labour processes . . . the ecology of a region . . . the given technology . . . (and the) social organization of labour utilization'.[10] A Cambridge thesis thus explains the communal holocaust in 1946 in eastern Bengal against the backdrop of a breakdown in the traditional economic 'symbiosis' between Muslim smallholding peasants and Hindu trader and talukdar creditors.[11]

What these projections unfortunately fail to recognize is the distinction between religiosity and communalism which, as I have tried to indicate in an earlier work,[12] is crucial for understanding the emergence and growth of the communal problem in India. Despite connections between the two, religious and communal identities are not identical. The former concerns personal allegiance to a set of practices and dogmas, often in search of a reward from the other or transcendental world. Communalism, on the other hand, entails individual commitment to special interests of a religious community for gaining worldly advantages at the expense of other communities. Religious violence is provoked by sectarian and doctrinaire differences; communal animosities are primarily motivated by conflicts over political power and economic resources. In this context I would consider communalism in India as a modern phenomenon, a product of colonialism. Instances of communal violence in pre-British period that Bayly cites[13] were actually more religious than communal.[14] It is also misleading to use interchangeably the categories of 'ethnicity' and 'communalism', as is often done.[15]

If we accept this analytical framework any discussion on the origin and development of communalism in India has to centre around, what I have called, the transition from community consciousness to communalism.[16] Community consciousness usually did not preclude the development of a strong syncretic tradition either at the popular realm or in the world of high culture. The world view of the people was ordered by local, largely inherited and socially enforced customs, some of which derived from, or were reinforced by awareness of the great traditions. Communalism *per se*, though, was a product of the nineteenth and twentieth centuries which saw the gradual manifestation of a sense of community in overtly separatist forms involving a degree of intolerance for those outside the communal boundary.

This transmutation of community consciousness to communalism, however, occurred at two levels: elite and popular. Following Sumit Sarkar we can thus delineate two spheres of communalism: elite communalism and popular communalism.[17] Of course, the two realms were not mutually exclusive. There were constant interactions between the two. The communal challenge in the Bengal politics of the 1940s that I propose to presently examine has been attempted in this specific historical configuration.

The Communal Challenge in Bengal's Institutional Politics

By the late 1920s the communal divide within Bengal's organized politics had become apparent. Commenting on its reflection in the Hindu and Muslim press a government report noted: 'No accusation was too low, no suggestion too mean if the object was to vilify the opposition party. Both sides made frantic appeals to past history. . . . Solemn warnings and fierce threats were accompanied by the impassioned appeals to their own supporters to be 'up and doing' in the communal cause.'[18]

Implementation of the 1935 Act providing for provincial autonomy based on separate electorate subsequently gave the Muslim elite the first real taste of provincial political power. The Communal Award of 1932 had already been condemned by the broadest spectrum of Hindu leaders for reducing their community to a position of 'permanent statutory inferiority'.[19]

This psychological blow was transformed into a material setback for the Hindu elite when the Krishak Praja Party-Muslim League coalition ministry initiated a series of social legislation.

In a situation where Muslims constituted more than 56 per cent of the total populace but lived under the socio-economic dominantion of Hindu zamindars (landlords) and mahajans (moneylenders) such pieces of legislation as the Bengal Tenancy Act (1938), Bengal Agricultural Debtors Act (1939) and Bengal Moneylenders' Act (1940) obviously affected the Hindu dominant economic interests. This provoked an opposition orchestrated along lines of Hindu solidarity. The other measure prompting communal bitterness in institutional politics was the Calcutta Municipal Amendment Act of 1939 which introduced separate electorates for Muslims and Anglo-Indians, reserved seats for Scheduled Castes and curtailed the prospects of Hindu employment in the Calcutta Corporation. Similarly, when the Bengal Secondary Education Bill (1940) sought to improve Muslim representation in secondary education by setting up a Board elected on communal basis, the Hindu educated elite felt threatened of being reduced to subservience. A significant increase in the Muslim share of government jobs following the rigid enforcement of the communal ratio further accentuated communal tensions in the realm of the organized political world in Bengal.

The Pakistan movement provided the final edge to Muslim separatism in the institutional politics of Bengal. Contesting the 1946 legislative elections on the single issue of Pakistan, the Muslim League captured 93 per cent of the Muslim constituencies and emerged as the single largest party with 119 out of a total of 250 seats. Attempts by sections of Muslim political opinion outside the League to develop Hindu-Muslim amity failed, and Bengal came to be governed by a League ministry under H.S. Suhrawardy on overtly communal lines. Aspirations of Bengali Muslims for a Muslim majority state in eastern India was no longer in doubt. It now had a firm political and institutional base. Meanwhile, at the all-India plane the League won all the 30 Muslim seats in the Central Assembly while the Congress secured 52 out of 62 general seats. This strengthened the League's claim to be the authoritative representative of Indian Muslims—a claim so long contested by the Congress. The subsequent 'League story' is well known: its rejection of the Cabinet Mission Plan and adoption of the Direct Action Programme of 16 August 1946 when the 'Muslim nation (was) to stand to a man behind their sole representative organization, the Muslim League, and be ready for a sacrifice'.[20]

Once the Pakistan movement gained ground, the Hindu leadership too no longer perceived the Muslim danger in merely religious terms but as a threat to their hitherto political dominance. The Pakistan ideology was counteracted by the slogan of *Akhand Hindusthan* (united India) with whose dissemination both the Bengal Congress as well as Hindu exclusivist political force—the Bengal Hindu Mahasabha—became involved. The Hindu press gave a formal call to oust the Muslim League government in Bengal, frustrate the Direct Action Day programme and raise volunteers for protecting Hindu rights and interests. The Hindu Mahasabha leader Shyama Prasad Mukherjee plainly told the Muslims that if they wanted to live in Pakistan they should 'pack their bag and baggage and leave India . . .'.[21] But when a separate Muslim homeland became a reality the Hindu public opinion in Bengal insisted on the partition of the province on religious line as the only guarantee for Hindu prosperity. Paradoxically, this was the view nursed both by the Hindu Mahasabha and the overwhelmingly Hinduized Bengal Provincial Congress Committee that had once strong secular pretensions.[22]

The Popular Base of Communal Challenge

Communalism within the institutional politics of Bengal in the 1940s was sustained by, what has been called, 'popular communalism'. I do not, however, subscribe to the view that this popular pressure from below had an autonomy of its own. Instead, both Muslim and Hindu communal solidarities at the grass root level were largely cemented by mobilization from the top.

The Muslim Assertion

Recent studies have demonstrated how the Khilafat and Non-Cooperation movements had led to the emergence of new leaders possessing strong connections with religious and social leadership of the Muslim peasantry, many of them being eminent mullahs (Muslim theologian usually in a mosque).[23] They made the Bengali Muslims more conscious of their interests and potency of their actions and organization. Muslim politicians effectively used the 'traditional structure of communal authority' and religious institutions and symbols to build their support base. Unlike 'the bhadralok-dominated Hindu voluntary associations, the local anjumans cut across divisions of class and status which proved to be 'readymade organizations for Muslim politicians'. The mosque particularly constituted a focus of loyalty and collective action. The mullahs could be motivated to deliver political messages to regular congregations; religious festivals enabled the aspiring politicians to display their zeal and devotion to the community.

Collaboration between Muslim politicians and the ulema was further strengthened in the 1940s.[24] 'Muslim samities' were formed throughout

Bengal to provide a common platform for the League and the ulema. Under their auspices Islamic festivals were organized, religious books and pamphlets were published, and a protest against the 'Hindu oriented syllabi' of the University of Calcutta was launched. Messages of the ulema were published in leading Muslim newspapers such as the *Millat,* their fatwas gained wide circulation. 'Today it has become *farz* for all Muslims to strengthen the Muslim League. . . .This is the command of the Quoran', was a common theme of the ulema message. The following ulema exhortation from a public platform in Mymensingh was typical: 'Islamic Tamaddun cannot exist without Islamic Hukumat. So this demand for Pakistan is based on the claim of justice. In the name of independence the Muslims cannot tolerate slavery of the Hindu Congress. . . . India should be partitioned into Pakistan and Hindusthan for the development of these two nations.'[25]

Yet, another contemporaneous development contributing to the popularization of Muslim communalist politics was the democratization of the Muslim League itself, accomplished primarily by the initiatives of the party's General Secretary Abul Hashim.[26] On the eve of the tumultuous days of 1946–7 the Bengal Muslim League had certainly become a 'mass-based organization capable of leading a sustained movement to attain its objectives'.[27]

It needs to be stressed also that this politicization of Bengali Muslims along communal lines was facilitated by the social reform movement of the late nineteenth century. By initiating a process of self-definition, self-classification and self-identification a vertical solidarity within the Muslim community had been created.[28] This in turn led to social alienation of the Muslim villager from his/her immediate Hindu neighbour with whom he/she generally shared a common pattern of rural life. A 'heightened consciousness of a separate cultural identity' made the Bengali Muslims feel that as Muslims they were required to be distinct from Hindus and to orient their manners, customs, personal and family names in accordance with Pan-Islamic norms. The 'focus of Muslim attention' became evident by the 1930s through a number of regional and cultural associations.[29] Areas such as Pabna, where Hindus and Muslims had for so long participated in each other's festivals, and Dacca which had been remarkably free from communal tensions, now became sites for recurrent communal confrontations on such issues as 'music before mosques'.

The Hindu Affirmation

The assertion of Muslim communal identity was matched by an avowal of Hindu self. Whether one was a reaction to the other is difficult to judge.

Probably the two went hand in hand. Unfortunately not much research has been undertaken to unravel the nature and dimension of popular Hindu communalism.[30] This may be partly because Hindu communalism is perceived to have never posed a viable threat to institutional politics in Bengal. But my own perusal of hitherto unutilized Intelligence Files of Bengal Police imparts a somewhat different picture.

It now appears that by the 1940s Hindu communalism could carve out an area for itself in the world of popular politics in Bengal. Certainly neither the Hindu Mahasabha nor the Arya Samaj nor the RSS was as powerful in Bengal as in north India. But a section of Bengali Congressmen did develop a strong sense of Hindu identity, especially in view of a perceptible threat from the Pakistan movement, which enabled the Hindu communalist forces to work often in collaboration with or through the Congress organization. Even Congressmen holding offices in municipalities openly supported Mahasabha activities. Police reports indicate 'Hindu sympathies' of some Congress members of the Bengal legislature too.[31] This was perhaps not unnatural because in the 1940s the space between communal and Congress politics in Bengal was not as determinate as it appears today from historical hindsight. Even in the all-India framework the relative strength of the Bengal Hindu Mahasabha in the post-Independence period was attested to by the fact that in the 1952 general elections out of the three Lok Sabha seats it won, two were from West Bengal.[32]

The leading lights of the Bengal Hindu Mahasabha were Shyama Prasad Mukherjee, N.C. Chatterjee, Ashutosh Lahiri, N.C. Chunder, Mahadhiraj of Kashimbazar and Maharaja Shashi Kanta Acharya. Financial support for the Party primarily came from Calcutta's Marwari mercantile community.[33] Influential north Indian Mahasabha leaders like Mahant Digvijayanath of the UP and the editor of *Sanmarga,* Satya Narayan Pande themselves came to Calcutta to ensure contributions from the city's wealthy Jaipurias.[34] According to a police estimate, the strength of Hindu Mahasabha volunteers in the beginning of 1940 was 125,000 whose main function was to organize the Hindu National Guard and 'carry on Sangathan (organizational) work' amongst different sections of Hindus.[35] Besides, the Party had two other mass fronts: the Hindu Students' Federation and the Mazdur Hindu Sabha. Such Hindu revivalist organizations as Hindu Shakti Sangha, Hindu Youth Dal, Hindu Sangathan Dal, Bharat Sevasram Sangha and Hindu Mission also lent helping hands to the Mahasabha.[36]

At a moment when the Bengal Muslim League was democratizing itself, the Mahasabha sought to develop an effective organization to disseminate its message of Hindutva. Local committees were formed at village, Union and district levels which had a channel of command with the provincial authorities.[37] Regular orientation camps were held in rural areas and mofussils to provide ideological clarity for the Mahasabha volunteers. Drills and training in sentry duties, musketry and use of lathi, sword and spear were combined with 'lectures on the aims and objects of . . . Hindu Sangathan and protection of Hindu rights'.[38] Written examinations were held and certificates awarded to successful volunteers.[39] The aim was to 'excite' the participants by recreating the lives of such 'Hindu achievers' as Shivaji, K.B. Hedgewar, B.G. Tilak, V.D. Savarkar, Swami Shradhanand, Dayanand Saraswati, Lajpat Rai and Ramdas Swami and totalitarian figures like Hitler, Mussolini and Chiang-Kai-Shek.[40] The texts prescribed for the volunteers are also revealing. They included *Unity of Cultures* by D.K. Kelkar, *Hinduism* by Savarkar, *Caution to Hindus* by Savitri Devi, *Danger of Pakistan* by Karandikar, *Harijan Problem* by Professor Mate, *History of Turks* by Bhave, *Literature on Hinduism* compiled by Hindu Bhandar of Nagpur, *History of Ireland* by Kelkar and short histories of Nazi Germany and Fascist Italy. Leaflets in the form of questions and answers on contemporary issues were distributed amongst the volunteers. Explaining the objectives of these training camps Shyama Prasad Mukherjee noted: 'At this supreme crisis that threatens the very existence of Hindus in this great province. . . . I feel the need for a well organized and disciplined body of youth who will fearlessly defend their rights and interests and the honour of our women folk.'[41]

N.C. Chatterjee, another Hindu Mahasabha stalwart from Bengal, reminded his party's volunteers of the need

for preaching the nationalist message of the Mahasabha and preserving the integrity of Hindusthan. . . . I had advocated Inter-Provincial and Inter-caste marriage in order to bring about Hindu solidarity throughout Hindusthan. The Hindu rank should not be thinned by the foolish notions of celibacy among the youth. They should preach the teachings of the Geeta. They should not cling to cowardice. It is their moral duty to fight aggressions and injustice in any shape or form. Hinduism has never tolerated a Monroe doctrine in religion and culture.[42]

In Murshidabad and adjoining districts RSS volunteers established libraries of books on Hinduism and Hindu heroes.[43]

The Hindu Mahasabha celebrated the birth and death anniversaries of leading Hindu personalities and commemorated 10 May, the day when the Sepoys rose in revolt in 1857, as Independence Day. Police reports indicate that local Congressmen and ex-revolutionaries like Bipin Ganguli and Deben De were enthusiastic participants on these occasions. Congressmen holding offices in municipalities, including the ex-Mayor of Calcutta, Sanat K. Roy Chaudhuri, as well as such personalities as the editor of *Bharatvarsha*. Phani Bhusan Mukherjee reportedly supported Mahasabha activities.[44] The Mahasabha rallies in Calcutta and districts were usually well-attended.[45]

When any area was plagued by natural calamities like flood the Mahasabha organized relief operations.[46] It appears from all available evidence that the Mahasabha particularly gained in considerable support and respect from the

Hindus of Bengal at the popular level through its relief activities during the man-made famine of 1943. Local Mahasabha committees conducted searches to recover surplus foodstuff which was distributed amongst the needy.[47] According to an estimate the Bengal Provincial Hindu Mahasabha in February 1944 was still serving 1,02,581 refugees from 183 centres.[48] Scanning through the *Hindu Mahasabha Papers* one is struck by the way the Party organized the supply of relief material from affluent Hindus and Hindu commercial organizations of Punjab, Lahore, Hardwar, Karnal, Gujranwala, Amritsar, Jalandar, Rawalpindi, Gokkar, Faridkot, Bhopal, Ferozabad, Delhi and Nagpur.[49] The Mahasabha could mobilize the students and youth for undertaking the relief work which should have widened its popular social base. The Party also tried to win the confidence of rural Hindu women by reconverting their compatriots who had been forcefully made to accept Islam.[50] But the lower caste Hindus generally appear to have preferred to rally around the Muslim League than the Mahasabha.[51]

As with the Muslims, the strengthening of political identity amongst Hindus was nourished by a rapid rise of revivalism at the popular level. In districts such as Pabna and Dacca local Hari Sabhas and Arya Dharma Pracharani Sabhas organized *yajnas* (public worship) and kirtans (devotional music) to generate solidarity within the Hindu community. The Marwaris in Calcutta formed Defence Societies to forestall attacks on Hindu property. A call was given to establish Hindu organizations in every part of Bengal. Local bodies such as the Hari Sabha of Pabna which had not been particularly anti-Muslim till the 1930s now became active in educating its followers on such communal rights as playing music in religious processions without any obstruction.[52]

The Pakistan Movement and the 'Communal Divide'

The Pakistan politics accentuated the polarization of Hindu-Muslim opinion in Bengal. Both the elite and rank and file within the Bengali Muslims found in Pakistan 'a bright future', although for different reasons. On the other hand the classic Hindu reaction to the notion of a separate Muslim homeland was expressed in a Hindu Mahasabha pamphlet of October 1944: 'We will never touch Pakistan in any shape or form with a pair of tongs.'[53] Interestingly, local Congressmen were found distributing such leaflets.[54] In fact, in many respects the tone of the Bengal Congress propaganda was not qualitatively different from that of the Mahasabha. The Bengal Provincial Congress Committee organized a campaign against the 'prostitution of the government authority' by the League to advance its political aims.[55] Two days before the Direct Action Day the Congress organized a 'provocative' rally of about 5,000 people in south Calcutta where Surendra Mohan Ghosh described the declaration of a public holiday on 16 August as an attempt to force the hartal on Hindus.[56] On the same occasion while K.S. Roy urged the audience to pursue normal business on 16 August, another speaker warned the Muslim League government that the people of Bengal who could 'ascend the gallows and brave the British bullets smilingly were not afraid of the hollow threats of the Muslim Leaguers' dangers.'[57] The League leaders alleged a 'nexus' between the Congress and Hindu Mahasabha to raise the fear of an impending Muslim violence and create 'an air of coming disaster on Hindus' in Calcutta and its outskirts.[58] Even if one is sarcastic about the League's contention, the fact remains that the Hindu mind had been inflamed against the Direct Action Day. A recent study has also indicated how the Arya Samaj propaganda in Bengal since the late 1930s had also sharpened the hostility of Hindu labouring classes towards their Muslim colleagues.[59]

The communalization of Bengal politics in the wake of the Pakistan agitation was reinforced by a process of legitimization wherein the actors derived legitimacy for their group actions. In developing this sense of legitimacy communal propaganda played an important role, a theme which I have sought to develop in a recent paper of mine.[60] Popular participation in communal politics in Bengal during the 1940s came to be primarily motivated by a kind of political legitimization. Muslim and Hindu leaders alike no longer coded their messages with religious or economic idioms, but sought to rally public opinion around the distinct political notion of Pakistan.

The general aim of Muslim propaganda literature was now to convince its readers that Muslims did not merely have a religious identity to self-determine their social affairs but, as the majority community in Bengal, had the political right to rule the province. The Muslim peasantry was thus encouraged not only to be defiant towards their Hindu zamindars but asked to join a general struggle to drive out the Hindus and establish a Muslim Raj. An Urdu circular issued by the Calcutta District Muslim League on the eve of the Direct Action Day expressed in no uncertain terms the political aim of the Muslim League thus: 'Let the blind see, the deaf hear and the dumb speak out that the Muslims are a living nation and will not rest till freedom is achieved.'[61] The *Asr-e-Jadid* in its editorial of 1 August 1946 did not hesitate to acknowledge that the Direct Action meant for the Muslims a political fight which implied 'violence'. The Muslim propaganda did continue to use religious idioms and symbols, but primarily to reinforce political notions and messages.[62]

Interestingly, in a revival of Pan-Islamic propaganda the Muslim League sought to impart an international flavour by presenting the Pakistan movement as a part of the general struggle of the Muslim community around the world for justice and equality. In this context the Muslims were urged not to trust the British who had become the enemy of the 'Muslims all over the world'. This anti-British ingredient in the Muslim League propaganda discourse was ironical since it came at a time when the Raj was successfully playing the Muslim card to weaken the resurgent anti-imperialist secular force.

The Hindu propaganda literature too, no longer perceived the Muslim threat in merely religious terms. Instead, it came to be viewed as a political danger to the hitherto entrenched Hindu political authority (as mentioned in previous chapter).

The communal tension on the eve of the Calcutta riot of 1946 occasioned the publication of a series of provocative Hindu pamphlets which brought out this dominant political tone of the Hindu propaganda.

Anonymous leaflets urged the Bengali Hindus to 'reassert themselves . . . forsaking their individualistic and selfish pursuits . . . (remembering) that Bengal where they are exploited by self-seeking robbers and traitors really belongs to them'.[63] The League was to be exposed as an organization violating the civil liberty of non-Muslim communities. The Bengal Congress President and the Bengal Hindu Mahasabha made a mockery of the Muslim League's claim to have become revolutionary when its role in the country's freedom struggle had been historically inglorious. In his circular of 7 August to all District Congress Committees the Bengal Pradesh Congress Committee Secretary Kalipada Mukherjee accordingly condemned the Direct Action Programme for strengthening the reactionery 'forces of the country which in ultimate reality will retard our achievement of national freedom'.[64] Interestingly enough, this period of propaganda 'warfare' was matched by a transfer of Hindu and Muslim leadership from local influential leaders to political personalities.

Evidently, the propaganda warfare first affected the educated section of both communities. But the message did percolate down to the subordinate social groups through pamphlets, leaflets, notices and religious congregations. Sometimes the original message got distorted in the process of transmission. It is not a mere coincidence that the most disturbed areas during a riot were those which had the highest circulation of such propaganda literature.

Communal mobilization from above need not, however, be overemphasized. As my own study on the riots show, there could be significant gaps between expectations, methods and frames of reference of the established leaders and the crowd who actually committed violence. Sometimes rumours of an anticipated change contributed to the creation of a popular mentality favouring an outbreak. For instance, the Muslim rioting crowd were encouraged by such rumours as the impending substitution of the British by an Islamic Raj or a British sanction for any rising against Hindus who had fallen out of official favour because of their nationalist aspirations.

Nevertheless, the fact remains that in the background of the increasing inroads of organized politics into the unorganized political realm on the one hand, and the growing communal orientation of organized politics on the other, communal politics in Bengal during the 1940s assumed an organized form but with strong popular roots. In fact, what occurred in Bengal during the 1940s was a 'psychological crystallization' of communal identity amongst Hindus and Muslims. Muslim and Hindu community consciousness did thus assume a distinct political identity.

The Communal Explosion

The 1946 legislative elections and the Partition Riots of 1946–7 clearly testified to a convergence of elite and popular communalism. Since I have already made a detailed study of these riots elsewhere, I need not go into their details.[65] The communal violence since the Dacca riot of 1941 relatively lost the class basis of the previous outbreaks. It became more organized and directly connected with developments in institutional politics, and consequently exclusively related to communal politics rather than class interests. The rioting crowd's emphasis was no more on economic gain but on revenge and humiliation of the members of the rival community. This rite of violence displayed communal animosity at its peak, thereby completing the process of dehumanization.

The communal hysteria of 1946–7 contributed to the creation of a convenient prelude to the partition of Bengal, nay India, along religious lines. Eastern part of the erstwhile Bengal presidency had an area of 35,298 sq. miles where Muslims constituted 74.7 per cent of the population. It became a part of Pakistan. Similarly, the western half of British Bengal encompassing 36,597 sq. miles and having a population whose 71.2 per cent were Hindus, became a federal unit of the Republic of India. While the communal warfare helped Jinnah to finally win the 'Muslim brief, the orgy of rioting reconciled a large section of Hindu and Muslim subordinate social groups to the idea of Pakistan. This political trend was reflected in the changed attitude of nationalist Muslims and the Congress leadership (except Gandhi and Abdul Gafoor Khan) whose secular stance gave way to an acceptance of Pakistan as the 'only real alternative'. Likewise, the Bengal Hindu Mahasabha abandoned its slogan of 'Akhand Hindusthan' (United India) and opted for the creation of a separate province within India comprising the Hindu majority areas in Bengal.[66] In his Presidential address at the Bengal Provincial Hindu Conference at Tarakeswar on 4 April 1947 N.C. Chatterjee thus explained his party's acceptance of the Partition:

Our demand for partition today is . . . to prevent the disintegration of the nationalist element and to preserve Bengal's culture and to secure a Homeland for the Hindus of Bengal which will constitute a National State as a part of India and will afford real protection to the [Hindu] minority in East Bengal. . . . If Bengal Hindus want to be saved from extinction there is only one alterative for them—to create a strong self-reliant National State in Bengal comprising all the Hindu-majority areas. . . .[67]

On the other hand, the communal violence of 1946–7, although not directed against the Raj, undermined the strength of the British administration. The Viceroy Wavell himself admitted in November 1946: 'We could not expect the same degree of cooperation and support from the officials...we formerly enjoyed.'[68]

The Bengal Governor remained constantly worried about the possibility of the grievance of each community against the other being 'diverted into anti-British channels'.[69] In this historical conjuncture where a reconciliation with the idea of Partition by a broad spectrum of Indian political forces converged with a heightened British feeling of insecurity the way was prepared for, what one scholar has aptly called, the 'passive revolution' of 15 August 1947.[70] Such a settlement, distressing to the secular and progressive nationalists, was surely satisfying for the departing colonial masters.[71] Henceforth, the Bengal Hindu Mahasabha primarily concerned itself with the rehabilitation of Hindu refugees from East Bengal on lands secured from Hindu zamindars. It also tried to mobilize public opinion for such demands as amalgamation of Bengali-speaking territories of Bihar with West Bengal, the establishment of a Military Academy in West Bengal for military training of Bengali youth, adoption of Bande Mataram as national anthem, recognition of Bengali as one of India's state languages, and repeal of the Zamindari Abolition Act.

Letters intercepted by the police indicate that in villages bordering the then East Pakistan the Mahasabha organized a social boycott of 'those having Muslim sympathy'. Lawyers, teachers and disillusioned members of nationalist organizations joined the Mahasabha.[72] Weeklies like *Swastika* and such dailies as *Hindu Vani* kept alive the Hindu propaganda. In the aftermath of communal troubles in East Bengal in February/March 1950 Calcutta was afflicted with an influx of Hindu refugees from East Pakistan, the figure of which rose to 31.42 lakh by the end of 1958.[73] While a small part of this influx could be housed in government transit camps, the overwhelming majority settled in squatters, colonies along the fringes of the city. This prompted the Hindu Mahasabha to demand a 'wholesale transfer of population between the two Bengals along the Punjab line'.[74] These months also witnessed a spate of Hindu riotings against Muslims living in north and central Calcutta. There was a deeply felt suspicion that these had been organized by the Mahasabha activists and such bodies as Hindusthan National Guard and Hindu Shakti Sangha.[75] It would perhaps not be irrelevant to mention that although the Mahasabha was a critic of the

Congress at the national level the Party opted to cooperate with the Congress government in West Bengal against the 'growing Communist menace'.[76]

Conclusion: The Legacy of the Communal Challenge of the 1940s

The communalization of Bengal politics in the decade preceding the Partition stultified the potentialities of a left alternative that had been expressed through a spurt of agitational politics in 1945–6, the days which have been aptly described as 'The Almost Revolution'.[77] The Sarat Bose-Suhrawardy proposal for a sovereign Greater Bengal never took off the ground, thanks to concerted opposition from the Congress and the Mahasabha alike.[78] The communal upsurge of 1946–7 directly led to the Partition of Bengal which 'engineered' the 'psychological fragmentation of national ethos', a feeling aptly reflected in the films of Ritwik Ghatak and novels of Manik Bandopadhyay, Tarasankar Bandopadhyay, Bijon Bhattacharya, Jyotirmoyee Devi, Prafulla Roy, Sunil Ganguli and Samaresh Bose.

The instant response of Calcuttans to the presence of Hindu refugees from across the border was one of intense hate and horror. Already a congested city, Calcutta was plagued by an acute housing shortage, rising price-level, unemployment and epidemics. At one level the inhabitants of the metropolis generally tended to avoid contacts with the 'dirty unwanted crowd'. On the other hand, the West Bengalis attempted to culturally distance themselves from the East Bengalis. The 'us' and 'they' syndrome was clearly manifest. Dubbed as *Bangals,* the East Bengal refugees were negatively stereotyped as troublemakers, indolent, obstructive and demanding. There are stories of how in schools the teachers of West Bengal origin would address students from the other Bengal as EBs, as if they were to be segregated in the same manner as TB patients. The differential identities of East and West Bengalis were represented in the sporting world too when two clubs of the city—East Bengal and Mohun Bagan—came to symbolize the East Bengali and West Bengali sentiments. A fragmentation of identity within the Calcutta Hindus themselves had thus taken place.[79]

At the same time tensions between those Muslims who stayed back in West Bengal and the Hindus remained. The average Hindu, especially in Calcutta, tended to view a Muslim with suspicion, as if he/she was responsible for the partition of the motherland—little appreciating the risk of political uncertainty that the Muslim had undertaken by staying back in his native soil. On the other hand, the average Muslim, faced with an abnormally tense atmosphere, fell back, perhaps unconsciously, on the idea of Pakistan as 'the safe haven'. These mutually antagonistic feelings manifested themselves in the communal riotings of 1948, 1950 and 1964. Mention may also be made of the considerable number of votes secured by the Jana Sangh, Hindu Mahasabha and Ram Rajya Parishad in the legislative elections of 1952. Even during the national rejoicing at the liberation of Bangladesh in 1971 a section of Muslims in Bengal could not reconcile themselves to the dismemberment of Pakistan.

Fortunately, however, the communal challenge and its legacy analysed here did not result in communalism gaining an entrenched space in post-1947 Bengal politics. This has been largely due to the triumph of the Left in Bengal. The temporary hegemony of communalism over ideology and politics in 1946–7 was substituted by a dialectical relationship between community and class once India and Pakistan emerged as independent entities in the comity of nations. Yet, communalism often intervenes between class and nationalist politics in Bengal, a fact rudely driven home by the violence that shocked Calcutta following the demolition of Babri Masjid in December 1992.[80]

We however, need to emphasize that communalism in Bengal, nay Indian, history has never been a static phenomenon. Nor can communalism be seen, as some scholars would have us believe, a field of natural spontaneous subaltern political activity.[81] Instead, in the specific historical situation of India communalism has a determined antagonism with nationalism. The expression of Hindu revivalism and Pan-Indianism in Bengal also alternated between expressions of lower-class discontent, and anti-imperialism. Not surprisingly, barely five months after the riots of August 1946 the Hindu and Muslim students joined in the 'Hands off Vietnam' demonstration, the tramway men waged a successful 85 day strike under Communist leadership and workers in the Calcutta port downed their tools on more than one occasion. Communalism in the history of Bengal and India requires to be seen as a developing process which culminated in an individual's perception of himself or herself as primarily Hindu or Muslim, often either prior to or during a riot, whilst at other junctures loyalties of class or locality may intervene to obscure this overt communal self-perception. A Bengali or Indian Hindu is hardly solely or even largely motivated by hostility towards his/her Muslim brethren except at brief moments of violence. The fact that the Bharatiya Janata Party could not with its slogan of Hindutva make a headway in the recent Assembly polls of north India is yet another example to demonstrate that communal identity cannot be a permanent and decisive category in Indian political discourse and praxis. The communal challenge in Bengal politics that I have tried to delineate requires to be viewed in this continuum.

Notes

1. R. Kumar, 'The Structure of Politics in Nehru Memorial Museum and Library, Delhi. India on the Eve of Independence', *Occasional Papers on History and Society*, Second Series, Number XVI.
2. S. Das, *Communal Riots in Bengal 1905–1947*, Delhi,1991.
3. See R. Melson and H. Wolpe, 'Modernisation and the Politics of Communalism: a Theoretical Perspective', in *The American Political Science Review*, vol. 64, 1970; R. Naidu, *Communal Edge to Plural Societies*, New Delhi, 1980; K.W. Jones, 'Communalism in the Punjab', *Journal of Asian Studies*, vol. 28, 1968.
4. P. Dixit, *Communalism: A Struggle for Power*, New Delhi, 1974; R. Kothari, 'Communalism in India: The New Face of Democracy', *Lokayan*, June 1984.
5. B. Chandra, *Communalism in Modern India*, New Delhi, 1984.
6. Ibid.
7. *Naiya*, Calcutta, no. 1, Baisakh-Asad 1399 BS.
8. G. Pandey, *Construction of Communalism in Colonial North India*, Delhi, 1990.
9. M. Hasan, *Nationalism and Communal Politics in India 1885–1930*, Delhi, 1991. Also see M. Hasan's excellent Introduction in M. Hasan, ed., *India's Partition: Process, Strategy and Mobilization*, Delhi, 1993.
10. H. Mukhia, 'Communalism and the Writing of Medieval Indian History: A Reappraisal', in *Social Scientist*, vol. II, no. 8, 1983. Also see R. Thapar et al., *Communalism and the Writing of Indian History*, New Delhi, 1969 and P.C. Joshi, 'The Economic Background of Communalism in India—A Model of Analysis', in B.R. Nanda, ed., *Essays in Modern Indian History*, Delhi, 1980.
11. S. Bose, *Agrarian Bengal: Economy, Social Structure and Politics 1979–1947*, Cambridge, 1986.
12. S. Das, *Communal Riots,* op. cit.
13. C.A. Bayly, 'The pre-history of Communalism? Religious Conflict in India 1700–1860', in *Modern Asian Studies*, vol. 19, no. 2, 1985.
14. I also question the contention that there existed in India 'a well-defined set of ideas and ritualized behaviours underlying the religious conflict between Hindus and Muslims'. See Chapter 1 of this book.
15. See B. De and S. Das, 'Ethnic Revivalism: Problems in the Indian Union', in K.S. Singh, ed., *Ethnicity, Caste & People: India and the Soviet Union*, Delhi, 1992.
16. S. Das, *Communal Riots,* op. cit.
17. S. Sarkar, *Modern India 1885–1947*, Delhi, 1983.
18. *Report on the Administration of Bengal 1926–7,* pp. 24–5.
19. S. Das, *Communal Riots,* op. cit., pp. 31–2.
20. I. Stephens, *Pakistan*, London, 1964, pp. 124–8; I.H. Qureshi, *The Struggle for Pakistan, Karachi,* 1965; H. Bolitho, *Jinnah: Creator of Pakistani*, London, 1954, p. 164.
21. *Bengal Legislative Council Proceedings* (hereafter *BLCP*), 1941, vol. lix, no. 6, p. 216. One is reminded of similar assertions by the present BJP leadership.
22. This becomes clear from the files of the Bengal Hindu Mahasabha and the Bengal Provincial Congress Committee preserved in the Nehru Memorial

Museum and Library, New Delhi. Also see Joya Chatterji, *Bengal Divided: Hindu Communalism and Partition, 1932–1947,* Cambridge, 1994.

23. See C. Sarkar, *The Bengali Muslims: A Study in their Politicization 1912–1929,* Calcutta, 1991, and P. Chatterjee, *Bengal 1920–1947:* The Land Question, vol. 1, Calcutta, 1984.

24. Md. E.H. Khan, 'Role of the Ulema in Bengal Muslim Politics 1937–47', *Clio,* vol. 1, 1983.

25. Cited in ibid.

26. For details see S. Das, *Communal Riots,* op. cit.

27. See ibid., pp. 164–5.

28. See R. Ahmed, *The Bengal Muslims 1871–1906: A Quest for Identity,* Delhi, 1981.

29. S. Das, *Communal Riots,* op. cit.

30. The only major exception is the path-breaking work of Joya Chatterji. See J. Chatterjee, *Bengal Divided: Hindu Communalism and Partition 1932–1947,* Cambridge, 1994.

31. Calcutta Special Branch Records (hereafter SBR). According to rules the file number cannot be cited.

32. B.D. Graham, 'Shyama Prasad Mookherjee and the Communalist Alternative', in D.A. Low, ed., *Soundings in Modern South Asian History,* London, 1968.

33. SBR.

34. Ibid.

35. Ibid.

36. Ibid.

37. *Hindu Mahasabha Papers* (hereafter *HMP*), Nehru Memorial Library, File-p-107.

38. SBR Records.

39. *HMP*, File-p-55, 1945.

40. Ibid.

41. *HMP*, File-p-147, 1946.

42. *HMP*, File-p-32, 1944.

43. SBR.

44. Ibid.

45. SBR; *HMP*, File-p-116. In Calcutta the Mahasabha rallies were usually held at Shradhananda Park, Deshbandhu Park, Beadon Park and Kumartoli Park.

46. Ibid. This was repeatedly noticed in the Sunderbans.

47. SBR.

48. *HMP*, Sub File 86; SB Files.

49. *HMP*, Sub File 86.

50. SBR.

51. Ibid.

52. S. Das, *Communal Riots,* op. cit.

53. *HMP*, C-60 Pt. II.

54. SBR.

55. Extracts from the Report by the Commissioner of Police, Calcutta, on the Political Situation and Labour Unrest, West Serial Home (Poll) Department,

Writers Building, Calcutta (hereafter EPC) ending 10 August 1946; G.D. Khosla Stern Reckoning: a survey of the events before and following the partition of India, Delhi, 1952, p. 55.

56. S. Das, *Communal Riots,* op. cit., Ch. 6.

57. Ibid., p. 167.

58. Ibid.

59. D. Chakrabarty, *Rethinking Working-Class History: Bengal 1890–1940,* Delhi, 1989.

60. See Chapter 2 of this book.

61. Cited in ibid.

62. For details see S. Das, *Communal Riots,* op. cit.

63. SBR.

64. Cited in S. Das, *Communal Riots,* op. cit.

65. For an analysis of the Partition Riots see S. Das, *Communal Riots,* op. cit., Chapter 6.

66. See S.P. Mukherjee's statement of 19 March 1947, HMP Subject File 142.

67. *HMP,* 107. 1948.

68. N. Mansergh, ed., *India: The Transfer of Power 1942–7,* vol. lX, Document 70, p. 128.

69. R/3/2/58, India Office Records (hereafter lOR) Bengal Governor to the Viceroy, 6 November 1946.

70. S. Sarkar, 'Popular Movements, National Leadership and the Coming of Freedom with Partition 1945–47', in *Economic and Politicial Weekly,* Annual Number, 1982.

71. This is evident from the comment of John Smith, the Private Secretary to the Bengal Governor, cited in S. Das, *Communal Riots,* op. cit.

72. We have mention in police records names like Surya K. Nag of Vidyasagar College, Biryabrata Sinha of the INA and Manoranjan Chaudhuri of Servants of Bengal Society and a Congress activist as local organizers of the Mahasabha and the RSS. SBR.

73. J. Chakravorty, 'The Refugee Problem in West Bengal: The Government, The Opposition, The People 1947–1955', M.Phil. thesis, University of Calcutta, 1986; J. Chatterji, *The Spoils of Partition: Bengal and India 1947–1967,* Cambridge, 2007.

74. Shyama Prasad Mukherjee Papers (hereafter SMP), Nehru Memorial Library, Subject File 162.

75. SBR.

76. SBR.

77. G. Chattopadhyay, 'The Almost Revolution', in *Essays in Honour of Prof. S.C. Sarkar,* B. De et al., eds., Delhi, 1976. Also see S. Das, 'The Politics of Agitation: Calcutta 1912–1947', in S Chaudhuri, ed., *Calcutta: The Living City,* vol. II, Calcutta, 1990.

78. N.C. Chatterjee explained the Mahasabha's opposition to the Greater Bengal Plan thus: 'Some people are talking of Greater Bengal. They suffer from greater delusion. No one will be happier than myself if we can build up a Greater Bengal as an integral part of Great India as a self-respecting unit of the Indian Federation. But if Greater Bengal means Greater Pakistan then it will be

insanity to accept such a plan. What right have you to bring in millions of Hindus under a Pakistan Regime and to ask them to commit harikari with you under a communal rule?', *HMP*, File-p-107, 1948.

79. I have discussed the impact of the refugee influx on Calcutta in 'The Great Calcutta Killing and the Partition of Bengal', in *Calcutta, 1905–1971: Au coeur des creations et des revoltes du siècle,* J.L. Racine, ed., Paris, 1997.

80. For an analysis of this riot see S. Das, 'Kalkatar Danga: Itihaser Drishtite'(in Bengali), *Desh,* 27 February 1993.

81. See the interview with G. Bhadra, *Naiya,* op. cit.

CHAPTER 4

THE 1992 CALCUTTA RIOT IN HISTORICAL CONTINUUM: A RELAPSE INTO 'COMMUNAL FURY'?

CALCUTTA'S FAILURE TO insulate itself from the communal hysteria that plagued the length and breadth of India in the aftermath of the demolition of Babri Masjid on 6 December 1992[1] came as a rude shock to the city's intelligentsia.[2] True, the Great Calcutta Killing of August 1946 had initiated a vicious circle of communal rioting in the subcontinent climaxing in the 'truncated settlement' of 15 August 1947.[3] The events of 1946–7 were viewed by left-wing intellectuals as a defeat of radicalism in post-Second World War Bengal politics. But the structural disarticulation between class and politics experienced during these Partition days was rapidly bridged in the western half of British Bengal that came to form a part of the Indian union. While other regions of India continued to be struck by periodic bouts of Hindu-Muslim violence, West Bengal remained relatively free of the communal virus. Calcutta, its capital city, emerged as the crucible of the country's left and democratic politics. The metropolis became the living embodiment of a composite and syncretic culture which enabled people of various castes and creeds to coexist with amity. This eclectic and secular tradition, however, received a jolt when, between 7 and 10 December 1992, the metropolis was thrown out of gear by large-scale organized rioting, the intensity of which was only second to the 1946 carnage. Many wondered if Bengal would be the new partner in 'cow-belt politics'.[4] Fortunately, this has proved to be an illusion.

Apparently, the December violence in Calcutta had marks of a communal outbreak. The disturbed areas were filled with cries of 'Alla ho Akbar' and 'Jai Ram'; mixed localities were usually fields of rioting; rumours of

*This paper was published in *Modern Asian Studies*, vol. 34, no. 2, 2000, pp. 281–306.

desecration of temples and mosques and molestation of women by members of the rival community gained wide circulation; in households or small gatherings the survivors from the Partition Riots recounted stories of those gruesome days which added fuel to the smouldering fire. We are yet to gain access to official papers on this spate of violence. A careful scrutiny of available evidence, however, indicates that although the 1992 outbreak was triggered off by the Ayodhya episode, it was qualitatively different from previous communal outbursts experienced in Calcutta. While the Great Calcutta Killing of 1946 was marked by an explosion of the politics of communal identity, the last outbreak rather reflected multiple layers of contradictions arising from not too perfect a process of urbanization in post-colonial Calcutta. An analysis of continuity and change in the pattern of Hindu-Muslim riots in Calcutta between 1946 and 1992 will perhaps bring out these differences.

Calcutta and the 'Communal Prelude' to the Transfer of Power

The first major Hindu-Muslim rioting in twentieth-century Calcutta occurred in 1918. Subsequently in 1926 and then in 1946–7 the city witnessed communal explosions. But these outbreaks were not similar in nature. The pre-1940 eruptions were relatively unorganized, autonomous of organized politics and reflected a strong class connotation, being essentially expressions of discontent amongst the city's subordinate Muslim population against the privileged Hindu social groups. But the 1946–7 turbulence was highly organized, overtly communal, linked with institutional politics, and manifested an explosive fusion of communal and national consciousness.[5]

The 1946 Calcutta riot occurred in the context of Muslim League's rejection of the Cabinet Mission proposals[6] and proclamation of a Direct Action Day on 16 August.[7] Despite opposition from the Bengal Congress, the Muslim League Chief Minister, H.S. Suhrawardy, declared a public holiday on 16 August and addressed an excited rally on that afternoon.[8] On the other hand, Hindu public opinion was mobilized around the *Akhand Hindusthan* (United India) slogan. The Congress leaders in Bengal were not necessarily Hindu communalists. But since most of the party's support came from Hindus, a section of the Congressmen imbibed a strong sense of Hindu identity, especially in view of the perceived threat from the Pakistan movement. Such mobilization along communal lines was partly successful due to a concerted propaganda campaign which, as I have demonstrated elsewhere, resulted in a 'legitimization of communal solidarities'.[9] Widespread

Hindu–Muslim rioting struck Calcutta between 16 and 19 August, leaving behind at least 4,000 dead and 100,000 wounded.[10] The worst affected region was the densely populated central northern sections of the city (Map 4.1). In the words of an English official, Calcutta was a 'cross between the worst of London air raids and the Great Plague'.[11]

The 1946 'Calcutta Killing' was unequivocally communal. Collective violence during the preceding Calcutta riots was directed against symbols

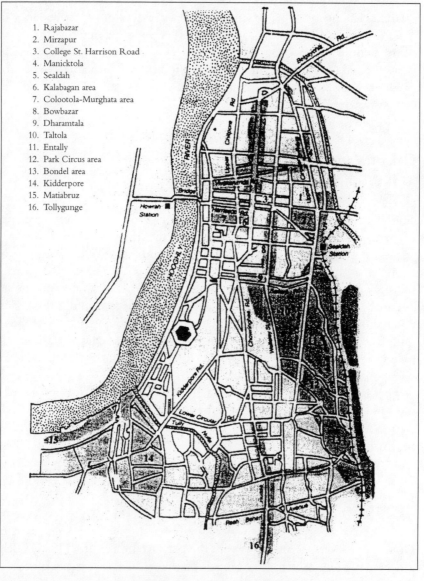

1. Rajabazar
2. Mirzapur
3. College St. Harrison Road
4. Manicktola
5. Sealdah
6. Kalabagan area
7. Coolootola-Murghata area
8. Bowbazar
9. Dharamtala
10. Taltola
11. Entally
12. Park Circus area
13. Bondel area
14. Kidderpore
15. Matiabruz
16. Tollygunge

MAP 4.1: Areas affected by riots in Calcutta in 1946.

Source: Reel 5 of 23, US State Dept. Files of Internal Affairs.

of class and colonial oppression. For British officials, the 1946 riotous crowd was 'menacing' too, but, to their relief, did not demonstrate any hostility either against the government or Europeans. While the rich Marwaris of central and north Calcutta were the main targets of the 1918 and 1926 rioters, the victims in 1946 were mostly subordinate social groups. This does not, however, mean property in shops and houses was not destroyed during the 1946 riot. But very few of the 'better classes' suffered physically. Women of both communities were also subjected to 'severe assaults', something which did not occur earlier on a large scale.

In the history of Calcutta's communal violence the lootings in 1946 acquired a distinct political dimension for the first time. This was evident from Muslim attacks on the establishments of Congress leaders, pro-Congress newspapers and such nationalist Muslims as the former Speaker of the Bengal legislature, Syed Naushar Ali. Yet another novel aspect of the Great Calcutta Killing was attacks and murders committed by small groups. The emphasis now was on revenge and control over the enemy's body; the aim was to cause the greatest possible humiliation, pain and suffering. In many respects the killings were conscious or unconscious imitations of particular rites of violence of the rival community. For instance, when young Hindu boys were killed inside a mosque a gruesome travesty of the Hindu ritual of sacrificing animals inside temples was performed. In the history of Calcutta there is no previous record of such sadistic violence when all rational norms were at a discount.

The other distinguishing feature of the 1946 riot was its organized nature. The Muslim League mobilized its frontal organizations to make the Direct Action Day a success, and once the riot started it used the government machinery to help its supporters. Amongst Hindus the Marwari merchants had purchased as 'a precautionary measure' arms and ammunitions from American soldiers which were later used during the riot. Acid bombs were manufactured and stored in Hindu-owned factories long before the outbreak. Interestingly, the Muslim and Hindu rioting crowd adopted similar strategies in perpetrating violence. The looted booty was carried to waiting lorries for transportation to a central place; shops were carefully marked with signs so that the crowd left untouched the establishments of their co-religionists; both League and Hindu activists used Red Cross badges to evade police detection. Perhaps at the height of antagonism the Hindu and Muslim rioting crowd became impregnated with cross-fertilization of ideas on collective conduct wherein one imitated the other—a trend noticed during the sixteenth-century Catholic-Protestant riots in France.

A broad element of continuity can, however, be noticed in the composition of the rioting crowd. Hindu and Muslim rioters still consisted predominantly of the lower social strata, especially the upcountrymen inhabiting the northern part of Calcutta. Goondas (toughs)—that umbrella term used in official discourse to denote a broad spectrum of social groups ranging from various marginalized groups to habitual criminals—emerged as organizers of violence once the riot gained in momentum.[12] Links between these goondas—Hindu and Muslim alike—and organized politics were clear. People who would not normally publicly associate themselves with such groups now consorted with them and followed their leadership. The only new ingredient amongst the 1946 rioters was the presence of Bengali middle class Hindus, who for the first time joined hands with their upcountry co-religionists in significant numbers.

Communal frenzy fomented by the Great Calcutta Killing spread to Noakhali, Tippera, Bihar, UP, and finally the Punjab. In Calcutta itself sporadic killings continued till the eve of Independence. Amidst this melee the inevitability of Partition gained a general acceptance.[13] Nevertheless, the aftermath of the 1946–7 riots occasioned the 'finest hour' in Gandhi's political career when the Mahatma refused to join the official hoisting of the tricolour in Delhi and preferred to spend time with the people of Calcutta to stem the tide of communal animosities.

Calcutta and the Communal Challenge in Post-Colonial Indian Politics

The departing colonial power as well as the new rulers of India and Pakistan had hoped that the Partition of the subcontinent along religious lines would restore amity between Hindus and Muslims. But this was a misplaced optimism—thanks to the recrudescence of riots in India and oppression of the Hindu minority population in East Pakistan. Communalism, however, failed to gain an entrenched space in post-1947 Calcutta politics. This can be explained partly by the mobilization of refugees settled in Calcutta around secular politics, and partly by the triumph of the Left in West Bengal. Yet, communal animosities did intervene between class and nationalist politics in West Bengal.[14] The first major riot to shake post-Independence Calcutta occurred in January 1964.

The 1964 Turmoil

The immediate context of the 1964 riot was the sudden disappearance of a holy relic from Kashmir's sacred Hazratbal mosque in the last week of December 1963.[15] A rumour gained ground amongst Muslims of the subcontinent that the desecration was a deliberate Hindu act. The communal undercurrent that resulted, first burst forth through Hindu-Muslim clashes in Jabbalpur (Madhya Pradesh). Almost simultaneously in early January 1964 serious communal violence affected the districts of Khulna and Jessore in East Pakistan, provoked largely by the Pakistan government's anti-India tirade over the Hazratbal incident. The Calcutta disturbance between 10 and 13 January needs to be situated in this context.[16]

The train of events began with the spread of reports of Muslim atrocities on Hindus in East Pakistan. Resentment of Calcutta Hindus had its first violent manifestation in the late hours of 8 January when some Muslim stalls in Sealdah (central Calcutta) were pulled down. On 9 January, meetings were held in different parts of the city to protest against the majority community's highhandedness on the other side of Bengal's national boundary. A large procession marched to the office of the Deputy High Commissioner of East Pakistan, demanding protection for the Hindu minority in East Pakistan, and punishment of those responsible who had spearheaded the disturbance in Khulna and Jessore. On this occasion processionists burnt effigies of the Pakistan President Ayub Khan. The crisis was precipitated when in the evening a procession, consisting mostly of Hindu students, voicing anger at the recent happenings in East Bengal, was unexpectedly attacked with sodawater bottles, lathies (sticks) and brickbats at an important crossing in central Calcutta.[17] An instant heightening of communal animosity followed. For it was automatically assumed that the procession had been assailed by Muslims of the locality. The same night a Hindu was stabbed to death.

On 10 January Hindu students of Calcutta schools and colleges boycotted their classes, organized rallies and then marched to the office of the Pakistani Deputy High Commissioner from various points of the city to express solidarity with their co-religionists in Khulna and Jessore. Police interception of such processions resulted in clashes with the excited crowd. The most unfortunate incident took place in Garia (south Calcutta) when police entered the precincts of Dinabandhu Andrews College, apparently to restrain a 'disorderly assembly', but got involved in a confrontation with the agitated gathering. Subsequent police firing claimed the life of Bhudeb Sen, a first year B.A. student. This part of the city had a sizeable presence of East Bengali refugees and the news of police action was instantly interpreted by them as a sign of the Bengal Government's lack of sympathy with the 'Hindu cause' in East Pakistan. The ensuing strain resulted in sporadic Hindu-Muslim clashes during the next two days.

Throughout 11 and 12 January disorder prevailed in the section of Calcutta bounded by Amherst Street, Sealdah, Taltola, Entally, Beniapukur, Beliaghata and Garia[18] (Map 4.2). Incidentally, some parts of this region were among the most badly hit zones during the Great Calcutta Killing. But in sharp contrast to that riot the violence this time was not characterized by clashes between two groups of rival communities. Instead, its dominant trend was arson, looting and secret stabbings. It is thus not surprising that

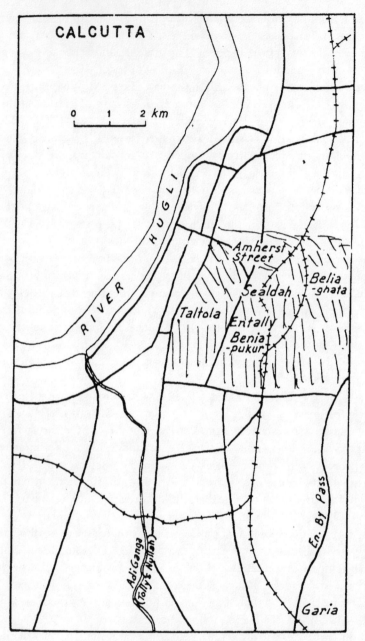

MAP 4.2: Areas affected by the 1964 riots.

while most of the deaths in 1946 were caused by rioting, in 1964 among the 82 who lost their lives 44 had succumbed to police/army bullets.[19] Nor was there any desecration of temples or mosques in 1964. Also there was no incidence of molestation of women. The 1946 rioters were connected with organized politics, but no such link can be discerned in 1964. Even the student protest which ended with communal rioting did not have any distinct political leadership, although such Hindu revivalist organizations as the Hindu Mahasabha constantly tried to foment communal discord.[20]

Some Hindu bustees (slums) in eastern Calcutta were ransacked during the 1964 riot. But generally Muslims bore the brunt of violence.[21] The worst to suffer were Muslim slums along the Sealdah-Ballygunge railway line, many of which were razed to the ground and their inhabitants driven out.[22] While 262 Muslims were injured during the riot, the corresponding figure for Hindus was 117.[23]

As in 1946, the Calcutta underworld was active during the 1964 riot. The crowd was armed with guns, rifles, revolvers, bombs and acid bulbs. Opposition leaders alleged police inaction when 'registered Hindu goondas' looted Muslim houses and shops.[24] Bengali middle class Hindus—whose participation in communal violence first surfaced seriously in 1946—also made their presence felt in the course of the riot. The impact of the riot in 1964 spilled over to the neighbouring districts of Hooghly, 24 Parganas, Nadia and Howrah which reminded one of how the Great Calcutta Killing was followed by the Noakhali-Tippera outburst.

In one significant respect, however, the 1964 episode marked a departure in the pattern of Calcutta's communal rioting. While the 1946 tragedy was rooted in the dialectics of Bengal's political process, the 1964 tumult was not only a fallout of a happening in far-off Kashmir, but a reaction to events across the border. Presumably, Pakistani agents even instigated the riot.[25] Once the news of Hindu suffering in Khulna and Jessore became public, the Deputy High Commissioner of Pakistan in Calcutta along with his officials frequented the city's Muslim areas reportedly to incite communal feelings amongst their co-religionists.[26] It is thus not without significance that on many occasions the Muslim crowd shouted 'Pakistan zindabad' (long live Pakistan).[27] The police suspected that firearms used by Muslim slumdwellers of central Calcutta were provided by Pakistani instigators.[28] Such rumours as the one that West Bengal was being incorporated within East Pakistan also caught the mind of a section of Calcutta Muslims, and drove them astray. It is difficult to assess the veracity of direct Pakistani complicity in provoking communal tensions in Calcutta in 1964. But the fact remains that the Calcutta episode was largely a response to communal incidents in East Pakistan. Provocative and misleading reports on the disorder in Calcutta were also published in Pakistani newspapers.[29]

Normalcy in Calcutta was restored on 13 January, but not before the military had been deployed to help the civil authorities; 6,870 persons were arrested in the city itself on rioting charges. The Union Home Minister had to fly down to Calcutta to supervise the restoration of order. The then opposition leader Jyoti Basu, however, criticized the police for its 'intelligence failure' and 'inept handling' of the situation.[30] Appointment of a judicial enquiry commission to probe the rioting was also demanded but the government refused.[31] This governmental rigidity and the failure to publish any official report on the events between 9 and 12 January left a lurking suspicion in many minds about the government's inability to rise to the occasion. Nevertheless, the 1964 riot did not reflect the same degree of overt communalism or organized looting witnessed in 1946. The impact of the 1964 violence on Bengali society was also not far-reaching, in sharp contrast to that of the Great Calcutta Killing which survives in the form of collective memories.

Anatomy of the 1992 Outbreak: Continuity or Change in the Pattern of Communal Violence?

Once the dust of the 1992 outbreak settled, it became increasingly doubtful if Calcutta's rioting crowd was driven solely by communal animosities. The demolition of the Babri Masjid did instil a feeling of insecurity amongst the city's Muslim communitiy. But the type of violence between 7 and 10 December did not indicate Muslim wrath against any and every Hindu of the city. Similarly, the Hindu crowd was not driven by an overarching anti-Muslim sentiment. The Calcutta Police chief himself testified to an absence of the 'classical pattern of rioting' in the form of stabbings, knife slashes and open collisions between rival communities, although stray cases of desecrating religious spots were reported.[32] In the words of a press correspondent, 'the common people of either community had not lost themselves in the frenzy'.[33] Like the 1964 outbreak, the emphasis of rioting in 1992 was not on physical assaults but on looting, arson and destruction of property. Molestation of women was not reported, although snatching of gold necklaces and bangles was not unknown. The 'brutalization of human consciousness', which had dominated the 1946 carnage and manifested itself in the recent post-Ayodhya outbreaks in Bombay (Maharashtra) and Surat (Gujarat), was not characteristic of the last Calcutta outbreak. Not unnaturally, the majority of those killed during this riot—the estimate of which varies between the official figure of 33 and an unofficial count of 50[34]—lost their lives from police/military firing, a feature reminiscent of the 1964 outbreak.[35] It is equally revealing that the 'traditional' riot zone of Calcutta—Rajabazar, Kidderpore, Kalabagan, Zacharia Street, Keshab Sen Street, Chitpur and Moulali (Maps 4.1 and 4.2)—remained outside the parameters of the 'unsettled zone' in 1992. Instead, the violence was concentrated in the city's south-west and eastern sectors comprising Metiabruz, Garden Reach, Park Circus, Tangra, Tapsia, Tiljala and Beniapukur slums[36] (Map 4.3). The social

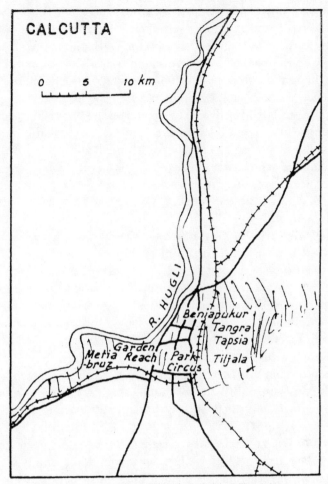

MAP 4.3: Areas affected by the 1992 riots.

context of this rioting was distinct too. The 1992 outbreak thus needs to be located within the trajectories of social transformation in contemporary Calcutta. Incidentally, unlike in 1946 and 1964, the violence in 1992 remained a strictly Calcutta affair. Even such sensitive districts in the state as Nadia, Murshidabad and Malda maintained communal amity.[37]

Within Metiabruz-Garden Reach itself a core area of rioting can be deciphered: Badartala, Bhangakhal, Kanchantala, Nimtala, Nadial Lichubagan and Kashyap Para. This enclave is predominantly Muslim. Hindus here constitute about 20 per cent of the populace. They mostly live in slums which their Bengali and Bihari Muslim neighbours torched and smashed to secure their evictions;[38] 447 families lost their homes.[39] Some slum-dwellers were burnt to death.[40] In the words of a press reporter: 'Metiabruz had all the appearance of a ghost town with the smouldering debris telling tales of the orgy of violence that had rocked this area. . . .'[41] The way attacks on police were coordinated to prevent their intervention on behalf of the victims revealed a high degree of organization. Telephone links with local police camps were snapped; attempts were made to blow up police pickets with gas cylinders. While rioting in 1946 continued throughout the day, the 1992 violence was inevitably committed in the late hours of the night.

Calcutta's eastern fringe affected by the violence—Tangra, Tiljala, Entally, Park Circus, Karaya and Taltala—experienced a systematic assault on Muslim slums in Bibibagan, Dhobiatala, Motijhil, and Meher Ali Lane, a large number of which were reduced to heaps of rubble. The modus operandi of the crowd was strikingly similar. It had 'the stamp of meticulous planning'. In all instances the rampage was initiated between 10 and 10.30 p.m. Each raid was generally of a short duration. Rioters entered the targeted areas in lorries or vans, armed with bombs, pipe-guns, lathies, rods and other lethal weapons. Red and green signals were used to direct the attacks.[42] On many occasions an organized dissemination of provocative rumours preceded the actual act of rioting.[43] A vernacular daily captured a typical rioting scene in east Calcutta thus: 'A shrill whistle. Immediately after that the sound of one or two bomb blasts, Within a few minutes the crowd group together and advance hurling bombs, setting the area ablaze and looting whatever comes in the way.'[44]

A correspondent of *The Statesman* (Calcutta, 10 December 1992) recounted the aftermath of a crowd running amuck: 'The fog swirled thick, the police helmets and shreds of glass left after an evening attack glinted under the street lamps'. *Ananda Bazar Patrika* (Calcutta) of 11 December 1992 portrayed Tangra, Tapsia and Tiljala thus: 'Burnt slums, streets appearing like scorched paddy fields, air filled with sounds of bomb blasts and thousands of people searching for shelter.' The same paper commented how such scenes reminded of many pictures of the recent Gulf War that had been beamed through the television. According to one estimate, 850 families of Tangra were displaced who sought shelter in a neighbouring slaughterhouse or a girls' school.[45] History, as a journalist of *The Telegraph* (Calcutta, 12 December 1992) remarked, repeated 'itself with a bitter twist' when ten families took refuge in the very house where Gandhi had gone on fast to stem the tide of communal disaffection in 1947.[46]

The then minister-in-charge of Information, Government of West Bengal, admitted that the manner in which the disturbance started almost simultaneously in the six thanas (police stations) of East Calcutta and slums were set ablaze with remarkable speed indicated the presence of 'an invisible hand' behind the turmoil.[47] This was true for the Metiabruz-Garden Reach sector as well. The police, too, viewed the riot as a part of a 'broader plot'.[48] Who was behind this conspiracy is difficult to identify. But it appears that 'promoters'[49] played a crucial role in inflaming the riot whose victims, as has been already indicated, were slum-dwellers.[50] Their obvious aim was to clear the bustees for construction projects.

Since the beginning of 1980, Metiabruz had developed as West Bengal's primary outpost of retail trade in garments. Metiabruz today resonates with the continuous chatter of sewing machines; every day, merchants converge here from all parts of the province to secure garments at wholesale prices. This economic prosperity gradually inflated real estate prices in the area, and currently the cost of one *kottah* (720 sq. ft.) of land range between Rs. 8 lakh and Rs. 10 lakh. A shop as small as 30 sq. ft. can yield Rs. 2 lakh.[51]

Responding to this phenomenal rise in the demand for space, a group of non-Bengali promoters had been trying to purchase old buildings, to construct multi-storeyed structures or modern airconditioned shopping complexes in their place and rent them out at a high rate.[52] Significantly, families such as those like Mahesh Agarwal's who did not succumb to this move had their houses burnt during the riot.[53] Similarly, shops whose Hindu owners remained determined to hold on to their forts, were gutted.[54] The expectation was that once such people were forced to abandon their establishments the realtors would have 'an easy way to rake in the fast buck'.[55]

In organizing the violence the promoters allegedly used their 'cosy links' with local politicians and prominent garment business owners.[56] But their real 'stormtroopers' were homeless Bangladeshi Muslim day-labourers.[57] Acquainted with the topography of the area, rioters 'kept entering the lanes and by-lanes, set houses ablaze, looted and escaped before the Army could intervene'.[58] The design of realtors yielded fruits. Descendants of such traditional Hindu landed magnates as Chandrasekhar Roy, Swapan Roy and Sundarlal Roy thus unequivocally told a journalist: 'No more. We will now sell our land and house and leave.'[59] Small grocers like Mahesh Agarwal, too, resolved to do the same.[60]

Rioting in Garden Reach was also connected with a lucrative land market. For the last five years this part of Calcutta had become the settling-ground for Muslim immigrants from Bangladesh and the neighbouring districts of Bihar. These migrants provide the manpower for the brisk smuggling trade centring around the Calcutta port which has enriched them. But their presence has caused a boom in the land market of this locality. Well-built housing complexes are fast coming up on both sides of the main road and the pressure on land continues to rise. Bustees like Lichubagan can alone provide new space for developmental projects. Incidentally, these were the prime targets of the violent crowd.

A convergence of commercial interests with religious fervor was equally explicit in eastern Calcutta. Dhobiatala bustee (also known as Dhobiatala Muslim camp)—housing 1,006 families—has its origin linked to the 1964 riot. Established to rehabilitate 48 riot-torn Muslim families, the number of its inhabitants rose by 1992 to 5,000, of whom 4,543 are Muslims, 450 Hindus and 7 Christians.[61] They make their ends meet as carters, rickshaw-pullers, ganja (marijuana) dealers and day-labourers. Situated along Calcutta's main sewerage canal, Mir Meher Ali Lane slum is extremely unhygenic into which are crammed an estimated 3,000 dwellers. Here the ratio between the two communities is almost equal, although Muslims tend to be compressed on the eastern side of the slum. Inhabitants of this bustee eke out their living either as construction workers or rag-pickers. Some work in factories.[62] Inmates of Bibibagan bustee, predominantly Muslims, are relatively well-off. Many of them are connected with rubber, plastic and leather manufacturing units.[63]

None of these slums had betrayed communal tensions in recent times. When on 9 December they were 'battered relentlessly by mobs on the rampage and smoke sneaked upwards from burning (huts) . . .',[64] the residents were naturally taken aback. The septuagenarian Abdul Rahim Khan, a witness to both 1946 and 1964 riots, exclaimed: 'I don't know what happened. Everything was so peaceful . . .',.[65] A clue to this riddle can, however, be found when the 1992 episode is viewed against the background of an increasing scramble for land following the growth of the tannery and leather industry in that locality. Not unnaturally, Dhobiatala bustee—encompassing at least 15 bighas of land whose occupants do not possess tenancy or possession certificates[66]—constitutes a prime site for estate developers. In the pre-riot days a group of promoters are thus said to have offered each dweller in Dhobiatala Rs. 20,000 as an incentive to desert their huts.[67] It is not a matter of sheer coincidence that during the December violence this bustee was disfigured beyond recognition. Even after order was restored, some drug pedlars tried to prevent the return of its residents[68]—a clear indication that the clearing of the bustee, more than anything, had been the primary objective of those who had organized the riot. Tenancy rights in the other two slums are relatively secured. But here too the rioters were primarily concerned with the expropriation of a predominantly Muslim population.

Many analysts have thus suggested a 'promoter-criminal-police nexus' behind the December violence.[69] Local 'anti-socials' and a section of the police were allegedly ready accomplices of promoters. In some cases old rivalry between 'anti-socials' themselves—unconnected with communal tension—sparked off violence.[70] The goondas, whose presence had been so marked during the Great Calcutta Killing, were significantly absent during the 1964 disturbances. But the 'anti-social element' was restored in the 1992 violence.[71] Commentators have sought to accord political identities to this underworld.[72] But such exercises have not produced convincing results. Metiabruz, Garden Reach and Tangra had become 'victims of the venality of a criminal syndicate . . . hand in glove with the administration and the powers that be over the years'.[73] Besides, undercover activities of Sikh terrorists, Kashmiri militants and Pakistani secret service interlopers had kept high the communal fervour amongst such sections of the metropolitan society.[74] It was these social groups which were primarily responsible for arson and looting during the December riot.[75]

What is, however, equally, and perhaps more, distressing is the reported ventilation of anti-Muslim feelings by some members of the Calcutta Police which is not only overwhelmingly Hindu but has a strong presence of upcountrymen. For instance, 150 Muslim youths arrested from Metiabruz were subjected to inhuman torture and forced to chant 'Jai Sri Ram'.[76] Communalization of the police and paramilitary forces had already taken place in the Hindi heartland, but West Bengal had kept herself free of it. Allegations of police joining the looting spree, remaining silent spectators and displaying communal preference—if true—should sound alarm bells for those who run the government in West Bengal.

In tune with all preceding Calcutta riots, the upcountrymen—Hindu and Muslim alike—were particularly restive in 1992. A separate study needs to be undertaken to explain the retention of a strong communal identity by this social segment. This can perhaps be accounted for by the fact that these upcountrymen have failed to integrate themselves with the ethos of Calcutta. For this again the cultural superiority complex beneath a secular exterior amongst the educated Bengali Hindu middle class is largely responsible. In this context the plight of Bihari Muslims—whose presence in Metiabruz-Garden Reach area has been steadily increasing owing to their influx from Bangladesh—deserves attention. Discriminated against as 'intruders', and denied opportunities of secure employment, they find solace from mullahs (Muslim religious preachers) and seek 'strength from strong kinship bonds which only religious loyalty can provide'.[77] The young among them get reconciled with 'rowdyism' as the only means of livelihood, becoming followers of local musclemen like Mughal and Jhunnu.[78] This segment of the Calcutta society expressed its social discontent by joining the December violence. A newspaper survey thus referred to a popular feeling that rioting was generally committed by 'non-Bengali Bihari toughs'.[79]

'Reactionary foreign powers' are also suspected of having provoked the disorder, aiming to destabilize the 'bastion of Leftism in the subcontinent'. For instance, pictures of 'burning Calcutta' transmitted by the BBC through the Star TV network on the night of 9 December proved highly provocative. Immediately after this television programme the riot spread with alarming alacrity. Reference has accordingly been made to a deliberate internationalization of the Ayodhya episode to undermine the national integrity of India.[80] Besides, Pakistan's secret service, the Inter Service

Intelligence, appears to have vitiated the communal relations in Calcutta through a 'whisper campaign'. The Special Branch of Calcutta Police had reportedly brought this fact to the attention of 'concerned authorities' and warned of an outbreak 'in certain pockets of the city if the Babri Masjid was damaged'.[81] But this warning went unheeded.[82]

The above discussion has hopefully demonstrated that the Calcutta outbreak of December 1992 was not necessarily a communal riot *per se*, although its eruption had a link with the tension following the demolition of Babri Masjid. A communal distemper was certainly present during those turbulent days. Stories of desecration of places of worship, capture of Lalbazar (Calcutta Police headquarters), heaps of dead-bodies lying on the streets, and cutting off one of women's breasts were systematically circulated to excite the sentiments of both communities.[83] While stories of the destruction of Muslim property antagonized the Muslims, the fear of losing their traditional authority aroused Hindu sensibilities. Yet, the actual nature of rioting did not manifest the heightened communalism of the 1946 variety. Neither can we detect the involvement of Hindutva and Muslim fundamentalist forces in the way it was experienced during the recent Hyderabad and north Indian riots.[84] Nor do we notice in Calcutta 'the foregrounding of the militantly communal women' which has been a 'sinister' aspect of the Hindutva movement in Upper India.[85]

What actually took place in 1992 was a land-grabbing riot under a communal garb.[86] The real estate developer-'anti-social' nexus sought to exploit the post-Ayodhya communal uneasiness in seizing stretches of land occupied by particular slums. While the riot left untouched the upper classes of either community, the subordinate Hindu and Muslim social groups were its prey. A Muslim slum-dweller of Tangra thus reiterated: 'They [looters] do not belong to any community. They are looters.'[87] Bustees were defaced, but prosperous buildings stood intact. The reverse had been the trend during pre-1940 communal riots in Calcutta, while in 1946 the rich and poor alike suffered from the carnage. A recent study has also demonstrated how the 'riot-hit areas generally coincided with the areas of the concentration of the informal sector' which provide the Calcutta poor with their main means of livelihood.[88] Moreover, if communalism alone had motivated the 1992 violence it should have spread to Calcutta's outskirts which 'are stated to be sputtering on a short fuse, thanks to the incessant inflow of refugees from across the borders, the bulk of them being Muslim'.[89] But this did not happen.

Even in the heat of rioting the communal animus in 1992 Calcutta was not pervasive. Press reports are replete with instances of courage—and conviction of people who considered preservation of human feelings more important than demolishing religious institutions. In Zacharia Street local Muslims resisted the desecration of an old temple; in Metiabruz five Muslim brothers saved 170 Hindu lives, risking the wrath of their coreligionists; in a workers' colony in Lichubagan, Muslims saved their Hindu colleagues by locking the gates and standing on guard; in Bibibagan Muhammad Sukur and Abdul Rashid left their own sleeping places on the pavement for a Hindu family; in Kamarhati (an outlying area of Calcutta) five young Muslim boys induced their community to frustrate an intended attack on the famous Vishalakshmi temple.[90] Joint Hindu-Muslim patrols were also organized to curb the spread of riot in Garden Reach.[91] The activists of local labour organizations in east Calcutta—especially those belonging to untouchable castes—resisted the strikes on bustees. Ramesh Tiwari, a leader of the Communist Party of India, sacrificed his life in trying to save the inmates of a burning hut. The former State Committee member of the Communist Party of India (Marxist), Nepaldeb Bhattacharya, was severely injured while restraining an excited crowd.[92] Again, 50 workers of a small factory in Ultadanga (east Calcutta) belonging to both communities organized a round-the-clock vigil of a local bustee and supplied foodstuffs and other essentials to its besieged inhabitants.[93] Joint efforts of secular and democratic parties succeeded in maintaining peace in many mixed and otherwise sensitive areas.[94]

Conclusion: Popular Consciousness and Communal Riots in Calcutta

This essay considers riots as eruptions which disrupt the normal tenor of life. Yet, they are significant entry points for analysis of social tensions in a historical continuum. Taking the Great Calcutta Killing of 1946 as a reference point I have thus tried to study in a comparative framework what is believed to be the worst riot in post-colonial Calcutta. Pandey's recent sophisticated intervention in the historiography of popular violence in modern India has rightly questioned some of the traditional assumptions.[95] The present argument is not in disagreement with this position. What is, however, unacceptable is the charge that the existing literature has tended to 'homogenize and normalize "national" cultures and histories'.[96] It is not an idle claim that a study of riots can bring historians closer to popular emotions, passions, and anguish with all its diversities. This 'historian's history' is not necessarily an exercise of homogenization but represents an 'attack on the unknown', a fulfilment of the historian's responsibility to unfold events and episodes in their minutest details. After all, reconstruction of popular perceptions of a riot has to be undertaken in the context of the structure of the violence itself.

I have shown elsewhere how the 1946–7 riots in Calcutta fractured Bengali consciousness at two levels: by crystallizing Hindu and Muslim identities on one hand, and reinforcing the 'us' and 'them' syndrome between West Bengalis (*Ghati*) and East Bengalis (*Bangal*) on the other. Even today, the 1946 riot is the yardstick, especially for its survivors, in assessing the intensity of communal violence of recent times. In 1946 communalization of politics reached its high point, damaging considerably the possibilities of a Left alternative that was slowly emerging from a spate of protest politics in 1945–6.[97] Once the Sarat Bose-Suhrawardy move for a sovereign Greater Bengal failed to take off, the second partition of British Bengal along religious lines appeared as the only available option.[98] In the wake of the Partition a large influx of Hindu refugees from East Bengal into Calcutta imposed a severe strain on the city's material resources and generated contradictions between the native Calcuttans and new settlers.[99] At the same time while a section of Calcutta Hindu elites was reluctant to accept the presence of Muslims amidst them, many Muslims of the province in their turn, perhaps without much thought, looked to Pakistan as a safe haven. The agonies of such fragmented consciousness are reflected in the films of Ritwik Ghatak and the writings of Bijon Bhattacharya, Atin Bandopadhyay, Sankar and Samaresh Bose.

Although not identical, the 1992 riot was no less shocking to sensitive minds. The distinguished literateur, Sunil Ganguly, expressed this anguish when he wrote: 'Can literature bring about social change? For a long time I have been writing against religious conservatism through poems, stories and novels. For this I have been condemned as a Muslim stooge. . . . Yet the task of the writer is to write, hoping that the mind of some can at least be transformed. But at this hour of crisis this belief itself tends to get lost.'[100]

For the Metiabruz businessman Shibnath Ghosh who lost all he had purchased for his daughter's marriage[101] or the 20,000 odd who took shelter in the slaughterhouse of east Calcutta where 'the rule of jungle prevailed at feeding time'[102] or the 18-year-old Yogesh from 'the squalor of the congested Lichubagan *bustee*' who had his right arm chopped off[103] or those who found their own neighbours as rioters, the fateful December days will remain everlasting haunting nightmares. Recapturing the feelings of female survivors of the 1984 anti-Sikh Delhi carnage a perceptive investigator notes what stood out in their consciousness was the dramatic transformation of their homes from a space they regarded as inviolable and protected from 'outsiders' to the very site of the killings.[104]

This must have been also the deduction of those women in Calcutta who saw their shanties demolished. Particularly painful was the appearance of cracks in traditional proletarian solidarity. Factory workers looted houses of their fellow mates or remained silent spectators when huts of their colleagues belonging to the rival community kept on burning.[105] The veteran Communist leader, Gita Mukherjee, repented how the workers of the Bengal Pottery who had held high 'the red flag flying' amidst the 1946 violence could not keep themselves aloof from the communal strife this time.[106]

Many social scientists contend that the real backdrop to the December explosion lies in a 'general decay of Calcutta'. Compared to Delhi, Bombay or Madras, Calcutta is today seen as a 'declining metropolis'. While Calcutta's population had registered a phenomenal rise, its economic prosperity and material facilities have relatively shrunk. In the words of one such analyst:

For sometime no new roads have been constructed. While new multi-storeyed constructions have come up and new complexes have been built either by demolishing old structures or by acquiring open spaces within traditional estates, neither water-supply system nor sanitation has been relatively developed. Thirty years ago those who belonged to middle class have now been pushed to the city's outskirts. The poor who live in the city's periphery are huddled in *bustees* along the railway track. Today the predominant section of Calcutta's middle class are non-Bengalis whose life-pattern is out of tune with the ethos of Bengali inhabitants (of the city).[107]

This social transfiguration, accompanied by an industrial decline, is believed to have caused an acute sense of deprivation amongst the city's subordinate social groups. Their despair was successfully exploited by some self-seekers in a communally surcharged atmosphere. It was thus not surprising that in Metiabruz the employees of three closed jute mills constituted the main support base for the 'local goons' who masterminded the riot.[108] In this context it has been remarked: 'The communal virus is not merely viewed in the context of power politics. Its root lies in a particular social failure and varied manifestations of popular struggles. ...'[109]

An underlying assumption in such a thesis is that communalism would appear in Calcutta as an inevitable by-product of a deep-rooted social crisis. It is, however, tempting to argue that such deprivations can also lead to a different kind of popular mobilization without the communal tinge. Besides, one's involvement with communal politics at a historical juncture does not necessarily preclude the possibility of his/her participation in class-based protest politics. The same person can be driven by communal hysteria at one point, while on other occasions he/she can be an active participant in anti-imperialist or class politics. History has shown that popular perceptions in Bengal are prisoners of indeterminate or unresolved tensions and sensations.[110] It is hardly conceivable that a Bengali peasant or a worker can be exclusively motivated by communal consciousness. If the 1992 disturbances revived public memories of the 1946 communal insanity, it also left behind memories of people forsaking communal identities and standing 'like an unassailable wall between the rioters and their prey'.[111] An Indian possesses multiple identities, and at a historical conjuncture one identity gains precedence over another. Not unnaturally, the imbalance created by the 1992 disorder was restored in due course.

Impressive rallies were held for communal peace and amity after the riot subsided, and working-class fraternity across communal lines has been revived. This changing mood of the city was succinctly expressed by a Muslim who had joined the riot when he remarked: 'What has happened has happened. Hindus and Muslims will have to live together.'[112] Significantly, while the survivors of the 1984 Delhi riot cannot still return to 'a semblance of normalcy',[113] the victims of the 1992 Calcutta violence have been largely rehabilitated. In fact, once the scar of rioting was healed and Calcuttans looked back in retrospect to the events between 7 and 10 December there was a general awareness of the true nature of the violence. It distinctly comes out from the admission of an ordinary Muslim citizen to a journalist: 'But we are aware it is the politicians who create these problems. We have nothing against Hindus. They are good decent people. But the politicians . . . light the fuse and then go and sit at home, secure. Nothing happens to them, we are the ones who suffer. The poor suffer all the time. . . .'[114]

This is the voice of reason in a normal state of mind and there cannot be a better lesson for a social scientist.

Notes

1. Babri Masjid was a historic monument built by the Mughal emperor Babar. Hindu fanatics believe that this was constructed on the ruins of a temple built to commemorate the birthplace of the mythical figure Ram. Led by the Bharatiya Janata Party the Hindu sectarian forces demolished this mosque on 6 December 1992 to build a Ram temple in its place. The worst spate of communal rioting in post-independent India followed this demolition.
2. *Sunday Mail* (Delhi) (hereafter *SM*), 20–6 December 1992.
3. This is how the decolonization process in the subcontinent is described where the departing colonial rulers transferred power to two successor states carved out of British India along religious lines—the predominantly Hindu India and the Muslim Pakistan.
4. The term 'cow-belt' is used to imply the Hindi heartland which has been the main ground of Hindu fundamentalist politics in independent India.
5. See Suranjan Das, *Communal Riots in Bengal 1905–1947*, Delhi, 1991 and 1993, for an explication of this thesis on the shift in the pattern of communal riots in British Bengal.
6. The Cabinet Mission led by the Secretary of State, Pethick-Lawrence, was sent by the British cabinet to India in March 1946 to discuss the framing of a constitution for India. It published its constitutional plan on 16 May 1946.
7. On this day Muslims all over India were urged to suspend their 'business' and resolve to end both the 'British slavery' and 'contemplated caste-Hindu domination' by establishing a separate Muslim state, Pakistan.

8. The Muslim League gathering on this day was 'the largest of its kind'. Estimates of its size vary from 30,000 to 500,000. See Suranjan Das, *Communal Riots,* op. cit., p. 171.

9. See ibid., Chapter 2.

10. For details of the 1946 outbreak see Suranjan Das, *Communal Riots,* op. cit., Chapter Six; and Suranjan Das, 'The Great Calcutta Killing of 1946', in *J-L Racine,* Calcutta, 1905–71: Au cceur des creations et des revoltes du siecle, Paris, 1997.

11. Cited in Suranjan Das, *Communal Riots,* op. cit., p. 171.

12. See ibid., Chapter 10.

13. This reconciliation with the idea of Partition was certainly not total. At the elite level, both Gandhi and Abdul Gafar Khan opposed the division of the country along religious lines. Recent studies have shown how, at the popular level, large sections of Muslims and Hindus opposed Partition. See Papiya Ghosh, 'The Discourse and Politics of *Qaum, Mazhab* and *Biradari* in 1940s Bihar', paper presented at the seminar on 'Northern India and Indian Independence', Nehru Memorial Museum and Library, 6–9 December 1993.

14. There were communal tensions in Calcutta in 1948 and 1950.

15. It is widely believed in the Muslim world that a piece of sacred hair of Prophet Muhammad was brought to Hazratbal mosque.

16. Unless otherwise stated this riot has been reconstructed from the accounts of *The Statesman* (Calcutta) (hereafter *ST*), *Amrita Bazar Patrika* (Calcutta) (hereafter *AB*), *Hindusthan Standard* (Calcutta) (hereafter *HS*) and *Ananda Bazar Patrika* (Calcutta) (hereafter *ABP*), I could also consult a short report on the disturbance compiled by the Intelligence Branch of Bengal Police preserved in Special Branch Record Room in Calcutta. No other official or unofficial report on the riot is available.

17. This is the crossing of Wellesley (now Rafi Ahmed Kidwai Road) and Blochman Street. For details see *ABP*, 10 January 1964.

18. This area comprised the four thanas (police stations) of Entally, Beniapukur, Amherst Street, Belliaghata and Taltala.

19. See the statement by the Minister-in-Charge of Home (Police), Government of West Bengal, Proceedings of the West Bengal Legislative Assembly [hereafter WBLAP], February-March 1964, vol. xxxviii, no. 1, p. 601.

20. *ABP*, 11 January 1992.

21. The two Hindu bustees that suffered were those in Motijheel and Linton Street.

22. See the submission by Barun De in *Pratidin* (Calcutta), 14 December 1992. According to the Intelligence Branch report cited earlier, 5306 huts/rooms belonging to both communities were victims of the riot.

23. *ABP*, 20 January 1964. However, an equal number of Hindus and Muslims lost their lives.

24. See the speech by Somnath Lahiri, WBLAP, pp. 84–5.

25. *ABP*, 18 January 1964. The Forward Bloc leader of the Bengal Assembly, Hemanta Basu, alleged the presence in Calcutta of a large number of Pakistani nationals without valid visas in full knowledge of the Calcutta Police. He felt that such persons had a hand in instigating the riot. See WBLAP, p. 73.

26. *ABP*, 16 January 1964.
27. Intelligence Report (see n. 16).
28. *ABP*, 18 January 1964.
29. *ABP*, 17 January 1964.
30. WBLAP, pp. 69–72.
31. Ibid., p. 881.
32. The Police Commissioner of Calcutta Tushar Talukdar's view is cited in the submission of Diptosh Majumdar, *The Telegraph* (Calcutta) (hereafter *TT*), 26 December 1992.
33. *The Hindustan Times* (Delhi), 15 December 1992.
34. See Shyamal Chakrabarti, 'Kolkatar Sampratik Danga' (Calcutta's recent riot), *Nandan,* January 1993 and 'Danga O Sampradaikata: Kayekti dalil' (Riot and communalism: some documents) in *Dangar Samay* (During Riot), ed. Milan Dutta, Calcutta, 1994, Section-II, pp. 18–19.
35. According to the official estimate, during the first two days of rioting, out of the 18 killed 10 died in police firing. See *Dangar Samay,* Section-II, p. 18.
36. 35 *thanas* in this region were affected by the riot.
37. *Ganasakti* (Calcutta), 8–11 December 1992; Also see Diptosh Mazumdar's submission in *TT*, 26 January 1992.
38. *Sunday Mail* (hereafter *SM*), 20–6 December 1992.
39. *Aajkal* (Calcutta), 18 December 1992.
40. *TT*, 26 December 1992.
41. *TT*, 9 December 1992.
42. This was experienced during the raids on the slums in east Calcutta. See the statement of local CPI(M) leaders cited in *Aajkal* (Calcutta), 11 December 1992.
43. For instance, on 9 December in Topsia two motorcycles toured the areas targeted for attack, spreading wild stories to incite communal passions. While Hindus told of Muslim aggression, the Muslims were aroused by rumours of Hindu misdeeds. See *Aajkal* (Calcutta), 11 December 1992.
44. *Pratidin* (Calcutta), 11 December 1992. Translation of the passage is mine.
45. The slaughterhouse, known as the Kilkhana slaughterhouse, is one of the largest of its kind, while the name of the school is Loreto School.
46. *Aajkal* (Calcutta), 18 December 1992.
47. *TT*, 13 December 1992.
48. *TT*, 11 December 1992.
49. This term is used in India to describe real estate dealers or developers.
50. *Aajkal* (Calcutta), 14 December 1992.
51. *ST*, 18 December 1992; *SM*, 20–6 December 1992.
52. *ST*, 15 December 1992.
53. *Dangar Samay,* Section-II, p. 10.
54. Ibid.
55. See the submission by Anirban Choudhury, *ST*, 18 December 1992.
56. Report by S. Dasgupta, *Business Standard* (Calcutta), 20 December 1992.
57. *Financial Express* (Delhi), 13 December 1992; *The Hindustan Times* (Delhi), 15 December 1992.

58. *TT*, 9 December 1992.
59. *Bartaman* (Calcutta), 14 December 1992.
60. Ibid.
61. *Kolkatar Danga: Akti Samikha* (Calcutta Riot: a survey) (*Nagarik Mancha*, Calcutta, January 1993), p. 7.
62. Ibid., pp. 7–8.
63. Ibid. p. 8.
64. *TT*, 12 December 1992.
65. *Financial Express* (Bombay), 14 December 1992.
66. *Kolkatar Danga*, p. 25. Despite the then Chief Minister's directives, the inhabitants of the bustee have been denied their legal occupancy right owing to bureaucratic wrangling. Ownership record of this bustee is also not reportedly available in Calcutta Corporation. According to one estimate, the market price of the 15 bighas over which the bustee stands is as high as Rs. 3 crore.
67. *SM*, 20-6 December 1992.
68. This was reported by Dr P. Jha, member of the Mayor-in-Council incharge of bustees of the Calcutta Municipal Corporation.
69. *SM*, 20–6 December 1992.
70. *Economic Times* (Bombay), 12 December 1992.
71. *TT*, 13 December 1992; Chakrabarty, *Kolkatar Sampratik Danga*; Arun P. Mukherjee, *Ayodhyakander Prekhite Paschimbanga o Police* (West Bengal and Police in the context of Ayodhya episode), *Nandan,* January 1993. As in 1946, this time, too 'respectable middle class residents' maintained close proximity with anti-socials for 'self-defence'.
72. *Kolkatar Danga; Chayayi December 0 Tarpar Danga: Kolkata 0 Anyatra* (Sixth December and After: Riots in Calcutta and elsewhere), Calcutta: March 1993.
73. *ST*, 9 December 1992.
74. *TT*, 22 July 1994.
75. In a self-critical tone the then West Bengal Chief Minister, Jyoti Basu, admitted the failure of politicians in combating communalism. He told a gathering in the Calcutta Book Fair: 'We politicians have tremendous responsibilities to maintain communal harmony and we have not perhaps always maintained that. Otherwise, how could the riots have taken place?', *TT*, 28 December 1992.
76. *TT*, 26 January 1993.
77. See the submission by Diptosh Majumdar, *TT*, 26 December 1992.
78. These two had become household names during the riot. They are believed to have masterminded much of the rioting and it took the police a long time to bring them to book.
79. *Bartaman* (Calcutta), 14 December 1992.
80. *Pratidin* (Calcutta), 11 December 1992. For an interesting analysis of the international press coverage of the Babri Masjid happening, see R. Bhattacharya et al., *Ayodhyaye Sampradaik Tandab o Antarjatik Sambadpatra* (Ayodhya communal carnage and international newspapers), *Nandan,* January 1993.
81. *TT*, 16 December 1992.
82. Ibid.

83. *Aajkal* (Calcutta), 11 December 1992; *Pratidin* (Calcutta), 11 January 1992; *Kolkatar Danga,* op. cit., p. 5.

84. For involvement of Hindu and Muslim fundamentalist forces in the recent riots outside Bengal, see G. Pandey, 'The Civilized and the Barbarian: The New Politics of Late Twentieth Century India and the World', C. Jaffrelot, 'The BJP in Madhya Pradesh: Networks, Strategies and Power', and J. Alam, 'The Changing Grounds of Communal Mobilization: The Majlis-E-Ittehad-Ul-Muslimeen and the Muslims of Hyderabad', in *Hindus And Others: The Question of Identity in India Today,* G. Pandey, ed., New Delhi,1993; S. Chandra, 'Of Communal Consciousness and Communal Violence: Impressions from Post-Riot Surat' in *Economic and Political Weekly* (hereafter *EPW*), vol. XXVIII, no. 36, 4 September 1993. For an analysis of inherent fascist trends within the Hindutva movement see S. Sarkar, 'The Fascism of the Sangh Parivar' in *EPW*, vol. xxviii, no. 5, 30 January 1993.

85. For this aspect of the *Hindutva* movement in north India see the perceptive analysis in T. Sarkar, 'Women's Agency Within Authoritarian Communalism: The Rashtrasevika Samiti And Ramjanmabhoomi', in *Hindus And Others,* G. Pandey, ed., op. cit.

86. The then Director-General of Police of West Bengal, Dr. Arun P. Mukherjee, admits this in his submission to *Nandan.* The Bombay riot of January 1993 also assumed the character of a 'land grabbing riot'.

87. *ST*, 13 December 1992.

88. I. Mukhopadhyay, 'Urban Informal Sector and Communal Violence: Case Study of 1992 Riots in Calcutta', *EPW*, 27 August 1994.

89. Submission by M. Bhattacharya, *Financial Express* (Delhi), 16 December 1992.

90. *Aajkal* (Calcutta), 9 December 1992; *ABP*, 9 December 1992; *TT*, 10 and 19 December 1992; *SM*, 20–6 December 1992.

91. *Kolkatar Danga,* op. cit., p. 19.

92. *Financial Express* (Delhi), 13 December 1992; *The Hindustan Times* (Delhi), 15 December 1992; *Ganasakti* (Calcutta), 10 December 1992.

93. *Financial Express* (Delhi), 13 December 1992.

94. Despite its anti-CPI(M) tone, *Kolkatar Danga,* op.cit., had to acknowledge this. Yet another anti-CPI(M) survey of the Calcutta episode, *Chayayi December O Tarpar Danga: Kolkata O Anyatra,* had to acknowledge the efforts of Leftist Councillors like Abdul Mannan, Abdul Ali and Abdul Khalek to check the violence.

95. G. Pandey, 'The Prose of Otherness', in *Subaltern Studies,* D. Arnold and D. Hardiman, eds., vol. viii, Delhi 1994.

96. Ibid., p. 190.

97. G. Chattopadhyay, 'The Almost Revolution' in *Essays in Honour of S.C. Sarkar,* B. De et al., eds., Delhi, 1976. Also see Chapter 7 of this book.

98. The Greater Bengal Movement was initiated by Sarat Bose and Suhrawardy to establish a sovereign Bengal, independent of either India or Pakistan.

99. See Chapter 3 of this book.

100. *ABP*, 12 December 1992.

101. *TT*, 9 December 1992.

102. *TT*, 13 December 1992.

103. *TT*, 10 January 1993.

104. U. Chakravarti, 'Victims, Neighbours and Watan: Survivors of Anti-Sikh Carnage of 1984', in *EPW*, vol. XXIX, no. 42, 15 October 1994.

105. For instance, Birla-owned Kesoram Cotton Mills lie close to Lichubagan bustee. But when the poor inhabitants of this slum were subjected to violence, the workers of Kesoram Mills kept a safe distance. Prominent trade unionists like Kamalapati Roy of the All India Trade Union Congress were surprised how 'a section of the workers are divided on the communal line', *Business Standard* (Calcutta), 12 December 1992.

106. *Bartaman* (Calcutta), 15 December 1992.

107. See the article by B. De in *Pratidin* (Calcutta), 14 December 1992, translation is mine.

108. This was acknowledged by local CPI(M) sources too. *TT*, 13 December 1992. Studies have established the relationship between social degradation and communal violence in Surat. See, for instance, P. Shah, 'Surat Riots: Degeneration of a City' in *EPW*, 30 Januasry 1993.

109. Barun De in *Pratidin,* op. cit.

110. See S. Das, *Communal Riots,* for a study of how until the last moment the political pendulum in twentieth-century British India had oscillated between mainstream nationalism, separatism and class politics.

111. This is how *ST*, 17 December 1992, describes the efforts of Md. Ayub Ansari and Qyabuddin Ansari—father and son—to save Hindu lives in Metiabruz.

112. Cited in the article by S. Sebastian, *TT*, 25 December 1992.

113. U. Chakravarti, 'Victims' in *EPW*, 15 October 1994.

114. *TT*, 25 December 1992.

CHAPTER 5

KNOWLEDGE FOR POLITICS: PARTISAN HISTORIES AND COMMUNAL MOBILIZATION IN INDIA AND PAKISTAN

IN LATE APRIL 2003, a number of historians working on India in the United States received an online petition against the appointment of Romila Thapar, a historian of ancient India, to the Kluge Chair at the Library of Congress. It may seem surprising that such an academic appointment can generate political heat in the expatriate Indian community. Yet the appointment sparked off an orchestrated political campaign on the internet. The petition, entitled 'Protest US Supported Marxist Assault Against Hindus', argues that Romila Thapar is responsible for cultural genocide against Hindus.[1]

The question that immediately comes to mind is: why do Hindu nationalists need to devote so much energy to combat the appointment of a historian engaged in research in 'classical antiquity'? The answer lies in the pamphlet itself. Hindu nationalists fear that a critical scrutiny of ancient Indian history will disrupt convenient myths about the origins of 'Hindu civilization'. They regard the earliest episodes of Indian history as sacrosanct and beyond critical empirical investigation, except for eulogistic self-glorification. For them, not only was ancient India a Hindu nation, but it remained unchanged from the time of the composition of the Vedic hymns (nearly one thousand years BC) to the advent of Islam in the Indo-Gangetic plain of South Asia (AD 1206).

Critical examination of ancient Indian civilization poses a threat to the idea of a monolithic 'Hindu nation' in India from time immemorial in its

*This article was co-authored with Dr Subho Basu, Department of History, Maxwell School, Syracuse University, USA, and was published in Max Paul Friedman and Padraic Kenney, eds., *The Past in Contemporary Global Politics: Partisan Histories*, New York, 2005.

unchanging modular form.[2] It was thus feared that the appointment of a nonconformist ancient Indian historian to a visible position within US academia would undermine the cause of Hindu nationalism in the West. The petition cited above, couched in a provocative rhetoric of cultural nationalism and suffused with anti-imperialist references, is a classic example of how the partisan use of the historian's craft can play a significant role in the politics of competing nationalism in South Asia.

As in other multi-ethnic Asian and African countries that experienced western colonialism, in the Indian subcontinent too, colonial interpretations of history have informed competing strategies of political mobilization during the struggle for freedom. But there was a qualitative difference in the use of history in mainstream nationalist politics and in sectarian politics. While the former primarily fell back on the 'Indian past' to counter the colonial discourse of the superiority of the West over the East, the latter—primarily religious nationalists, both Hindu and Muslim—used history to generate a monolithic identity of religiously based nation-states in a decolonized South Asia. In the postcolonial period, against the background of the political turbulence surrounding diverse trajectories of the two successor nation-states—democratic India, with a Hindu majority but supposedly secular, and Islamic Pakistan—partisan history has continued to play a role in political rhetoric and strategies of mobilization.

This essay explores how Hindu and Muslim nationalists have invoked history in the Indian subcontinent both during and in the aftermath of the freedom struggle. These partisan histories have their origins in the way colonial rulers viewed India, as a complex mosaic of static, unchanging, and conflicting well-defined ethnic communities; the British perceived their role as a neutral umpire controlling these hostile and competing communities. Drawing on colonial historiography that celebrated such essentialized categories of religious, caste, linguistic and ethnic identities, Hindu and Muslim nationalists developed competing versions of nationalism premised on the belief that Hindus and Muslims constituted two distinct nations that could not coexist.[3] While Hindu nationalists looked to transform Hindu civilization into an exclusivist nation-state, their Muslim counterparts invoked a modular partisan past to justify the separatist movement for a Muslim homeland in the shape of Pakistan, and then to provide an ideological legitimacy for an essentially Islamicized militaristic nation-state. This is how, as the essay hopes to demonstrate, history itself became the site of power struggles based on religious nationalism in South Asia.

Colonial and Nationalist Historiography

In a classic statement of a Eurocentric philosophy of history, the German philosopher Hegel, otherwise an admirer of Indian civilization, asserted that

India had no history, in contrast, for example, to China, or of course Europe. The underlying assumption here was that whereas Europe, the birthplace of modernity, has a well-defined historical consciousness, the formerly colonized non-European world actually comprised people without historical consciousness.[4]

Most British historians in colonial India were important bureaucrats who extended their historical assumptions into the strategies of governance, thus carefully transforming their discourses into a new epistemological system of the past to project colonial power and domination. Drawing upon Persian texts, early colonial rulers introduced in the English language survey histories that became a biography of the Indian civilization.[5] In these works, the periodization of Indian history followed the contemporary European ideals of three stages of historical evolution—classical antiquity, dark medieval era, and the post-renaissance modern period. The only difference in the Indian context was that the tripartite epochal division of history became linked with the religion and nationality of ruling elites. Ancient India was referred to as the Hindu period, ignoring the periods of complex religious systems. In a similar fashion, medieval India was identified with Muslim rule, although there were powerful non-Muslim rulers in that period as well. The Muslims in India were also treated as a monolithic community, as if all of them were migrants and invaders, claiming descent from the Arabs, Turks, Afghans, and Mughals.[6] The colonial phase of Indian history, in turn, was looked upon in colonial historiography as a harbinger of universal modernity through evangelicalism, western science, philosophy, and rationality.

Colonial historical writings also concentrated on the story of Hindu resistance to 'Muslim rule'. Historical sources were also compiled in a manner to drive home this point, as is best illustrated in Elliot and Dowson's *History of India as Told by Her Own Historians* (London, 1866–7). This collection of bardic tales and a romantic reconstruction of Rajput and Maratha rebellions against Mughal rulers presented as authentic academic history captured the imagination of newly rising Hindu middle classes, and became a source of antagonism between Hindus and Muslims.

Another aspect of this discordant Hindu–Muslim relationship in colonial historiography was the semiotics of sexuality. For example, one tale collected by a nineteenth-century British scholar told of the lust of Alauddin, a powerful Muslim monarch, for a beautiful Hindu Rajput queen, and hence his desire to conquer the Hindu Kingdom. This contributed to a stereotype of Muslims as rapists, and Hindus as passive, docile, and submissive.[7] The text romanticized the collective suicide of Hindu women to evade the lustful Muslim men, and thus justified the burning of women on funeral pyres of their husbands. Women were denied individuality and choice, and were posited as the representatives of the community's honor. The image of masculine Muslim and effeminate Hindu became the source of anxiety for Hindu nationalists, who in response preached a militarized spirituality for Hindus.[8] This quest for militarized spirituality gave birth to Hindu nationalist organizations to combat putative 'Muslim aggression'.

Colonial historiography also racialized Hindu identity. In this, it followed comparative philology, which asserted similarities between Sanskrit and ancient Germanic and Latin linguistic structures, positing a common origin of Aryan civilization in India, Iran, and Western Europe.[9] In a detailed investigation of the origin and impact of this history, Vasant Kaiwar wrote:

The study of Indo-European languages across the whole space of Europe and South-West and South Asia established the idea of diffusion of the master culture and civilization of the Aryans from a central homeland. In this model, Greece and India served as the opposing poles of the dialectic of world history. Both were neatly detached from their local contexts and attached to a central diasporic model, with classical Greece anchoring a triumph list account of European history, and India—after a brief romantic flirtation with the notion of an Oriental renaissance— illustrating a story of decline and degeneration, except in India itself, where the Aryan model and ideas generated by the Oriental renaissance could be mobilized behind conservative agendas of national renaissance.[10]

Partisan History and Hindu Nationalist Discourse

As the rise of mass nationalism against the Raj was equally matched, in the early twentieth century, by an intense Hindu–Muslim communal divide, both Hindu and Muslim nationalists developed competing narratives of the history of their respective communities. The lead in this direction came from the founding ideologue of Hindu nationalism—Vinayak Damodar Savarkar. Nurtured by the tradition of masculine Hindu radicalism and informed by brahmanical social conservatism that rejected the moderate, cosmopolitan, and constitutional politics of the dominant Congress Party, Savarkar became involved with revolutionary politics during his student days in India and England, which led to frequent imprisonment. He wrote a nationalist account of the 1857 Revolt, celebrating it as the First War of Indian Independence. Following the breakdown of Hindu–Muslim solidarity, which had been cemented around the Khilafat-Non-Cooperation movement and the subsequent communal violence, Savarkar emerged as a prominent organizer of the Hindu nationalist party, the Hindu Mahasabha.

Through his writings Savarkar went beyond the traditional invocation of Hindu sensibilities and created the ideological foundation of the Hindu supremacist movement by arguing for the desemitization of Indian culture.

He developed the concept of Hindutva (Hinduness), which stipulated that Indians could be those whose *pitribhumi* (land of their ancestors) and *punyabhumi* (land of their religion) lay within the territory of British India. Since Muslims and Christians supposedly regarded Arabia and Palestine as their holy land, they could not claim the rights of citizenship.[11] By the same logic the communists, indoctrinated with their atheism and proletarian internationalism, were to be denied Indian citizenship. Such an idea of an exclusivist Indian citizenship was further explicated by another Hindu nationalist theoretician, M.S. Golwalkar, who categorically stated that non-Hindus could never be Indian citizens.[12] Savarkar believed that the idea of Hinduness could not be defined in clear terms, but it could be summed up as the entirety of the history of Indian civilization. In *The Six Glorious Epochs of Indian History*, which many of his followers regard as an elucidation of the survival strategy of the Hindu race and nation, Savarkar even praised the persecution of Buddhists in ancient India:

Pushyametra and his generals were forced by the exigency of the time, when the war was actually going on, to hang the Indian Buddhists who were guilty of seditious acts, and pulled down monasteries which had become the centres of sedition. It was just punishment for high treason and for joining hands with the enemy, in order that Indian independence and empire might be protected. It was no religious persecution.[13]

He also categorized Ambedkar, the leader of the Dalit (untouchable) movement in India, as a 'man burning with hatred against Hinduism'. When Ambedkar advised his followers to embrace Buddhism to escape from the Hindu caste system, Savarkar claimed that Buddhism aggravated untouchability in ancient India. He employed the colonial stereotype of aggressive Muslim tyranny in medieval India: 'Intoxicated by this religious ambition, which was many times more diabolic than their political one, these millions of Muslim invaders from all over Asia fell over India century after century with all the ferocity at their command to destroy Hindu religion which was the life blood of the nation.'[14]

Savarkar did not merely present Muslim men as lustful, but depicted rape and molestation of Hindu women as deliberate ploys adopted by medieval Muslim rulers to demoralize Hindu resistance. Mohamad Tavakoli-Targhi has coined the term 'hate mysticism' to describe Islamic radicals' anger with the West and modernity.[15] Savarkar's hate mysticism formulated a discourse of Hindu supremacism that obliterated the boundary between evil and good, and saw the world from an instrumentalist, nationalist political understanding.

It is this instrumentalist understanding of the Indian past that prompted Savarkar and his associates to admire and praise German Nazism and Italian fascism. On many occasions, he stated that Hitler was the best for Germany. Savarkar and the Hindu Mahasabha celebrated the revival of Aryan culture in Germany. The Nazi newspaper *Volkischer Beobachter* reported on Savarkar's speeches in exchange for the promotion of Germany's anti-Semitic policies.[16] Despite his admiration of Hitler and Germany, Savarkar supported the idea of the establishment of Israel not only in accordance with his theory of nationalism, but he also saw in the Jewish state a bulwark against the Islamic Arab world.[17] A combination of masculine nationalism and hate mysticism transformed Savarkar's doctrine into an Indian version of aggressive religious nationalist political philosophy.

Much of the Hindu ultranationalist history was political rhetoric that in its attempt to inferiorize others did not bother about evidence. Professional historians of India before and after Independence raised questions about the evidential basis of such historical writings. Yet, in popular imagination legends could easily pass for history; thus, it is often difficult to clearly distinguish not just between history and mythography, but also between history and hate literature.

Muslim Nationalism and the Use of History

The Hindu nationalist discourse naturally provoked a Muslim nationalist response, although the latter was not as systematic and organized as the former. Muslim nationalist discourse essentially stressed the emergence of the Muslim community in India as an exclusivist political entity, quite distinct from the majority Hindu community; the demand for a separate homeland for Muslims in the form of Pakistan followed logically from this discourse. The idea of Pakistan originated in England when Choudhary Rahmat Ali (1895–1951) coined the term Pakistan as a homeland for the 30 million Muslims inhabiting British India in a memorable pamphlet 'Now or Never; Are We to Live or Perish Forever?' The homeland movement for Indian Muslims that developed under the stewardship of the Muslim League leader Mohammad Ali Jinnah was largely based upon constitutional bargaining, and informed by a modernist dream for parity of Indian Muslims with the Hindu majority within India. In the tradition of South Asian politics, constitutional categories were transformed into political entities through careful emotional investment. This political mobilizational strategy required a powerful rhetoric of the other, fear psychosis, and romantic historical narrative. In tune with Hindu nationalist rhetoric, this line of thought was crucially linked to the idea of two monolithic and homogeneous religious communities coexisting in a situation of nearly perpetual conflict, and sometimes in uneasy peace. This rhetoric constituted the foundational myth of the Islamic state of Pakistan.

Though British India was predominandy non-Muslim, the largest numbers of Muslims in the world were concentrated in the Indian subcontinent. Muslim South Asians, like their Hindu counterparts, never constituted a monolithic homogeneous community. They were internally divided by language, caste, and even different forms of religious practices. However, in north India, particularly in the Indo-Gangetic heartland, the Muslim service elite of the Mughal Empire shared a common memory of successive Muslim empires. Even in the twilight years of the Mughal Empire, they exercised a stranglehold over government jobs and legal professions. The gradual erosion of the Mughal Empire and the Indian princely states undermined the social and economic status of this service elite.

The uneven nature of the progress of colonial modernity, the emergence of new Hindu service elites and competition for limited resources caused a growing feeling of insecurity for this elite. The rise of enumerated identity through the census and growing assertiveness of Hindu nationalism further escalated the sense of uncertainty that enveloped this community. Many Muslim elites sought to adopt colonial modernity and embraced colonial education; concerned about Hindu majoritarian tendencies within Indian nationalist politics, some sought protection through separate electorates and safeguards for Muslims in access to jobs and education. The traditional Muslim intelligentsia—primarily the learned ulema—however, found it difficult to accept the so-called march of modernity. They increasingly turned toward pan-Islamism and accommodation with Indian nationalism. These binary categories of modernist and traditional intelligentsia are undoubtedly problematic and do not always neatly dovetail with social formations.

With the rise of mass nationalism after World War I, the pan-Islamists joined hands with Gandhian nationalists. This temporarily displaced constitutionalists like Jinnah. But they came back to the limelight as methods of Gandhian mass politics failed to immediately dismantle the Raj. Jinnah now sought to play upon the fears and aspirations of the minority Muslim elite of the heartland. It is here that the nostalgia for the Islamic past was recreated, and the sceptre of Hindu domination was presented in a threatening manner. To rally the much-divided Muslim provincial politicians in the majority provinces into an all-India platform, Jinnah placed stress on federalism, and the protection of the interests of Muslim majority provinces. This gave him a powerful position as the 'sole spokesman' of the Indian Muslims.[18] Yet the brittleness of Muslim politics constantly plagued Jinnah's project and he thus sought solace in the Muslim League's Pakistan Resolution of 1940. The resolution imagined in distinct terms India's two largest religious communities—Hindus and Muslims—as nations, and demanded that areas where Muslims were numerically in a majority should be grouped to constitute an 'Independent State States' in which the constituent units would be accorded considerable autonomy. The historical negotiations over the transfer of power from British to indigenous hands and the subsequent communal strife were presented by Muslim nationalists as a vindication of the assertion in the 1940 resolution that Hindus and Muslims constituted two monolithic religious nationalities, which could not coexist within one territorial unit. The idea of Pakistan could not thus accommodate any historical reading that could suggest a shared cross-communal identity.

Both Hindu and Muslim nationalist discourses cited above had thus fallen back upon a colonial historiography that rejected multiple identities in subcontinental society based on occupation, language, caste, social hierarchy, and religion. Religious nationalisms premised their master narratives of Indian history on the notion of competing religious identities in Indian society. As we have seen, Hindu nationalist discourse advanced the theory that Muslim invaders destroyed Hindu civilization, created a tyrannical form of government, and caused backwardness in Indian society and economy, opening a path for British colonization. But the Hindutva theory, equating Indian culture with Hindu culture, is ahistorical, since what we know today as the Indian culture is an amalgam of several strands—Hinduism, Islam, Christianity, Zoroastrianism, Persian, Greek, Roman, Parthian, Scythian, and so on. In fact, the theory of Hindutva goes against the eclectic nature of Hinduism itself. In its pristine form, Hinduism is a heterogeneous admixture of diverse practices, rituals, and cults, lacking a rigid structure and organized neither around a single text nor a church. But complexities of historical events were sacrificed on the altar of partisan history for the sake of ideological construction of a homogeneous Hindu nation resisting a monolithic Muslim imperial state. Similarly, the Muslim nationalist dictum ignores unique features of Indian Islam, which has appropriated many rituals of other religions in India, including Hinduism, so much so that one scholar has spoken of Islamic syncretism in the subcontinent.[19] Even today Muslim villagers often worship the same deity with their Hindu neighbours either for a good harvest or to fight epidemics. Numerous instances can be cited of Muslims participating in Hindu festivals and vice versa. Muslim religious figures also contributed much to the development of the Bhakti movement in medieval India that brought together Vedantic and Islamic thinking.

Despite the ahistorical nature of these Hindu and Muslim nationalist discourses, by the 1940s they had brought about a political stalemate in the progress toward independence, as communal fears and apprehensions were channelled against specific individuals, institutions, objects, and symbols. The Pakistan movement and its Hindu nationalist counterpart occasioned in India what Scribner has called, in the context of the German Reformation movement, the process of negative assimilation, wherein the common person became convinced of the Tightness of the 'evangelical cause', and therefore felt compelled to support the movement.[20] This set the stage for the decolonization process in South Asia, in which the departing colonial rulers divided the subcontinent into two successor states along religious lines before quitting the region.

Partisan History and Political Mobilization in Postcolonial South Asia

The closing years of colonialism in the subcontinent were marked by a series of devastating human tragedies: the painful exodus of Indian refugees from Burma in the wake of Japanese invasion, the ruthless suppression of the 1942 August Revolution, and the man-made Bengal famine of 1943 that took a toll of nearly three million lives. The exit strategy from the Indian empire worked out well for India's former imperial rulers, but not for Indians themselves. A conservative estimate indicates that nearly 14 million people were rendered homeless refugees, nearly 500,000 people perished, and 250,000 women were raped and mutilated in the tragic run-up to the Partition of the subcontinent on 15 August 1947. These statistics, as Gyanendra Pandey has shown, do not capture the nature of human tragedy associated with the Partition saga.[21] The brutalization of human consciousness that occurred during that tumultuous period informed the writings of poets, literary figures, historians, and political activists in subsequent decades. In fact, the Partition became the most common reference point for the history in postcolonial India and Pakistan.

To Hindu nationalists, the Partition validated their historical assumptions. They viewed the event as an evidence of Muslim failure to accept India as their fatherland and blamed the ruling Congress party and the 'effeminate' Gandhian variety of non-violent nationalism for creating a situation that enabled the British to impose a 'truncated settlement'. The assassination of Gandhi by a Hindu nationalist was one such expression. Hindu nationalist rhetoric saw Congress leaders as appeasers of the Muslim minority through their ideology of 'pseudo-secularism'—evident, for example, in attempts at a democratic solution to the Kashmir problem. Hindu nationalist discourse gradually developed a cultural nationalist project to create a unified corporatist political organizational structure for Hindus, through such bodies as the Bharatiya Jana Sangh (later Bharatiya Janata Party, hereafter BJP), the Rashtriya Swayamsewak Sangh (hereafter RSS) and the Vishwa Hindu Parishad (hereafter VHP).[22]

From the beginning, the writing of Indian history became the ideological battleground between RSS-sponsored organizations and the Indian nation-state under stewardship of the India's first prime minister, Jawaharlal Nehru. While Nehru imagined a new India in terms of social justice, cultural pluralism, and political democracy, Hindu nationalists fell back on Savarkar's dream of a Hinduized state polity. But once the modernist developmental model of the state failed to deliver the promised progress and India fell victim to what has been called 'dynastic democracy', the newly enfranchised marginal social groups registered their presence in national politics through regional political forums; in the long run, this helped Hindu nationalist forces to gain a foothold in Indian federal politics.

The BJP-Ied Hindu nationalist block ensured its political ascendancy by carefully orchestrating the Ramjanmabhumi[23] movement in the 1980s. This movement aimed to liberate from Muslim stranglehold the birthplace of the Hindu mythical king Lord Rama by removing a mosque called the Babri Masjid that had been built in 1528, allegedly on that sacred spot. The movement—projected as an expression of both Hindu religiosity and Hindu national pride—evoked a passionate explanation of history that combined myths and legends with partisan historical analysis and even archaeological data. In an environment of growing distrust of the ruling Congress party and the political establishment associated with it, the movement instantly captured the imagination of upper caste and lower middle-class Hindus. The late 1980s was also a period of growing assertiveness of backward castes, which demanded affirmative action to bolster their growing political and economic clout. Alarmed by such developments, India's Hindu upper and lower middle classes extended their support to the Ramjanmabhumi movement. The result was a tectonic shift in Indian politics.

The Ramjanmabhumi movement used new technologies such as audio and video cassettes to spread the message of Hindu nationalism. It employed a language of visceral hatred against India's Muslim minorities. Women leaders of the VHP employed the most powerful and populist anti-Muslim rhetoric, grounded in a Hindu interpretation of the Indian past. The most powerful examples of such leaders were Sadhvi Rithambara and Uma Bharati, both of whom were sanyasins—female monks who take the vow of chastity. Hinduism regards women's sexuality as both powerful and dangerous.[24] A celibate woman could sublimate her femininity and be free from the constraints of social restrictions and could thus command the respect of the people for her sexual purity and emancipated social position. These women criticized the Indian political establishment for being 'eunuchs', submitting to Muslita pressure. Rithambara constantly referred to Muslim threats to ordinary Hindu women and their sexual purity, and evoked memories of the pre-Partition communal turmoil. In her speeches she referred to the Partition as the vivisection of mother India, describing the present Indian political map as a country without arms. In her speeches, she employed such melodic couplets as: 'Muslims, like a pinch of sugar, should sweeten a glass of milk; instead, like lemon, they sour it. What they do not realize is that a squeezed lemon is thrown away while the milk that has been curdled solidifies into paneer [cheese]. So Muslims have two choices, either to live like sugar or like wrung lemons.'[25]

Such verses thus implied that the Muslims were to choose between assimilation with Hindus and death. Uma Bharati, the other woman leader of the VHP, was more explicit in referring to Muslims, such as in a 1991 election speech:

Declare without hesitation that this is *Hindu rashtra*, a nation of Hindus. We have come to strengthen the immense Hindu shakti [force] into a fist. Do not display any love for your enemies. The Qur'an teaches them to lie in wait for idol worshippers, to skin them alive, to stuff them in animal skins and torture them until they ask for forgiveness. . . . [We] could not teach them with words, now let us teach them with kicks. . . . Tie up your religiosity and kindness in a bundle and throw it in the Jamuna. . . . A non-Hindu who lives here does so at our mercy.[26]

The Ramjanmabhumi movement successfully generated a wave of anti-Muslim hatred that culminated in the pulling down of the Babri Masjid on 6 December 1992. The incident provoked an orgy of communal riots across the length and breadth of the country. Members of Muslim and Christian minorities were targeted and murdered systematically through carefully orchestrated mob frenzy. A partisan use of Indian history remained at the centre of the Hindu nationalist movement as its leaders expanded their targets to several other 'controversial' Muslim religious places supposedly constructed by Mughal emperors to subjugate Hindu aristocracy. Riding on the crest of Hindu nationalism, the BJP-led National Democratic Alliance wrested power in New Delhi, holding power until May 2004.

In a bid to buttress its ideological hegemony, this BJP-led government embarked upon an ambitious project to rewrite history textbooks for school children with a distinct Hindu bias.[27] To prove the genesis of Indian society as Vedic Hindu, even the Indus Valley Civilization was claimed 'to have been authored by the Vedic Aryans', although this is 'untenable on the existing linguistic evidence'.[28] Many documentation projects that had been initiated by such institutions as the Indian Council of Historical Research were abruptly terminated on grounds of anti-Hindu and Left bias. This bid to revise history—not unlike the Nazi abuse of archaeology in the 1930s to prove the Aryan origins of the German race[29]—constituted the core of the Hindu nationalist project, in its battle for control over the ideological meaning of the nation-state. In waging this battle, the BJP-led regime not only adopted the Hindutva discourse of Savarkar, but also the modular structure of history formulated by colonial historiography. At a time when the scope of historical enquiry is being expanded to include the study of economics, technology, state formations, environment, gender, and other subaltern identities, the Hindutva revision of history falls back upon dated colonial historiography. Even the naming of new weapons added to the military arsenal; satellites launched with Hindu names reflected the Hinduization efforts of the then BJP-led political establishment. History was sought to be used to imprison Indians with a mindset of communal hatred and the idea of a monolithic and exclusivist Hindu past.

This Hindu nationalist establishment in New Delhi used rituals and symbols to restore Savarkar, who provided the theoretical foundations for contemporary nationalist political mobilization, to the centre stage of modern Indian political thought. On 26 February 2003, the then president of the Republic of India, A.P.J. Abdul Kalam, unveiled Savarkar's portrait in the Central Hall of the Indian Parliament. Since Savarkar was not simply the ideological founder of Hindu nationalist movement but was believed to have been involved in conspiring the assassination of Gandhi,[30] the entire opposition in Parliament boycotted the unveiling. While Hindu nationalists celebrated the ceremony, the event generated diverse forms of protest. No less a person than the former naval chief Admiral Vishnu Bhagwat openly expressed his doubts about the patriotism of the Hindu nationalist leader. In retaliation, the cadres of the Shiv Sena, a local Hindu nationalist organization, physically attacked him. Hindu nationalist organizations even demanded that state governments (the federative units of the Indian union) should install the portrait of Damodar Savarkar in state legislative assemblies.

Even before the unveiling of Savarkar's portrait in the Indian Parliament, the government in New Delhi had performed another symbolic act to rehabilitate the Hindu nationalist leader in the Indian political psyche. On 5 May 2002, the then home minister L.K. Advani renamed the Port Blair airport in the Andaman Islands as Veer [Valiant Hero] Savarkar Airport. Savarkar himself had been a political prisoner in the Andaman prison, a place similar in symbolism to Robben Island Prison in South Africa; Hindu nationalists sought, in this way, to establish their claim to Indian nationalism. The very reference to Savarkar, however, provoked a nationwide criticism from the former Andaman inmates, who questioned the credentials of 'Veer' Savarkar as a true soldier of the freedom movement. Evidence was cited of petitions by Savarkar to the British government in 1911 and 1913 (during his prison sentence) seeking pardon from the British government and allegedly pledging loyalty to the imperial ruler. The 96-year-old Bhagat Singh Bilga, a freedom fighter and a former Andaman inmate, slammed the central government for naming the airport after a person who, he claimed, flinched before the British authority and aptly condemned the episode as a 'dishonour' to those freedom fighters who suffered inhuman torture in the Andaman jails but never flinched.[31] The act of renaming the airport, and the hanging of a portrait thus became occasions for political and ideological battles over the history of the nationalist movement in India.

History was also a powerful tool for the managers of the Pakistani state and its military leaders as they constructed Pakistani nationhood after August 1947. Pakistani nationalism had evolved in the Indian subcontinent not primarily as territorial nationalism that could draw upon territorial patriotism suffused with ethnoreligious meanings, as was evident in the case of the Hindu nationalist discourse. This put the founding fathers of Pakistan in a difficult situation. Historically speaking, the centre of Indo-Islamic power lay in the north Indian Gangetic plain, in the fertile region between the Yamuna and Ganga rivers, and had never been located in the region that came to constitute Pakistan. The imperial cities of the Indo-Islamic empires such as Delhi, Agra, and Lucknow were located in the heart of India. In fact, to the great irritation of Pakistani leaders, the managers of the Indian nation-state made subtle symbolic claims to the Mughal heritage by holding Independence Day celebrations in front of the Red Fort, a palace constructed by the Mughal emperor Shahjahan between 1618 and 1647. This made it difficult for the Pakistani ruling elites to use the grand Mughal architectural heritage to reclaim symbolically the subcontinent's imperial Islamic past.

Partisan history premised on Muslim nationalist discourse of the days of nationalist struggle became more important in Pakistan because of the absence of political legitimacy for its military rulers. Intense regional feuds, the absence of an overarching shared notion of history, and confusion over the main ideological content of the nation-state (i.e. Islam versus a secular Muslim identity), also contributed to the importance of history in political conflict. To vindicate the stand that Pakistan was a nation of South Asian Muslims, the founding fathers of the state adopted Urdu as the national language, although no Pakistani community, except for the immigrants from the Indian states of Bihar and Uttar Pradesh, spoke Urdu as their first language. The idea of Bengali as the language of non-Muslims implied a homogeneous Muslim identity.

The colonial notion of racial inferiority of the indigenous non-Aryan population now returned in the language of Pakistan's military dictators. Indeed, General Ayub Khan, the military ruler of Pakistan (1958–69), wrote that the Muslims probably belong to the very original Indian races. … They have been in turn ruled by the caste Hindus, Moghuls, Pathans, or the British. In addition, they have been and still are under the considerable Hindu cultural and linguistic influence. As such, they have all the inhibitions of downtrodden races and they have not yet found it possible to adjust psychologically to the requirements of the newborn freedom.[32]

The irony is that it was Ayub Khan who trampled the newly formulated constitution of Pakistan in 1958 through a military coup and ushered in an era of rule by handpicked members from the military, who talked about the newfound freedom of the nation. Yet what is more noticeable here is the echo of colonial historiography and the belief that the supposed pre-Aryan inhabitants of India constituted inferior vanquished nations. So deep was the belief among Pakistani military officers that Bengali Muslims were 'converted Hindus' without a clear understanding of the purity of Islamic faith that one of them claimed during the 1970–1 civil war: 'This is a war between the pure and the impure. . . . The people here may have Muslim names and call themselves Muslims. But they are Hindu at heart. We are now sorting them out. . . . Those who are left will be real Muslims. We will even teach them Urdu.'[33]

This ideological conflation of religion, language, and masculine Muslim purity drove the Pakistani army to commit horrendous atrocities upon the Bengali people. Yet the denial of equal status to Bengali—a language with heavy inputs of Sanskrit words and reflecting a shared Hindu-Muslim culture—spoken by the Muslims in East Pakistan exposed the brittleness of the Pakistani state and directly contributed to the loss of East Pakistan, which became the sovereign state of Bangladesh. The emergence of Bangladesh undermined the legitimacy of the two-nation theory that relied on a nationalism exclusively based on religious identity.

Nevertheless, Pakistani officials continued to approach history as a frozen instrumental discipline. The subjection of history to state regulation has undermined its independence from the struggle for political power. In state-sponsored history textbooks in Pakistan, the study of Indian history becomes worthwhile only after the establishment of 'Muslim rule'. Muslim invasions from the seventh century onward are thus celebrated as the beginning of the process of the establishment of a Muslim nation in South Asia. The expansion of Muslim empires is portrayed as the triumph of Islam over Hindu India. Certain Muslim monarchs like Akbar, who are celebrated in Indian textbooks for their religious tolerance and syncretic beliefs, are ignored, while monarchs such as Aurangazeb, who are vilified in Indian textbooks for their Islamic bigotry, are praised in Pakistani texts for their piousness. History came to be written and projected primarily from the perspective of a nation-state and its need to produce a religious nationalist identity. In an interview with *The Times of India*, the noted Pakistan historian Mubarak Ali was quoted as saying:

history writing had suffered in Pakistan because of fanaticism. Anyone writing against the ideology of Pakistan is liable to be jailed for 10 years, according to the Pakistani Ideology Act of 1991. It is also not possible to write against M.A. Jinnah, the founder of Pakistan. . . . He said history writing had not developed as a discipline in Pakistan because of such problems. History writing was confined to writing of textbooks and articles in newspapers. . . . History books in Pakistan traced the two-nation theory to the time of Akbar who was blamed for the downfall of the Mughals. Akbar was not even mentioned in school books. However, Aurangazeb was praised.[34]

The unleashing of a fresh dose of Islamization of Pakistan by General Zia ul-Haq, who ruled Pakistan under martial law from 5 July 1977 till his death in a plane crash on 17 August 1988, intensified the use of the rhetoric of religious nationalism in history writing in Pakistan. The Afghan crisis and the radicalization of Islam had a further impact on the domestic politics of Pakistan. Today, in the post-11 September world, Pakistan is still in the eye of the Islamic fundamentalist storm. It is thus no surprise that in 1998 the upgraded Pakistani ballistic missiles—which, with a range of 2,700–3,000 km., can target virtually all important Indian establishments—were named Ghauri, after the twelfth century general Muhammad Ghori, who conquered Delhi in 1206. Partisan history could be powerful enough to convince today's generals to repeat history with upgraded nuclear weapon systems. Yet Pakistan exists today as 'Nationalism without a Nation', failing to resolve the competing ethnic claims of Punjabis, Sindhis, Mohajirs, Baluchis, and Pakhtoons.[35]

Conclusion

One can raise the question as to whether a historical piece can be anything but partisan, since we can no longer speak of a purely objective and value-free historical discourse.[36] It has also been argued that all history is contemporary history, given the fact that the understanding of a historian is shaped by the age in which he lives. Yet, following E.J. Hobsbawm, we can make a sharp distinction between subjective partisanship in historical literature and partisan history per se. Whereas the former 'rests on disagreement not about verified facts, but about their selection and combination, and about what may be inferred from them', the latter is essentially a recording of the past to serve particular political interests based neither on established methodological canons nor reliable evidence.[37] The colonial, Hindu, and Muslim nationalist discourses considered above fall in the second category. Such histories provide legitimacy to sectarian political action and provide fuel to the formation of contested national identities.

The identity of victim and the desire for revenge so informs partisan history that, with state sponsorship, it can become a real disruptive force. In the hands of its partisan practitioners, the study of history is no longer concerned with an exploration of knowledge. Rewriting history is essential to keep in touch with the advancing frontiers of knowledge, but rewriting for partisan purposes as experienced in India and Pakistan for imprinting the ideologies of ruling regimes, the notion of Hindu rashtra in the case of India and Islamic fundamentalism in the case of Pakistan, transforms history into an instrumentalist discipline. It is also important to recognize, as indicated above, that such historical writings were products of colonial modernization. This very colonial project has survived in the form of religious nationalist ideologies trying to foster essentialized religio-ethnic identities both before and after the colonial period. The modern globalized structure of politics plays a crucial role in sustaining and disseminating such religious nationalism. Thus, it is not without significance that the rising strength of religious nationalism in both India and Pakistan has been contemporaneous with the blatant subjection of the two states to the force of globalization. This is perhaps because, as Romila Thapar aptly remarks: 'The new communities created by globalization are supposed to be modern but where modernization fails them they use religious identities as a cover for a barbaric cult of terror and fear.'[38] Both in India and Pakistan, this process has been sustained by the financial support of their residents settled abroad.

The victims in each case have been democracy, secularism, social equity, and justice. Yet democracy can provide a cure for the extremes of religious nationalism. This became evident when in India the ruling BJP-led Hindu fundamentalist coalition that had engaged itself in popular mobilization through its modular partisan history was defeated in the fourteenth parliamentary election of May 2004. In the parliamentary election, the electorate, contradicting all predictions of the victory of Hindu nationalists and their ability to mobilize people through their modular partisan history, passed a verdict in favour of an alliance of secular and democratic forces. It reveals that in a democratic society, despite the readymade attraction, partisan history could become a trap for its proponents as well.[39]

Notes

1. Available at http://www.petitiononline.com/108india/petition.html. The petition reads, in part: 'she is an avowed antagonist of India's Hindu civilization. As a well known Marxist, she represents a completely Eurocentric world view. I fail to see how she can be the correct choice to represent India's ancient history and civilization. She completely disavows that India ever had a history. . . .The ongoing campaign by Romila Thapar and others to discredit Hindu civilization is a war of cultural genocide.'

2. Benedict Anderson uses the notion of 'modular'—i.e. capable of being transplanted in diverse social terrains with varying degrees of self-consciousness—in his discussion of print capitalism and the formation of 'imagined communities'. Anderson argues that nationness, as well as nationalism, are cultural artifacts of a particular kind. See Benedict Anderson, *Imagined Communities: Reflections on the Origin and Spread of Nationalism*, London, 1993; Partha Chatterjee questions

this 'eurocentric' idea, arguing that the notion of a modular imagined community reduces Asians and Africans to perpetual passive consumers of a modernity emanating from European and American sources. See Partha Chatterjee, *The Nation and Its Fragments: Colonial and Postcolonial Histories*, Princeton, 1993, pp. 4–5.

3. See Gyan Prakash, 'Writing Post-Orientalist Histories of the Third World: Perspectives from Indian Historiography', in *Mapping Subaltern Studies and the Post Colonial*, Vinayak Chaturvedi, ed., London and New York, 2000.

4. For a detailed discussion of the theme, see Eric Wolf, *Europe and the Peoples without History*, Berkeley and Los Angeles, 1997.

5. Examples are James Mill, *The History of British India*, J. Elemes, ed., London, 1820; Sir William Jones, *Discourses delivered before the Asiatic Society and miscellaneous papers on the nations of India with an essay by Lord Teignmouth*, London, 1824 (5 vols.); and Vincent Arthur Smith, *The Oxford History of India*, Delhi, 1981. On this historiography, see Romila Thapar's submission on 'History as Politics' available at www.indiatogether.org/2003/ may/opl-history.htm.

6. Recent research, in fact, has shown that a substantial majority of Indian Muslims were converts from Hinduism. It has also been argued that contrary to colonial projection of the clash between Muslim invaders and indigenous power blocks in terms of religious conflict, the issue at stake was primarily territory, political power, and status. See Romila Thapar, 'History as Politics'.

7. Discussed in Purushottam Agarwal, 'Savarkar, Surat and Draupadi: Legitimising Rape as a Political Weapon', in *Women and the Hindu Right: A Collection of Essays*, Tanika Sarkar and Urbashi Butalia, eds., New Delhi, 1996.

8. See Indira Chowdhury, *The Frail Hero and Virile History: Gender and the Politics of Culture in Colonial Bengal*, New Delhi, 1996; and Sikata Banerjee, *Warriors in Politics: Hindu Nationalism, Violence, and the Shiv Sena in India*, Boulder, 1999.

9. See Thomas Trautmann, *Aryans and British India*, Berkeley and Los Angeles, 1997.

10. Vasant Kaiwar, 'The Aryan Model of History and the Oriental Renaissance: The Politics of Identity in an Age of Revolutions, Colonialism and Nationalism', in *Antinomies of Modernity: Essays on Race, Orient, Nation*, Vasant Kaiwar and Sucheta Mazumdar, eds., Durham and London: Duke University Press, 2003.

11. V.D. Savarkar, *Hindutva: Who is a Hindu?*, Delhi, 1989.

12. M.S. Golwalkar, *Bunch of Thoughts*, Bangalore, 1996.

13. V.D. Savarkar, *The Six Glorious Epochs of Indian History*, Delhi, 1984, p. 85. Quoted in Purushottam Agarwal, 'Savarkar Surat and Draupadi', p. 44.

14. V.D. Savarkar, *The Six Glorious Epochs*, pp. 129–30, quoted in Purushottam Agarwal, p. 48.

15. Mohamad Tavakoli-Targhi, *Refashioning Iran: Orientalism, Occidentalism and Nationalist Historiography*, Oxford, 2001.

16. Christophe Jaffrelot, *The Hindu Nationalist Movement and Indian Politics, 1925 to the 1990s*, London, 1996.

17. For a detailed explanation of Savarkar's appreciation of Nazi Germany and fascist Italy, see Marzia Casolari, 'Hindutva's Foreign Tie-Up in the 1930s: Archival Evidence', in *Economic and Political Weekly*, 22 January 2000. Also see

Chetan Bhatt, *Hindu Nationalism Origins, Ideologies and Modern Myths*, Oxford, 2001, pp. 105–8.

18. Ayesha Jalal, *The Sole Spokesman: Jinnah, the Muslim League and the Demand for Pakistan,* Cambridge, 1994.

19. Asim Roy, *The Islamic Syncretistic Tradition in Bengal*, Princeton, 1983; also see his *Islam in South Asia: A Regional Perspective,* New Delhi, 1996.

20. See Suranjan Das, *Communal Riots in Bengal 1905–1947*, Delhi, 1990.

21. For an excellent analysis of the violence that accompanied the Partition of British India in 1947, and the memory and 'shifting meanings and contours' of that violence, see Gyanendra Pandey, *Remembering Partition: Violence, Nationalism And History In India,* Cambridge, 2001.

22. The RSS, founded in 1925, is an organization aiming to establish a Hindu value system in India. Dr. K.B. Hedgewar is considered its founding father. The Viswa Hindu Parishad was founded in 1964 with the following objectives: to establish connections with Hindus settled outside India, to reintegrate within Hindu society all those who had once cut themselves off from it, and to spread Hindu values. Both these organizations are part of the broader Hindu fundamentalist front in India, known in political parlance as the 'Sangh parivar'. See Thomas B. Hansen, *The Saffron Wave: Democracy and Hindu Nationalism in Modern India,* Princeton, 1999, chap. 3.

23. For an overview of the movement see Sarvepalli Gopal, ed., *Anatomy of a Confrontation: The Babri Masjid–Ramjanmabhumi Issue,* New Delhi, 1991.

24. Amrita Basu, 'Feminism Inverted: The Gendered Imagery and Real Women of Hindu Nationalism,' in *Women and the Hindu Right,* Tanika Sarkar and Urbashi Butalia, eds., op. cit., pp. 162–3.

25. Ibid., p. 163.

26. Quoted in Thomas B. Hansen, *The Saffron Wave,* op. cit., p. 180.

27. See Krishna Kumar 'Continued Text' and Rashmi Paliwal and C.M. Subramanium 'Ideology and Pedagogy,' in *Seminar,* 400, December 1992, pp. 17–19, 34.

28. Romila Thapar, 'History as Politics', op. cit.

29. Ibid.

30. See A.G. Noorani, *Savarkar and Hindutva: The Godse Connection,* New Delhi, 2002. See also the review of the book by P.K. Datta, in *Frontline,* vol. 20, no. 8, 12–25 April 2003.

31. See *Deccan Herald,* 24 November 2002.

32. Quoted in Philip Oldenburg, 'A Place Insufficiently Imagined: Language, Belief and the Pakistan Crisis of 1971', in *Journal of Asian Studies,* vol. 44, no. 4, 1985, p. 724.

33. Anthony Mascarenhas, 'Genocide,' in *Sunday Times of London,* 13 June 1971.

34. Interview by Vidyadhar Date, *The Times of India,* 29 January 1999.

35. Christophe Jaffrelot, ed., *Pakistan: Nationalism without a Nation?,* New Delhi and London, 2002.

36. This is well elucidated in E.H. Carr, *What is History?,* Harmondsworth, 1964.

37. Eric Hobsbawm, *On History,* London, 1990.

38. Romila Thapar, 'History as Politics', op. cit.

39. The Indian National Congress-led United Progressive Alliance government that assumed power in New Delhi in 2004 under the premiership of Manmohan Singh positioned itself in favor of secular democratic politics. This government was supported from outside by the 61-strong Left group in the 543-member lower house of the Indian Parliament (Lok Sabha).

CHAPTER 6

CALCUTTA IN TURMOIL: APRIL 1919

The recent disturbances in Calcutta ... definitely point out that sedition and anarchy, which were primarily confined to the young men of the educated community, are finding a large number of recruits from amongst the masses as well.
—Home (Poll B) August 1919, nos. 315–19, National Archives of India, weekly report of Director, Central Intelligence, 7 July 1919.

T HAT WAS HOW a contemporary Bengali political detainee assessed the implication of the anti-Rowlatt Act turmoil in Calcutta between 11 and 13 April 1919. Unfortunately, however, in the existing historical literature on Rowlatt Satyagraha the significance of this unrest has gone unnoticed. This is partly because the disorder in Calcutta was relatively mild in the all-India context. While nine people were killed during the disturbances in Calcutta, the figure for the Punjab was 228, for Delhi 12 and for Ahmedabad 28.[1] Not unnaturally, the British official spokesman was content: There were no outrages of the same character in Calcutta, the disorder lasted only a few hours, there was no necessity for the introduction of martial law, there were no summary trials.[2] Similarly, while introducing the best available volume on Rowaltt Satyagraha, Ravinder Kumar expresses surprise how 'Calcutta ... remained quiet in 1919, despite its great reputation for being the liveliest city in India'.[3] But Calcutta did retort against the Rowlatt Act in its own way and the turbulence connected with it, as the present submission seeks to demonstrate, was an important chapter in the history of agitational politics that continues to be so characteristic of Calcutta.

*This essay was published in *Bengal Past and Present*, vol. 112, nos. 214–215, pts. 1 and 2, 1993.

The Backdrop to the Turmoil

The Rowlatt Satyagraha, as Ravinder Kumar aptly remarks, was the 'first countrywide agitation to be launched against the British government and it transformed nationalism in India from a movement representing the classes to a movement representing the masses . . .'[4]. The 'same unmistakable signs of unrest' that had affected the people in Bombay, Delhi, Lahore or Central Provinces were present in Calcutta. The city shared the general all-India post-war grievance: while the Indian political and educated elite had strained their economic resources to fight for England in the First World War, the Raj retaliated by the repressive Rowlatt Act which resulted in their scepticism about the Montagu-Chelmsford scheme, and convinced them about the need for a 'broader' movement.[5] On the other hand, the Khilafat question had turned the Calcutta Muslims against the British government. Gandhi's call for the Satyagraha in 1919 resulted in a fusion of these various layers of discontent. The potentialities of a major political upsurge were revealed when a Calcutta daily commented that if the Calcuttans had been armed like the Irish 'this unrest would have by this time developed into a rebellion . . .'.[6]

Frequent references are also found in official records to 'scheming revolutionaries' in Calcutta[7] and many contemporary officials ascribed the 'current political crisis' to the influence of Bolshevism.[8] The British were certainly overreacting. The 1917 revolution had such a traumatic effect on the British bureaucracy that any 'violent threat' to the Empire's stability was looked upon as a Bolshevik conspiracy. To quote an official comment: 'The danger of Bolshevism to India lies not in a military victory of Bolshevik arms, but in the insidious effects of Bolshevik propaganda. This propaganda is always directed towards the exploitation of social grievances . . . [which] are so serious . . . [that] . . . the propaganda become[s] formidable.[9]

Micro-level studies have unravelled how 'passions' excited by the Rowlatt Satyagraha 'had little to do with formal organisation'.[10] Instead, Gandhi has been shown to 'have relied upon local discontents to draw various classes and communities into a movement of protest against the British Government'.[11] The same was largely true for Calcutta.

The period preceding the April outburst in Calcutta witnessed a rising price-curve of the daily necessities,[12] the situation being further complicated by increasing cases of food adulteration.[13] Certain social developments on the eve of the tumult also made sections of the Calcuttans restive and the Gandhian Satyagraha in Calcutta, as in other cities, drew upon 'local' discontents to unite classes and communities into a movement of protest against the British government.[14] References may, for instance, be made to the distress of a large number of slum-dwellers of north Calcutta who had their huts demolished for 'improvement schemes' without being properly rehoused by the Calcutta Improvement Trust.[15] Again, the months preceding the turbulence were 'exceptionally unhealthy' in Calcutta, the mortality rate reaching the highest figure to be recorded since 1907.[16] Calcutta Corporation's measures to tackle this problem of public health were hopelessly inadequate and widespread public anger was evident. A government report itself admitted that the victims—most of them Muslims—were found 'talking about their grievances in shops, *masjids* and homes'.[17] The Satyagraha provided a means of expressing such popular grievances.

Material discontent alone could not have generated a political climate conducive to a popular outburst. But an ideological disapproval of the Raj combined with socio-economic discomfort created a strong public distemper in 1919 Calcutta. Nationalist newspapers, both English and vernacular, published articles on the 'un-British rule', economic nationalism and heightened racialism which must have affected at least the educated sections of the society.[18] Provocative leaflets in popular language were distributed in different parts of the city immediately before the outbreak.[19] An active propaganda campaign also popularized the charisma of Gandhi which made the Mahatma's image a 'rallying point' for popular mobilization. Interestingly, the area most affected by the turmoil experienced largest circulation of 'provocative leaflets' in Hindi and Bengali.[20]

In tune with the rest of India, the Calcuttans had observed 6 April as the protest day against the Rowlatt Act. The northern part of the town wore a deserted look from the very morning, and in the afternoon a 10,000 strong crowd was addressed by C. R. Das at the maidan. But no 'untoward' incident happened. The news of Gandhi's arrest on the 10 April near Delhi, however, had an electrifying effect on the sensitive psychology of the Calcutta crowd, and normal life in the city came to a halt in the next three days.

From the early morning of the 11th (Friday) shops in the entire northern belt of Calcutta—encompassing Strand Road, Harrison Road, Chitpur Road, Canning Street and Cornwallis Street—remained closed; crowds collected in street corners and persistently interferred with tramcars and other traffic. The same was experienced on the 12th and 13th.[21] Processions singing national songs and shouting 'Bande Mataram' and 'Hindu-Musalman ki jai' paraded the main thoroughfares. Often the processionists ended their walk by taking a dip in the Ganges. Any attempt by the police to restore order incited clashes with the crowd. In fact, as soon as patrols appeared they were pelted with bricks, stones and other missiles, causing injuries to the police personnel. By the afternoon of the 12th the Bengal Governor feard that matters were slipping beyond control and called in the army. Order was restored on the 14th, but not without resorting to firings by the police and the army.[22]

The Anatomy of the Turmoil

Unlike the riots which preceded and followed it—communal and non-communal alike—the April outbreak did not experience any lootings. Instead, its predominant characteristic was the expression of anti-European feelings. Actual cases of assaults on Europeans in 1919 might not have been numerous.[23] But the intense anti-European mentality of the restive crowd was clearly manifest. Europeans were made to disembark from trams, buses and private vehicles and walk to their destinations.[24] Sikh drivers boycotted their English employers and the European quarter of the town remained without vehicles for at least two days. At all important crossroads Europeans were forced to take off their topees (hats worn by Europeans) and proceed bareheaded, and such actions were invariably accompanied with loud cheers and shouts of 'Gandhi ki jai'.[25] European women were chased by the frenzied crowd which often occasioned police intervention.[26] At Chitpur Road in central Calcutta, a man running with a topee was readily greeted with appaluse and nationalist slogans.[27] Sometimes when the Europeans tried to force their vehicles through the crowd they faced physical assaults.[28] The hostility faced by Europeans in general becomes evident from the following experience of one of them:

On reaching the Chitpur crossing, I found myself in the midst of a small crowd of about fifty persons. Two or three amongst them ordered me to take off my hat and make my way up to Chitpur. There were loud laughters behind me, so I put my hat on again ... I was [then] hurled against a shop-window, my hat was snatched off my head, somebody slapped my face, I was struck with a stick on the shoulder, and kicked ... but suddenly the people moved off, and I saw that a police patrol car had come. . . .[29]

European hotels were another favourite target of the crowd. Particular mention may be made of the ransacking of the Bristol Hotel in central Calcutta.[30]

Anti-Europeanism went hand in hand with the ventilation of anti-government sentiments. One way of demonstrating this feeling was found by closing the shutters of Indian shops and business establishments.[31] There is hardly any indication of the use of threat or force for keeping the shops closed. Rather, the shopkeepers displayed, as the *Nayak* noted, 'a strong undercurrent of self-restraint and self-sacrifice'.[32] The 1919 agitation, the same paper remarked, 'was not the product of ease-loving *babus,* but of the self-sacrificing people'.

The police, the most visible manifestation of the Raj which the Satyagraha was challenging, became a natural target of the crowd fury. At different points along the central and northern parts of Calcutta the police parties were pelted with bricks, stones, lumps of wood and soda water bottles from housetops.[33] The Deputy Commissioner Wilson and Assistant Commissioner Cook were themselves injured while combating a gathering of youths—'mostly Muslims with a sprinkling of Marwaris'—at Zakaria Street on the 12 April.[34] On the same day a turbulent crowd in Howrah attacked a police picket and set its cars on fire.[35] The extent of popular antagonism against the police is borne out by the following account from a correspondent of the *The Englishman* (14 April 1919).

On Harrison Road men armed with scaffolding bamboos ran up to the vehicle shouting *Nai Jane Dega* (We shall not allow you to go). The European sergeant replied, *Jaye-ga, Hut Jao* (shall go, move away) . . . (Instantly) the crowd closed round us (the police) and stones began to fly rattling on the body and hood of the car. The men with the bamboo thrust them in front of the car . . . there were shouts of *Mar Sala* and *Mar dalo* (Beat them). . . .

The police officers in such circumstances were usually saved only by the dexterity of the drivers of their vehicles.

Other incidents can be cited as examples of a general resentment against the police.[36] For example, in north Calcutta the crowd greeted a person who was running across the road carrying a battered white helmet of the 'type worn by police themselves'. On another occasion a tall man holding aloft a 12–feet-long bamboo stood in the midst of the road, refusing to allow any police patrol to pass. This made the crowd cheer him with shouts of 'Gandhi ki jai' (victory to Gandhi). Isolated attacks on the police were also common. For example, two constables while escorting an Oriya prisoner were stopped by a crowd who demanded the release of the convict. When the policemen refused, they were beaten up and the prisoner was rescued. The two constables had to be hospitalized.[37] The turbulent crowd also intervened in the attempts by the Fire Brigade personnel to put down fire.[38]

In combating this crowd fury the police did not hesitate to use all available techniques. In some areas they even dropped 'dacoity wire netting' to prevent the crowd from 'advancing further'.[39] The *Amrita Bazar Patrika* (16 April 1919) reported how Indian public figures like Babu Sarju Prasad Singh, a member of the Executive Committee of the India Home Rule League, were subjected to police high-handedness when they sought to restrain the crowd. Very often unprovoked firing was resorted to. On the 12th at the Howrah-Chitpur Road junction the police, for example, discharged volleys of shots towards the upper storeys of the houses of such prominent people as Protap Narayan Roy, leaving at least thirteen 'in a pool of blood'.[40] The *Amrita Bazar Patrika* (16 April 1919) reported on the military's firing of 'bullets . . . on the upper part of the body of the wounded contrary to the usual humane practice'.

Disruption of the transport system also symbolized the anti-establishment consciousness of the recalitrant crowd in Calcutta. Trams, buses, taxis, private cars, hackney carriages, etc., were forced off the road to throw the city's life out of gear. Initially persuasive measures were adopted by the demonstrators but when they failed force was applied, vehicles being attacked with missiles of all sorts and passengers dragged out.[41] Cases of the snatching of moneybags from tram conductors were also reported.[42]

The Calcutta tumult was characterized by an exceptional Hindu-Muslim fraternity without which the anti-British assertions would not have been as strong as was noticed in those days of April 1919. Muslims and Hindus of all shades—Bengalis, Marwars, upcountrymen—joined the processions in 'tens and thousands'. At a meeting in the Maidan the Muslims and Marwaris were found embracing one another.[43] The Marwari priests put vermilion marks on the foreheads of the assembled Muslims: the Hindus cried 'Ali Ali'; national songs were sung in processions and rallies; Muslims lent their voice to *Bande Mataram*.[44] In large gatherings, drinking water was delivered from the same lorries to Hindus and Muslims alike, and shouts of 'Hindu Mussalman ki jai' filled the air.[45] In an unprecedented move a joint Hindu-Muslim meeting was also held in the afternoon of the 11 April 1919 inside the Nakhoda mosque, addressed amongst others by Hira Lal Gandhi, the son of the Mahatma.[46] One Muslim speaker, Syed Ahmed Hossain, reminded the gathering that the closure of shops would 'not go too far' if the government employees continued to join their offices. The meeting ended on a dramatic note with a Marwari priest raising the cry of 'Sultan ki jai'.[47] Of course, such scenes of Hindu-Muslim 'comradeship' was a common feature of the Rowlatt Satyagraha in other cities.[48]

The Crowd

The spread of the disturbance was associated with a change in the nature of the political leadership on the ground. The initial rallies adopting the Satyagraha pledge was of a 'composite' nature, comprising lawyers, teachers, students, merchants as well as 'the ordinary men in the streets' whom C.R. Das preferred to address as the 'Daridra Narayan' (the poor is god). Marwaris, Bhatias, Gujratis, Hindusthani durwans of Burrabazar and Punjabi and Sikh taxi drivers were particularly prominent.[49] An index to the nature of the Hindu crowd at this stage is provided by the Nakhoda mosque gathering of the 12th, nearly half of whom were Bhatias, Marwaris, Jains and uncountry Hindus.[50] Similarly, the Beadon Square rally on the same day reportedly contained 67 per cent upcountry Hindus of various castes.[51]

It is thus not unnatural to find the prominence of young upcountrymen, mostly aged between 18 and 35, in the list of the wounded and arrested.[52] An official report disdainfully refers to them as 'chokras' (young boys).[53] The upcountry street urchins between 15 and 30 years of age were also active in making the passengers disembark from buses and trams.[54] The following statistics represent a sample indicator of the crowd which became increasingly associated with actual violence.[55]

TABLE 6.1: Casualties (killed and wounded) in
Calcutta Disturbances on 12 April 1919

Name	Caste	Age	Address	Remarks
(A) PERSONS DEAD FROM POLICE/MILITARY FIRING ON HARRISON ROAD				
Chandra Pal Singh	Hindu (upcountry)	40	183 Harrison Rd.	
Sagar Mull	Hindu	35	17 Rup Chand Roy St.	
Ramesh Ch. Mukherji	Hindu	18	12 Patuatola Lane	
Unknown person	Hindu	27		
Nemai Chand	Hindu	25	68–1 Bartolla St.	
Brijlal Bhatia	Hindu	30		
Puran Mull	Hindu	30	57 Khengraputty	
Dukharam Ahir	Hindu	19		
(B) PERSONS with NON-FATAL INJURIES FROM FIRING ON HARRISON ROAD				
Sewakaram Bias	Upcountry Hindu	24	37 Armenian St.	
Peer Bux	Muslim	35	Armenian St.	
Ram Dular Tewari	Upcountry Hindu	27	61 Cross St. or 20 Khengraputty	
Mali Ram Brahmin	Upcountry Hindu	28	1 Goenka Lane	
Purusottam Ahir	Upcountry Hindu	24	Jagannath Ghat	

A sharp contrast between the previous Swadeshi and the 1919 crowd needs to be emphasized here. While the former had a predominance of bhadraloks,[56] that social group was conspicuous by its absence in 1919, except in some stray incidents involving interference with the transport system.[57] The Beadon Square rally of the 11th reportedly contained only 25 per cent Bengali Hindus and there was, what the Chief Secretary to the Bengal government noted, a 'remarkable absence of Bengali (Hindu) students who generally form a large element in a Calcutta mass meeting ...'.[58] The *Nayak* alleged that none of the Bengali Hindu leaders had signed the Satyagraha vow;[59] the *Dainik Basumati* repented how the enthusiasm of the upcountry Hindus had 'cast us [the Bengali Hindus] into the shade ...'.[60]

A detailed study needs to be undertaken to explain the relative non-involvement of Bengali Hindu bhadraloks in the 1919 outburst.

On the other hand, the Marwaris, hitherto renowned for their 'peaceful avocation', surprised the Bengal government by their participation in the Rowalatt Satyagraha.[61] In his weekly report of 7 July 1919 the Director of Central Intelligence thus remarked on the active Marwari participation in the Calcutta disturbances: They [Marwaris] joined the crowds; they wrote and published leaflets and handbills; asked their durwans and other employees to join the sacred cause; helped in organizing volunteer groups and paid for initial expenses.[62] Some Marwaris even paid the security amount on behalf of the *Amrita Bazar Patrika* which had been prosecuted for 'inflaming popular passions against the Rowlatt Act'. Prominent Marwaris also took the initiative to form a Civil Rights Committee that raised money in aid of the riot victims.

This Marwari involvement in the Calcutta turmoil made the Governor Ronaldshay search for an explanation.[63] A sizeable section amongst the Marwaris was believed to have been impressed with an idea that a common cause with the Muslims could have a 'restraining influence' on cowslaughter of which they were the most vociferous Hindu critics. At the same time, noted Ronaldshay, the Mahatma was viewed as a 'supporter of . . . orthodox Hindu aspirations' which made the Marwaris readily rally around the Gandhian call. Moreover, the Marwaris had reacted sharply against the government's new Excise-Profits Tax whose 'searching methods of enquiry' adversely affected their economic pursuits. Ronaldshay refers to 'wildest rumour' of government's determination to take 'Rs. 2.8 out of every Rs. 5 that a person possessed' and the anguish against the Raj that followed from it prompted the Marwari participation in the disturbance. Whatever might have been the 'true reason' for their participation, the presence of the Marwaris and Bhatias among the 1919 turbulent crowd was such that *The Times* spoke of a 'Marwari rebellion' in Calcutta.[64] The Chief Secretary to the Bengal government also characterized the disturbance as an affair of the non-Bengali population of northern Calcutta.[65] The Bengal Governor himself accused the Marwaris and Bhatias for having provoked violence.[66]

It is, however, difficult to dissect the components of the Muslim rioting crowd because of the lack of available data. It appears that both Bengali and non-Bengali Muslims, especially of the lower social order, were active. Among the Muslims present at the Nakhoda Mosque meeting of the 12th April, the majority were 'illiterates'.[67] The Muslim inhabitants of central and north Calcutta *bustees* [slums], whom the officials disdainly categorised as 'low class Muhammadans' were singled out by the police as 'notorious' in 'stone throwing incidents'.[68] Butchers were also prominent in the Muslim crowd.[69]

Most contemporary observers referred to a gradual shift in the initiative for action to the 'ordinary people', particularly the upcountry Hindus and Muslims.[70] The government itself acknowledged 'breaking of the monopoly control over political agitation by a handful of educated persons' and admitted that 'the dumb had become voiced'.[71] This popular 'radicalism', however, displayed an irresistible tendency to seek 'shelter behind the Mahatma's banner', a trend which, as recent studies have shown, manifested itself throughout the period of Gandhian nationalism.[72] The on-the-spot organizers of such 'radical shift' were by and large the subordinate social groups, and established leaders asked themselves how this could have been possible.[73] The *Calcutta Samachar* commented that the Calcutta event had exploded the myth 'circulated by the Anglo-Indian press that the untouchable and illiterate do not know what political agitation is . . .'.[74]

The Crowd–Leader Dichotomy

Increasing participation by members of the lower social strata in the 1919 Calcutta outburst contributed to the spread of the unrest. It, however, alarmed the established leaders—Hindu and Muslim alike—who now issued manifestos condemning the disturbances.[75] The Indian Muslim Association and the Committee of Central Muhammadan Association even questioned the righteousness of allowing non-Muslims to preach from the pulpit of the Nakhoda mosque.[76] Similarly, the Marwari Association and the Marwari Chambers of Commerce expressed 'deep . . . pain and sorrow at the disturbance' and affirmed 'their loyalty to the government'.[77] Some Marwari leaders disclaimed the responsibility of their community as a whole for the disturbances and 'alleged that those Marwaris who had taken part in them were an insignificant number of men of the lowest class'.[78] The Moderates also disliked 'the degeneration' of the Satyagraha[79] and their leader S.N. Banerjee 'unhesitatingly' approved of the Governor Ronaldshay's plan to censure the *Amrita Bazar Patrika* for 'pouring poison into the mind of the youth of the country . . .'.[80]

All these demonstrate a crowd/leader dichotomy, a contrast between the attitude of the leaders and of the crowd. The two leading contemporary Bengali figures in organized politics, C.R. Das and Byomkesh Chakravarti, were never interested in a calculated 'breach of peace'. In their audience with the Governor on 4 April they promised to exercise 'discretion' so that their speeches remained 'moderate in tone, short, devoid of provocative language'.[81] Both had confessed to the Governor that they did not even support the 'idea of requesting people to close their shops'.[82] The Governor also drew comfort from the fact that the plan of forming a Committee to frame a list of laws which were to be disobeyed had not materialized in Bengal.[83] But, as has been indicated above, once the subordinate social groups came out on the streets, they could not be made to play the restricted role which the leaders of institutional politics had chalked out for them. Very often the leaders of organized politics were pressurized by the crowd to undertake actions against their own convictions. For example, Byomkesh Chakravarti repented to the Bengal Governor how he was 'compelled' to address the historic joint Hindu-Muslim gathering in the Nakhoda mosque, 'although he had no desire to do so'.[84] This was an apt illustration of the dilemma in which the leaders of organized politics were placed—their resentment at the 'mob' 'going out of hand' but their inability to impose checks at that juncture.

The irony of the situation, was exposed when Byomkesh Chakravarti conceded the 'duty of all law-abiding citizens to support [the] Government in putting down [the] disturbance', but added in a sombre vein that 'he must go some way with the organizers or demonstrators (i.e. the subordinate social groups) or they would simply throw him over and any authority or influence he had with them would disappear'. Chakravarti even went to the length of praising the police action which had 'hitherto . . . been all that could be desired and they had sedulously refrained from provocation'. He also agreed to plead with 'the people' for the resumption of normal business since 'Mr. Gandhi was not under arrest but was free to move as he wished in the Bombay Presidency'.[85]

Certainly the Moderates such as Byomkesh Chakravarti ultimately had their way and such 'repeated brakes' on 'mass pressures' were experienced throughout the nationalist movement.[86] Yet, short-lived popular initiatives and points of contradictions between organized institutional politics and the world of unorganized and perhaps relatively autonomous popular actions were by themselves noteworthy, and their implications need to be worked out. The outbreak of popular radicalism in Calcutta was particularly important as it came only days after contemporary observers had expressed surprise at the 'lack of excitement' in that city when Bombay and other areas were considerably agitated over the passage of the Rowlatt Act.[87]

Conclusion: The April Turmoil and Agitational Politics in Calcutta

The Calcutta outburst, then, demands attention not merely as an episodic event or as a behaviourial condition at a given point of time. Instead, it is possible to view it as a contributing point in the historical process that converted the once prized city of the Raj into a crucible of the politics of protest which not only fuelled the nationalist struggle but was also directly connected with the evolution of a radical political culture in Calcutta. Throughout the nationalist movement the colonial government had to confront in Calcutta hartals, riots, insurrections, demonstrations and rallies, the incidence of which significantly increased after the second decade of this century. The 1919 outburst shared the basic features of popular violence with its immediate predecessor, the Swadeshi Riot of 1907, and the long chain of militant outbreaks of subordinate social groups that followed. Expressions of anti-European feelings, attacks on the police as the most palpable instrument of the Raj, the disruption of the communication system to dislocate the normal functioning of the state apparatus and the crowd–leader dichotomy, which characterized the April violence, were replicated in future outbreaks connected with mainstream nationalism, revolutionary terrorism, as well as working class and youth radicalism which reached a climactic point in 1945–6, celebrated by a historian as 'The Almost Revolution'.[88]

The secular and anti-imperialist trend in popular politics in Calcutta, of which the 1919 outburst forms an important chapter, was not, however, a unlinear development.[89] Instead, it was interspersed with doses of communal rioting which I have tried to delineate in my work on *Communal Riots in Bengal 1905–1947*. The communalization of Bengal politics, reaching its climax with the Great Calcutta Killing of August 1946 and the spate of riotings that followed, certainly implied a crucial setback for the secular and anti-imperialist spirit of political Calcutta.

The communal carnage could not, however, destroy the equally weighty force of secular anti-imperialism in Bengal politics. When we look back from the vantage point of the 1940s into the politics of the earlier decades, we find that until the last moment the political pendulum in Calcutta, or even in Bengal, swung between nationalist and separatist politics. But during the 'prelude to the Partition', as we know, mainstream Congres nationalism lost much of its Muslim political support and a section within it developed a strong Hindu communal identity. Consequently, Calcutta came to suffer from a rather desperate introversion of consciousness, and the Bengali psyche was gripped by an obsessive sense of uncertainty about whether it would go to Pakistan or not. This sense of pain and anguish was compounded by the influx of refugees and its inability to integrate with the national mainstream after the truncated settlement of 1947. Nevertheless, the structural disarticulation between class and politics that was seen during the Partition came to be rapidly bridged in the post-August 1947 days, as is evident from the strength of the organized Left in the political life of West Bengal.

At another level the 1919 Calcutta turmoil remains a living example of how at a particular conjuncture regional barriers could be transcended to create nationalist linkages. An explication of this trend has become specially important as a possible counterpoise to the thesis that fragmented identities of caste, community or kinship, and not national or class identities, had been the determining factors in Indian history.[90] In a recent fundamental and sophisticated intervention in Indian historiography, Partha Chatterjee[91] has effectively 'reimagined' nationhood in India. The basic presupposition of the treatise is the notion of community, distinct from the 'single determinate, demographically enumerable form of nation'. Partha Chatterjee contends that 'anti-colonial nationalism creates its own domain of sovereignty within colonial society well before it begins its political battle with the imperial power'. The emergence of the nation-state in India was contemporaneous with the subjugation, appropriation and marginalization of the fragmented identities which characterized, what Chatterjee calls, the spiritual domain of social institutions and practices. Chatterjee is convinced that these fragments not only resisted the totalizing project of nationalism but represented 'richer ways of imagining a community'.

The 1919 anti-Rowlatt disturbances in Calcutta, however, brought to the fore nationalist assertions across narrower parochial identities. The Intelligence Branch papers record in unequivocal terms the 'general sympathy' of the Calcuttans for the 1919 disturbances.[92] To quote *Amrita Bazar Patrika* (12 April 1919):

Another remarkable feature apparent even to the meanest intelligence is the fact that the spirit of nationalism . . . has filtered down to the substrata of the society. Hithertofore, the cravings for reforms were confined to the few intelligentsia of the country and the masses were apathetic to it. But now the whole community, even the neglected *'Daridra Narayan'* or the 'proletariat' if we may call them so, have now come to realise the situation and have responded to the call of the country. . . .

Perhaps the *Amrita Bazar Patrika* was being over-enthusiastic. But the fact that *The Englishman* (14 April 1919), by no means a nationalist organ, cited the remark as an evidence of resurgent nationalism demonstrates that the British administration had been unnerved by the way events were cutting across regional and sectarian barriers to create a more powerful form of anti-colonial agitation.

Thanks to a strict press censorship, the news of the Jallianwala Bagh massacre reached Calcutta a little late. But once the story became public, popular indignation ran high, although no violent outburst occurred. Secret 'preachings' in the outlying mill areas urged the Muslim workers to 'lay aside all differences and join Marwaris . . . if all castes joined it would be impossible for Government to deal with them'.[93] This propaganda campaign was undertaken by such 'expert' Muslim preachers as Mohammed Azeem, Mohammad Azimullah and Mohammad Kudratmulla who had originally hailed from 'upcountry' but had settled down in north Calcutta.[94] Police reports refer to group meetings in Calcutta slums, particularly in the predominantly Muslim ones, to acquaint the people of Dwyer's misdeeds. These gatherings were invariably addressed by, to use Police vocabulary, 'unknown characters', obviously implying relatively unimportant main-stream nationalist figures. Rabindranath Tagore renounced his knighthood to protest against the Jallianwala Bagh massacre. The letter that Tagore wrote to the British government on this occasion reflected 'the anguish of the Bengali intellectual community. It was also in the aftermath of the Jallianwala Bagh tragedy that the Calcutta Punjab Sabha was established. It organized local meetings and distributed leaflets to mobilize public opinion against 'the Punjab wrongs'.[95] One of the organizers of the Sabha, Gopal Das, was a disciple of Lajpat Rai and was known to the Police 'for the virulence of his anti-Government and extremist opinion'.

While finalizing this article, I came across a number of IB files on the labour situation in 1919 Bengal which indicated instrances of a convergence between labour and nationalist consciousness. The files contain references to a number of labour agitations where slogans demanding economic justice were raised along with condemnation of the Jallianwala Bagh killings. I have cited elsewhere such conjunctures between popular protest and nationalist politics in Bengal around mainstream nationalist stirrings, notably during the Quit India movement.[96] The 1919 Calcutta disorders perhaps anticipated this trend. The way Calcutta responded to a happening in distant Punjab demonstrated how a sense of national identity could be generated amongst a people when pitted against the 'other', and in this case the killers at Jallianwala Bagh represented the 'other',

Nations can be 'constructs' or 'imagined communities'.[97] But the process of construction of national identity in opposition against the colonial ruler during liberation movement is not necessarily similar to what is experienced in 'nation-building' under postcolonial regimes. In the course of the anti-colonial struggle when a nation seeks to come to its own there remain strong possibilities for the merger of narrow identities to fight an alien rule. The subordination of local, regional or ethnic identities by the superimposition of 'unity from the top' in the interest of a national ruling class becomes particularly prominent after the nation-state has been formed.[98] The political turmoil in Calcutta in April 1919 was an event in the continuum of the anti-colonial movement which culminated in the creation of two independent states in the subcontinent. It was a tragic finale and India after that date was a substantially changed entity.

Notes

1. Home (Poll B) August 1919, nos. 253–4, National Archives of India (hereafter NAI). The figures for wounded in the Rowlatt violence were 9 in Calcutta, 29 in Delhi, 123 in Ahmedabad and 33 in the Punjab.

2. See the statement by Sir William Vincent, *Proceedings of the Indian Legislative Assembly,* 12 September 1919.

3. Ravinder Kumar, ed., *Essays on Gandhian Politics: The Rowlatt Satyagraha of 1919,* Oxford, 1971, p. 7.

4. Ibid., p. 4.

5. *The Hitavadi* (Calcutta), 25 April 1919, Report on Native Newspapers (hereafter NNR) no. 18 of 1919, p. 357, para-56, West Bengal State Archives (hereafter WBSA) .

6. *The Bengalee* (Calcutta), 16 April 1919, NNR no. 17 of 1919, p. 355, para-58, WBSA.

7. *The Nayak* (Calcutta) 18 April 1919, NNR no. 23 of 1919, p. 341, para-81, WBSA.

8. *The Nayak* (Calcutta), 10 April 1919, NNR no. 23 of 1919, p. 312, WBSA; *The Bengalee* (Calcutta), 26 April 1919, NNR no. 18 of 1919, p. 356, para-65, WBSA.

9. Home (Poll) A, December 1919, nos. 1–7, NAI, p. 11.

10. See D.E.U. Baker, 'The Rowlatt Satyagraha in the Central Provinces and Berar', K.L. Gillion, 'Gujrat in 1919', J. Masselos, 'Some Aspects of Bombay City Politics in 1919', D.W. Ferrell, 'The Rowlatt Satyagraha in Delhi', and R. Kumar, 'The Rowlatt Satyagraha in Lahore', in Ravinder Kumar, ed., *Essays,* op. cit.; Also see H. Singh, *Gandhi Rowlatt Satyagraha And British Imperialism,* Delhi, 1990.

11. Ravinder Kumar, op. cit., p. 6.

12. *Index Number of Indian Prices 1861–1918,* Department of Statistics, Government of India, Calcutta, p. 1, para-4.

13. *The Dainik Basumati,* Calcutta, 23 April 1919, NNR no. 35 of 1919, WBSA.

14. Ravinder Kumar, ed., *Essays,* op. cit., see the Introduction.

15. *Report on the Administration of Bengal 1918–1919* (Part II), pp. 48–9, para-226.

16. Ibid., p. 49, para-240. The death rate rose to 35 per 1,000, the infant mortality being 200 per registered deaths.

17. Weekly Report of the Director, Central Intelligence, 7 July 1919, op. cit.

18. For an indication see *Amrita Bazar Patrika* (hereafter *ABP*) of the period.

19. File-Home (Poll) B May 1919, Progs. 514–15, Appendix-A, NAI.

20. *The Englishman* (Calcutta), 15 April 1919.

21. J.H. Kerr Chief Secretary, Bengal, to the Secretary, Home, India, no. 176–P-D dated 29 April 1919, Home (Poll) B May 1919, nos. 514–15, NAI.

22. Ibid.; *The Englishman* (Calcutta), 14 April 1919.

23. File-Home (Poll) B May 1919, nos. 514–15, op. cit.

24. Ibid.

25. Ibid.

26. Ibid.

27. Ibid.
28. File-Home (Poll) Deposit October 1919, no. 33, NAI.
29. Ibid.; See also *The Englishman* (Calcutta), 14 April 1919.
30. *The Statesman* (hereafter *ST*), 8 April 1919.
31. File-Home (Poll) B May 1919, nos. 514–15, op. cit.
32. *The Nayak* (Calcutta), 12 April 1919, NNR no. 16 of 1919, p. 313, para-65.
33. *ST*, 8 April 1919.
34. File-Home (Poll) B May 1919, nos. 514–15, op. cit.
35. Ibid.
36. Ibid., especially the report of G.D. Pinder Agent, Bank of Bengal, Burrabazar Branch.
37. *ST*, 8 April 1919.
38. From Clarke, Police Commissioner, Calcutta to the Chief Secretary, Bengal, 14 April 1919, op. cit.
39. *The Englishman* (Calcutta), 14 April 1919.
40. File-Home (Deposit) October 1919, no. 33, NAI.
41. File-Home (Poll) B May 1919, nos. 514–15, op. cit.
42. File-Home (Poll) Deposit, October 1919, no. 33, op. cit.
43. *The Bengalee* (Calcutta), 8 April 1919, NNR no. 14 of 1919, WBSA.
44. Ibid.; File-Home (Deposit) October 1919, no. 33, op. cit.
45. *ABP*, 7 April 1919.
46. File-Home (Poll) B May 1919, nos. 514–15, op. cit.
47. Ibid.
48. Ravinder Kumar, ed., *Essays,* op. cit.; *The Bengalee* (Calcutta), 8 April 1919, NNR no. 14 of 1919, WBSA.
49. File-Home (Poll) B May 1919 nos. 514–15, op. cit.; *ST*, 16 April 1919; File-Home (Poll) Deposit, no. 46, July 1919, NAI.
50. *The Nayak* (Calcutta), 18 April 1919, NNR no. 16 of 1919, p. 65, *The Bengalee* (Calcutta), April 1919, NNR no. 15 of 1919, pp. 287–8, WBSA; File-Home (Poll) B May 1919, nos. 514–15, op. cit.
51. Ibid.
52. File-Home (Poll) B May 1919, nos. 514–15, op. cit.
53. File-Home (Poll) Deposit October 1919, no. 33, op. cit.
54. Ibid.
55. Ibid.
56. *The Rowlatt Report* on the revolutionary movement (1918); Hiren Chakrabarti, *Political Protest in Bengal: Boycott and Terrorism,* Calcutta, 1992; Sumit Sarkar, *The Swadeshi Movement in Bengal*, Calcutta, 1975 .
57. File-Home (Poll) Deposit October 1919, no. 33, op. cit.
58. File-Home (Poll) B May 1919, nos. 514–15, op. cit.
59. *The Nayak* (Calcutta), 8 April 1919, NNR no. 16 of 1919.
60. NNR no. 15 of 1919, p. 288, para-24, WBSA.
61. Mss. Eur. D523/30 India Office Library (hereafter IOL). Ronaldshay to Montagu, 19 May 1919.
62. Weekly Report of Director, Central Intelligence, 7 July 1919, op. cit.
63. Mss. Eur. D523/30, IOL, op. cit.

64. NNR no. 20 of 1919, p. 408, para-65.
65. File-Home (Conf) 299/1919, serial-3, WBSA.
66. NNR no. 17 of 1919, WBSA.
67. File-Home (Poll) B May 1919, nos. 514–15, op. cit.
68. Ibid.
69. *ST*, 13 April 1919.
70. Ibid.
71. File-Home (Poll) B May, nos. 514–15, op. cit.
72. Sumit Sarkar, *Popular Movements and 'Middle Class' Leadership in Late Colonial India: Perspectives and Problems of a 'History from Below'*, Calcutta, 1983; Shahid Amin, 'Gandhi as Mahatma: Gorakhpur District, Eastern UP 1921–22', in *Subaltern Studies*-III, Ranajit Guha, ed., Delhi, 1984 .
73. File-Home (Poll) B May 1919, nos. 514–15.
74. *Calcutta Samachar,* 8 April 1919.
75. J.H. Kerr, Chief Secretary, Bengal to the Secretary, Home, Government of India, op. cit.
76. Ibid.
77. Ibid.
78. Ibid.
79. *ST*, 18 April 1919.
80. Mss. Eur. D 609/1, IOL, *My Bengal Diary,* vol. I, pp. 224–5.
81. Mss. Eur. D 609/1 IOL, *My Bengal Diary*, op. cit.; Mss. Eur. D 523/30, Ronaldshay to Montagu, 14 April 1919.
82. *My Bengal Diary,* op. cit.
83. Ibid.
84. Ibid.*,* pp. 221–3.
85. From Clarke, Police Commissioner, Calcutta, to Chief Secretary, Bengal, 14 April 1919, op. cit.
86. Sumit Sarkar, *Popular Movements,* op. cit.
87. *My Bengal Diary,* op. cit., p. 216.
88. Gautam Chattopadhyay, 'The Almost Revolution', in *Essays in Honour of S.C. Sarkar,* Barun De et al., eds., Delhi, 1976 .
89. For an analysis of this trend, see Chapter 7 of this book.
90. See the volumes of *Subaltern Studies.*
91. Partha Chatterjee, *The Nation and its Fragments: Colonial and Postcolonial Histories,* Delhi, 1993.
92. IB records, Cal SB Branch, see diary of 10 May 1919.
93. Ibid., see diary of 3 May 1919.
94. Ibid.*,* WBSA, see file 221/19.
95. Weekly Report of Director, Central Intelligence, 14 July 1919 Home (Poll) B August 1919, nos. 315–19.
96. *Ganasakti* (Calcutta), 10 August 1993.
98. Benedict Anderson, *Imagined Communities: Reflections on the Origin and Spread of Nationalism*, London, 1983.
99. See Suranjan Das and Barun De, 'Ethnic Revivalism: Problems in the Indian Union', in *Ethnicity, Caste and People,* K.S. Singh, ed., Delhi, 1992.

CHAPTER 7

THE POLITICS OF AGITATION: CALCUTTA 1912–1947

ONCE BENGAL BECAME the stamping ground of English colonialism in the subcontinent, Calcutta and its hinterland rapidly emerged as the main nucleus of British economic interests in the country. The prominent position that the city came to enjoy under the Raj was demonstrated by the concentration of industries there, the level of shipping which passed through its port and the vast hinterland given over to the production of tea, coal and jute, nurtured in funds and in spirit from Calcutta itself. The city also developed as the melting pot of Eastern and Western culture. When the Raj sought to impart Western education, Calcutta was the experimental site: the new Western-educated middle class rapidly made Calcutta the cultural capital of the subcontinent.

Yet this prized city of the Empire was to become a crucible of agitational politics that greatly contributed to the ending of the Empire. From the 1860s, Calcutta became a focal point of what has been called the 'politics of association', culminating in the establishment of the Indian National Congress in 1885. When Lord Curzon announced his infamous partition of Bengal in 1905, Calcutta responded enthusiastically to the anti-Partition agitation which gained in 1911 the limited success of rejoining the fractured Bengali-speaking community. But 1912 again altered the balance of Bengali morale. The transfer of the capital from Calcutta to Delhi indicated the British determination to evade future challenges to its authority. Although essentially a 'bhadralok movement', the anti-Partition Swadeshi agitation witnessed the first attempts at labour mobilization on a significant scale. On the other hand, the defeat of the Partition scheme came as a rude shock to the Muslim elite, which had its first taste of political power with the

*This essay was published in Sukanta Chaudhuri, ed., *Calcutta: The Living City*, vol. II, Calcutta, 1993.

formation of East Bengal and Assam as a separate province. This resentment was the fountainhead of Muslim separatist politics in Bengal. Agitational politics in Calcutta from 1912 till 1947 reflected all these trends: mainstream nationalism, the militancy of subordinate social groups, and communal animosities. I shall endeavour to show the interactions between these levels of popular politics in Calcutta.

The Roots of Political Militancy

There were strong historical reasons why Calcutta, born as a nucleus of British imperial economic interests, should have been transformed into an important centre of political militancy. Paradoxical as it might seem, the cause lay in the economic expansion of Calcutta itself. The dominance of European capital was reflected in a strong feeling of 'racial antipathy' towards the Indian residents. As Rajat Ray has put it: '. . . in Calcutta it could not be asserted, as was claimed of Madras, that friendly relations existed between the two [European and Indian] races. . . . Because the stake of British capital was so large in Calcutta and its hinterland, racial antagonism was also all-pervasive there.'[1]

Racialism was encountered in Calcutta at various levels. Englishmen slapped, kicked and whipped the 'natives' and addressed them as 'niggers' and 'swine' without any hesitation. Murderous assaults on Indian servants were common. Indian men and women were frequently thrown out of railway carriages. Calcutta was dotted with exclusive European clubs whose doors were closed to the 'natives'. Appeals for redress were of no consequence as the licence for English arrogance was 'virtually built into the judicial system'. Indians did not always suffer racial oppression without protest. As early as 1893, *The Englishman* complained of increasing signs of resistance: Europeans are insulted, abused and jeered at by the lowest type of natives, and if they retaliate, they are set upon by a mob. The bitterness born of such mental antagonism exacerbated the intensity of Calcutta politics.

The growth of organized politics in Calcutta was also connected with a particular social development in the nineteenth century: the emergence of an educated middle class among the Bengali *bhadralok*. They provided the initial support for running a colonial state, but were soon at odds with the prevalent views of administration. Exposure to liberal-democratic bourgeois values through Western education, a flourishing press, voluntary associations and political pressure groups gave the *bhadralok* an ideological orientation that went against the grain of the 'power relationships' on which the earlier colonial administration had been reared. 'As a result', writes J. McGuire, '(the *bhadralok*) would become a more progressive, though not united, force by forging strong ties with classes more central to capitalist development. Their common ground would be defined by opposition to the colonial state in so far as it represented the interests of British capital.'[2]

The failure of the ablest *bhadraloks* such as Umeshchandra Banerji ('Woomesh Chunder' or W.C. Bonnerji) and Surendranath Banerji, to move up in the administrative hierarchy owing to sheer racial barriers drove the educated middle class to demand a more effective system of power-sharing. *Bhadralok* militancy acquired a new dynamism with the anti-Partition movement, an agitation which had a strong *bhadralok* base but significant popular ramifications. The transfer of the capital in 1912 dried up major sources of government jobs and patronage, causing further erosion of the *bhadralok's* role in colonial administration. Simultaneous to this came a general stagnation of *bhadralok* economic entrepreneurship. Material deprivation went hand in hand with the *bhadralok's* increasing exposure to political discourse of all sorts—Gandhian, nationalist in both liberal and extremist veins, and communal—leading to his future involvement in the Congress movement, revolutionary terrorism and Hindu revivalist politics. At the other end of the elite political spectrum, the Muslims—who lagged far behind the Hindus in the race for shrinking government jobs and patronage—took recourse to separatist politics: a tendency patronized by the British to foster their policy of 'divide and rule'.

Parallel developments at the popular level reinforced these trends in Calcutta's elite political world. The administrative and economic pull of Calcutta had attracted migrants from its hinterland as well as other provinces, giving the city a cosmopolitan character. By 1901, the proportion of Calcuttans speaking Bengali had fallen to 51.3 per cent, while that of Hindustani speakers rose to 36.3 per cent. At the start of the century, two-thirds of the city's population was Hindus; of the rest, 30 per cent were Muslims. According to another estimate of the same period, nearly 75 per cent of Calcutta's inhabitants could be classified as 'poor', including migrants working as labourers, artisans, and petty traders. Living conditions for these subordinate social groups were appalling. Ill-paid, subjected to economic and racial assaults, and deprived of state protection, they lived in insanitary crowded bustees (slums).

Although belonging to the same economic stratum, the various social groups retained their individual religious and communal identities. Recent historians have thus emphasized the need to look at the 'community' rather than the 'class' consciousness of the embryonic industrial labour force in late-nineteenth and early-twentieth-century Calcutta. The anthropologist Nirmal K. Basu also remarked: 'The overlap in culture has been too small: class has not succeeded in dissolving linguistic or regional ties, or even in obliterating cultural differences to any appreciable extent.'[3]

Nevertheless, these subordinate social groups remained a volatile element and a support base for political militancy in Calcutta. Given the fragmented nature of their identities, it is perhaps not so surprising that they were active participants both in united anti-imperialist struggles and internecine communal conflicts.

Economic pressures often provided other and more immediate motivations for militancy: for instance, the dislocations following from the First and Second World Wars or the 1930s depression. The man–made Bengal famine of 1943, which took away 1.17 million lives in one single year, did not provoke any popular protest but nonetheless unsettled the balance of Calcutta society. 'Famine victimization', as Paul Greenough's study has revealed, not only destroyed lives; it wrecked the moral and social bonds of the poorer citizens.[4] Contemporary accounts provide enough evidence to construct a picture of the 'social fate of famine beggars' who were looked down upon as 'befouled, inauspicious and set apart from the rest of the society'. Tarakchandra Das describes how the destitutes would search for vegetable skins and rotten fruit: 'They collected the former from the streets and the latter from near about the fruit stalls in the markets. The receptacles of street garbage were regularly haunted. . . .'[5]

The dehumanizing impact of the Famine led to a brutalization of human consciousness that perhaps prepared Calcutta for the communal killings of August 1946. The subsequent trauma of the Partition of India, and the influx of Hindu refugees from East Pakistan (now Bangladesh) with little to fall back upon—a theme brilliantly documented in the films of Ritwik Ghatak—created a new reservoir of strength for Calcutta's political world, a source which provides much of the sustenance for current agitational politics that still have their epicentre in the city.

A Historical Outline of Calcutta's Agitational Politics

1912–1920

The post-1912 years anticipated many of the later trends in popular politics in Calcutta. The First World War dislocated the economic balance and led to more acute conflicts of view between the Indians and the British, particularly with regard to the drain of wealth, deindustrialization, rising revenue demands and the stultification of indigenous commerce and industry. While revolutionary terrorism continued unabated, moderate Calcutta politicians like Bhupendranath Basu (1859–1924) favoured the adoption of any course that would lift the Congress out of the rut into which it had fallen. Calcutta responded favourably to the 1916 Lucknow Pact by which the Congress sought to secure Hindu–Muslim unity from the top through a bargain reached with the Muslim leaders over distribution of legislative seats. But the communal element in Calcutta politics soon surfaced when in 1918 the city experienced the first major Hindu–Muslim riot of the present century.

The 1918 outbreak disrupted normal life in Calcutta from 9 to 11 September. Although it bore some appearances of a Hindu–Muslim conflict, it also revealed shifting levels of violence. The riot was provoked by communal issues such as the disrespect shown to the Prophet by a leading daily newspaper; but it lapsed into the collective violence of working-class Muslims against such symbols of class and colonial exploitation as the Marwaris, the Europeans and the police, who were seen as the main beneficiaries and upholders of the new contradictions opened up by the First World War. Significantly enough, the established Muslim leadership allied with the colonial authorities to restrain the escalating popular violence.

In 1919, Mahatma Gandhi launched a movement against the severe restrictions on civil liberties imposed by the Rowlatt Act. Calcutta's participation in the Rowlatt Satyagraha of 1919 represented the City's effective initiation into mainstream nationalism under Gandhian leadership. The sources of Calcutta's discontent reflected an all-India trend: anger against the repressive Rowlatt Act, promulgated despite Indian support to the British War efforts; popular Muslim resentment at the British treatment of the Caliphate (Khilafat); widespread economic discontent caused by a rising price-curve and general depression resulting from the War. Gandhi's call for a movement against the Rowlatt Act helped to unite the varying strata of popular dissatisfaction. The Mahatma's arrest on 10 April near Delhi finally brought the Calcuttans onto the streets. Normal life in the city was disrupted from 11 to 13 April 1919.

Barely six months after the September communal riots, April 1919 witnessed remarkable Hindu–Muslim fraternity. Hindu, Bengalis, Marwaris and upcountrymen marched together with Muslims in processions, singing national songs and shouting *Vande Mataram*. In public rallies, Marwari priests put vermilion marks on the foreheads of Muslims while the Hindus lent their voices to shouts of *Ali Ali*. A joint Hindu–Muslim meeting was even held inside the Nakhoda mosque, addressed amongst others by the Mahatma's son Hiralal Gandhi.

Expressions of anti-government feelings were marked in the Rowlatt Satyagraha. There were few physical attacks on Europeans, but certain aspects of popular action revealed the intense anti-European psychology of the crowd. Europeans were made to disembark from trams, buses and private vehicles, and were forced to take off their topees and proceed bareheaded; European women were chased by crowds shouting 'Gandhi ki jai'. The police, as another visible manifestation of the Raj, also became a natural target of collective violence. Police parties were pelted with bricks, stones, lumps of wood and aerated-water bottles. Police posts were set on fire. *The Englishman* (Calcutta) of 14 April 1919 describes a typical scene:

On Harrison Road men armed with scaffolding bamboos ran up to the vehicle shouting *Na ijane dega* [We shall not allow you to go]. The European sergeant replied *Jaye-ga, Hut jao* [We shall go, move away], . . . [Instantly] the crowd closed round [the police] and stones began to fly, rattling on the body and hood of the car. The men with the bamboos thrust them in front of the car. . . . There were shouts of *Mar Sala* and *Mar dalo* [Beat them].

The spread of the disturbance was associated with a shift in the leadership. While the initial rallies adopting the Satyagraha pledge were of a 'composite' nature comprising lawyers, teachers, students, merchants and 'the general populace', the initiative for action gradually passed to the 'ordinary people', especially the upcountrymen—Hindus and Muslims alike. The government itself acknowledged the breaking of the monopoly control over political agitation by a handful of educated persons and admitted that the dumb had become voiced. The *Kalikata Samachar* (Calcutta, 8 April 1919) commented that the events in Calcutta had exploded the myth 'circulated by the Anglo-Indian press that the untouchable and illiterate do not know what political agitation is . . .'. But even this popular radicalism tended irresistibly to shelter behind the Mahatma's banner.

This increasing participation from the lower social strata caused the riot to spread. The established leaders, both Hindu and Muslim, grew alarmed and issued manifestos condemning the disturbances. The Indian Muslim Association and the Committee of the Central Muhammadan Association even questioned the decision to allow non-Muslims to preach from the pulpit of the Nakhoda mosque. The Moderates—the section of Congressmen believing in constitutional agitation rather than the new 'passive resistance'— also disliked the degeneration of the Satyagraha, and their leader Surendranath Banerji (1848–1925) 'unhesitatingly' approved of Governor Ronaldshay's plan to censure the *Amrita Bazar Patrika* for 'pouring poison into the minds of the youth of the country'.

September 1920 saw the next important event in Calcutta's participation in the Congress nationalist agitation. The occasion was the Special Session of the Indian National Congress in the city. It was resolved to initiate, under Gandhi's leadership, a non-cooperation movement to support the Khilafat agitation, started in 1920 by Muhammad Ali and Shaukat Ali to move the British Government over its Turkish policy; to demand the punishment of Sir Michael O'Dwyer and other officials for the Jallianwala Bagh massacre and other 'Punjab wrongs' during the Rowlatt Satyagraha; and to press for the establishment of *Swarajya* to 'vindicate national honour'. The Non-Cooperation Movement, says Sumit Sarkar, was possibly the point of greatest strength and unity in the entire history of the national movement in Bengal.[6] Nationalist lawyers such as Chittaranjan Das (1870–1925) renounced lucrative practices; others like Netaji Subhas Chandra Bose (1897–1945?) refused to take up a career in the colonial bureaucracy; students left schools and colleges to court arrest in their hundreds. Women in large numbers followed Basanti Debi (1880–1974), the wife of Chittaranjan Das, to enrol themselves as Congress volunteers for the first time, and such subordinate social groups as Muslim boatmen and millhands were brought into mainstream nationalism. The successful hartal against the visit of the Prince of Wales on 17 November 1921 marked the height of the Non-Cooperation movement in Calcutta. To quote a contemporary account:

[Calcutta] looked like a deserted city. All Indian shops, bazars, markets, including the great business quarters, were closed. There was no tram, nor any sort of vehicular traffic in the streets. . . . All mills were closed and the millhands occupied themselves with singing *bhajans* [religious songs] and taking ablutions in the river. . . . The European business offices had to stop work owing to the absence of the Indian staff. The Courts and Government offices had similarly to close down. . . . In the night the greater part of the town was in darkness as no lights were lighted. . . . It was remarkable how the Goliath of Western civilization, the London of the Far East . . . could come to a sudden stop led by the finger of the man thousands of miles away.[7]

Even the police was affected by the rising tide of nationalism: many members resigned and a senior official lamented disaffection among his men.

1921–1929

Gandhi's sudden withdrawal of the Non-Cooperation agitation following the killing of 22 policemen by a violent mob at Chauri Chaura in UP, and the systematic government repression of nationalist organizations, put a sharp brake on popular militancy in India. Mass agitational politics in Calcutta too suffered from a general decline and fragmentation. While the established leaders of the Bengal Congress frittered their energies away on factional squabbles and Calcutta Corporation politics, a section of disillusioned educated Calcutta youth found an outlet through acts of revolutionary terrorism. This reached a climax in January 1924 when Gopinath Saha (1906–24) shot dead an Englishman named Day instead of his real target, the hated Calcutta Police chief Charles Tegart. But the repressive Bengal Ordinance of October 1924, together with the failure of the terrorists to ensure sustained social support, reduced the spate of revolutionary actions at least till the 1930s.

Calcutta politics lost its mass nationalist thrust once the Khilafat movement petered out. This may lead one to ask: was Calcutta prone only to all-India agitational initiatives? It is difficult to answer this question. But the fact remains that the ebb in nationalist agitations coincided with increasing communal tensions in Calcutta. This was amply manifested in 1926 in three successive bouts of Hindu-Muslim riots: from 2 to 14 April, 22 April to 8 May and 11 to 25 July. The immediate cause of the first outbreak was the playing of music before a mosque. The second was prompted by a street brawl in central Calcutta. The third was connected with a number of Hindu processions.

These riots displayed many similarities with the 1918 outbreak. The Muslim wrath was focused on the Marwari and Bhatia merchants; the transport system and police remained favourite targets of collective violence; temples and mosques were desecrated on a large scale; shops dealing with consumer goods continued to be the main objects of the looters. The participating crowd again mostly comprised upcountry Hindus and Muslims of the lower social strata.

Yet a certain change could be noticed in the pattern of violence in 1926. This was apparent in greater organization and planning. The Hindu crowd used the houses of their political leaders as bases of operation; the Arya Samajists dressed as Muslims and made 'feigned' attacks on Hindus to incite the latter; Muslims in central Calcutta bustees were encouraged to rise up by the beating of drums. Significantly, the growing violence was accompanied by the emergence of local leaders among such subordinate social groups as carters, butchers, boatmen, doorkeepers, sweepers, coachmen and other men 'on the spot'. As during earlier riots, both Hindu and Muslim leaders condemned 'the violence' and issued appeals to the 'brains and organizations behind the scenes'.

However, Calcutta witnessed a resurgence of nationalist politics after 1927. Following the repugnant appointment of the all-white Simon Commission in November 1927 to review the Indian political situation, hartals and joint Hindu-Muslim demonstrations displaying black flags and shouting 'Go back Simon' became regular occurrences in Calcutta. Sir John Simon's arrival in Bombay on 3 February 1928 was received with a hartal; protest rallies were held in all the Calcutta Corporation wards urging the people to boycott British goods. This anti-Simon agitation marked the formal entry of Calcutta students to mainstream nationalism and began, as Sumit Sarkar puts it, the period of 'youth conferences and associations, and rising demands for complete independence and radical social and economic changes'.[8] Commenting on the 'unprecedented success of the hartal', *The Forward* of 4 February remarked: '[It] gave the people a faint vision of Swaraj when they would be masters in their own household.' *The Vishwamitra* also noted in the same vein on 6 February: '[The hartal showed that] the aspiration and political ambitions of a country cannot be repressed by violence or brute force.'

Contemporary newspapers are replete with accounts of police repression of this resurgent nationalism. But the 'protest mentality' instilled among the people could not be suppressed—a fact amply demonstrated during the forty-third session of the Indian National Congress held at Calcutta on 29 December 1928. Perhaps for the first time in the history of the Congress, nearly 20,000 workers and peasants independently marched to the site of the session 'to assert their right' under the Congress banner. The Congress session had to be adjourned for an hour and such personalities as Jawaharlal Nehru, Subhas Chandra Bose and even Gandhi had to address the gathering and accept the following resolution: 'We, the workers and peasants of the land, shall not rest till complete independence is established and all exploitation from capital and imperialism cease. We do call upon the National Congress to keep that goal before them and organize the national forces for that purpose.'

Such popular interventions not only indicated the rising expectations of the people but also contributed in widening the base of the Congress. Thus, throughout 1928–9 the two 'leftist' leaders of the Congress—Jawaharlal Nehru and Subhas Bose—addressed a large number of youth conferences in Calcutta, urging the audience to learn from the youth movements in Europe and calling the attainment of independence the prelude to a 'communistic society'.

Not surprisingly, Subhas called 1928–9 the 'most encouraging' year. He instilled revolutionary zeal in a considerable number of Calcutta youths and demonstrated it by organizing during the 1928 Congress session a paramilitary parade of his volunteers with himself on horseback as General Officer Commanding. To quote Tanika Sarkar: 'With Bose as the President of the Bengal Provincial Congress Committee, the hold of the more militant youths on the organization increased noticeably and the distinction between radical young volunteers and actual revolutionary terrorists was often blurred.'[9]

The agitational mood of Calcutta was also demonstrated during the All-Bengal Khadi Exhibition of October 1928 through patriotic magic lantern shows, anti-government posters, dagger play and the display of pictures of nationalist heroes. When Gandhi was arrested while presiding over a public bonfire of foreign cloth in the city, a militant agitation took form over the boycott of foreign cloth. Hindus and Muslims of all social categories from labourers to Marwari traders, as well as upper and middle class women, became involved in the movement.

1930–1937

The Civil Disobedience movement of 1930 began slowly in Bengal, thanks to factional squabbles within the Bengal Provincial Congress Committee and the preoccupation of provincial leaders with Calcutta Corporation politics. Subsequently, however, the movement acquired a remarkable intensity from its own impetus. Jawaharlal's arrest on 15 April and Gandhi's imprisonment in early May brought the Calcutta crowd out onto the streets. Students fought the police; tramcars, other vehicles and fire engines were burnt; Europeans were assaulted. These incidents, signalling a total departure from non-violent principles, were also notable for the widespread participation of transport workers, among them were many Sikhs, Oriya coolies and upcountry carters. A boycott of football matches and film shows was also advocated so that the people would not be diverted from Civil Disobedience; at least two Calcutta soccer clubs, the Aryans and Mohan Bagan, cancelled some fixtures. As in other parts of the country, this process of radicalization alienated the propertied classes and largely contributed to Gandhi's compromise with the Raj in the Poona Pact of 1932.

This settlement came as a severe jolt to Hindu political interests in Calcutta. Under the new scheme, Hindu representation in the Bengal legislature was perceived to have fallen far below what was considered appropriate to their cultural and economic advancement. This sentiment was shared by all sections of Hindus, as appears from a petition signed by a whole range of personalities from Rabindranath Thakur (Tagore), Praphullachandra Ray and Sharatchandra Chatterji to Jugalkishore Birla and Rai Jatindranath Choudhuri. The Hindu Mahasabha was quick to capitalize on this sense of Hindu deprivation, which strengthened Hindu identity on the one hand and produced a poor response in Calcutta when Gandhi renewed the Civil Disobedience movement in 1932.

The first half of the 1930s also witnessed perhaps the last phase of revolutionary terrorism in Calcutta. In 1930 Dalhousie Square, seat of the chief government offices, was rocked by bombs, and the Writers' Buildings or Secretariat was itself raided by Binaykrishna Basu (1908–30), Badal Gupta (1912–30) and Dineshchandra Gupta (1911–31)—the revolutionaries after whom the Square has now been renamed. Charles Tegart, the Police Commissioner, himself escaped an attempt on his life that year. In 1932 Bina Das (1911–86), a young woman student, fired at Governor Jackson during the convocation of University of Calcutta. Another memorable day for revolutionary terrorism was 24 May 1933 when the three most wanted terrorists—Nalini Das (1910–34), Dinesh Majumdar (1907–34) and Jagadananda Mukherji—fought a revolver battle with the police from a house in Cornwallis Street before surrendering themselves.

Revolutionary terrorism certainly shook the confidence of the administration; but it also perturbed the mainstream nationalists. By 1934 the government had more or less successfully suppressed the main threat from the revolutionaries, who nevertheless left behind a source of inspiration for future generations in their struggle for a more just society.

A striking feature of the nationalist agitations in Calcutta in the 1930s was the substantial participation of women. They marched in the funeral procession of Chittaranjan Das, which clashed with the police. Women picketed foreign cloth and liquor stores and joined rallies and processions, suffering imprisonment and police atrocities in the process. In their search for suspected ringleaders, the police did not even hesitate to enter college buildings and beat up women students and teachers. Such repressive measures could not, however, halt the growing political consciousness of Calcutta women. To quote *Advance* (21 August 1930):

The alacrity and self-sacrifice with which the Indian woman has stepped forward from the cosy seclusion of the purdah into the din and turmoil of the world outside is a remarkable phenomenon in India. . . . Ladies belonging to the highest and most respected families . . ., old ladies of 70 and young girls of 16 have vied with each other to prove to a world struck with wonder and with awe that Indian nationalism is not an offspring of questionable origin, but born and nurtured in the ancient bosom of a great Mother, who had in her own youth rocked the cradle of civilization.

The new self-awareness among Calcutta women also found expression in attempts to develop a collective female identity among women at large. The rising consciousness of Calcutta's women in this period has been treated elsewhere in this volume.

The labouring class also left their mark on Calcutta politics in the late 1920s and early 1930s. The Calcutta scavengers, dock and transport workers, railwaymen and millhands were particularly active in ventilating their class grievances. Tanika Sarkar[10] has shown how in times of labour violence 'symbols of ritual and occupational degradation could be turned into weapons of strength'. For instance, when in April 1928 striking Hindu women scavengers clashed with Anglo-Indian police sergeants, they hurled pots of excreta at the latter, making them flee tearing off their uniforms and vowing never to return until they got permission to fire.

Instances of cross-professional solidarity among the Calcutta working class were also manifest. Thus in April 1933, after the police had fired on a crowd of striking Calcutta dustmen, hundreds of carters and labourers of various descriptions came out on the streets in protest and paralysed road traffic. Two labour strikes were particularly successful. First, the 1929 strike in the jute mills forced the abandonment of a plan to extend working-hours from 54 to 60 per week. Again, in April 1930 the carters had demonstrated against an official move to prohibit the transport of goods during the afternoon. Barricades were constructed with carts to paralyse all city traffic, forcing the government into a compromise settlement.

Some scholars emphasize the 'autonomy' of such subaltern actions as the carters' strike. But the carters' movement was not necessarily divorced from all organizational networks and mediations. Communist activists such as Abdul Momin (1906–83) took a leading part in organizing the carters and other labouring groups; *chowdhris* such as Ramlagan Singh also had links with local Congress Committees. Secret meetings were held in leaders' houses, and volunteers sent to estimate the number of carters killed or wounded by police firing.

In fact, it was in the 1930s that the Communists established their hold over labour politics in Calcutta, if not Bengal. The 'Left' within the Congress under Subhash Basu and Jawaharlal Nehru did appeal to workers 'to unite, organize and join hands with the Congress' through open rallies, as at Calcutta in October 1937. But the trade union movement in and around Calcutta remained under the leadership of the Communist Party of India (CPI) and other leftist groups, where leaders like Abdul Halim (1904–66), Somnath Lahiri (1909–84), Ranen Sen and Muzaffar Ahmed (1889–1973) first rose to prominence. The greater appeal of the Communists over the Congress-Khilafat combination can be partly explained by the conscious effort of early Communists to declass themselves from their petty *bhadralok* background, and the dissemination of Communist ideology through propaganda literature and populist campaigns.

1937–1947

The legislative elections of 1937 brought about a temporary decline of mainstream nationalist forces in Calcutta politics. No party won an absolute majority; the Muslim League joined the Krishak Praja Party to form a coalition ministry under Fazlul Huq (1873–1962). This enabled the Muslim League to consolidate its position in institutional politics. Within the Congress itself, the ouster of Subhash Basu in 1939 after his clash with Gandhi at the Tripuri session resulted in right-wingers and astute Gandhians, such as Praphullachandra Ghosh and Kiranshankar Ray (1891–1949), assuming charge of the Bengal Congress. There was also an ebb in subaltern militancy, perhaps because the Communist Party, having been declared illegal, had to operate as an underground organization. The only instance of a strong popular agitation was the successful movement of July 1937, when at the instance of various students' organizations, a spate of hartals, demonstrations and rallies were held in Calcutta to demand the release of political prisoners. The Bengal Government ultimately arrived at a compromise by releasing all political prisoners except those serving long-term sentences.

The outbreak of the Second World War dramatically changed the Indian political situation. Calcutta could not remain untouched. The city shared the general national grievance that the Viceroy had unilaterally declared India's participation in the British War effort without consulting any Indian political party. The German victory at Dunkirk and the fall of France began a new trend among certain Bengali politicians to exploit the British predicament by forging alliances with the Axis powers. This found most concrete expression in Subhash Basu's dramatic escape from Calcutta and his formation of the Indian National Army (INA) to liberate India with Japanese help.

The successful advance of the Japanese to Rangoon in February 1942 brought the War to the very borders of India. Mobilization of popular Indian support was indispensable for the British War effort. This induced the Raj to offer new political concessions which provided the immediate perspective for the Cripps Mission of 1942. But the Cripps offer failed, and in August 1942 Gandhi made the final call to 'Do or Die'. The Quit India movement in Bengal is usually believed to have assumed a primarily rural character. But Calcutta also witnessed a series of successful hartals from 10 to 17 August. Even in upper-class and European quarters of the city, there were acid-bulb attacks on tram passengers, and processions came out regularly shouting 'Ingrej Bharat Chharo' (Englishmen, quit India) and protesting against the presence of American troops.

Calcutta experienced a resurgence of popular agitational politics in 1945–6, the years which have been aptly described by Gautam Chatterji as 'The Almost Revolution'. Already in July 1940, a broad anti-imperialist front of the Congress, the Muslim League and the Communists had organized a successful movement to remove a monument erected at Dalhousie Square (now B.B.D. Bag) in memory of J.Z. Holwell, the main proponent of the maliciously exaggerated story of the Black Hole of Calcutta. The victory of the democratic forces in the Second World War, the emergence of socialist regimes in Eastern Europe, the new resurgent trend in the People's Democratic Revolution in China, the anti-colonial upsurge in South-East Asia and the Labour Party's victory in the British parliamentary elections—all these fired the popular imagination throughout India, and Calcutta was no exception.

The turning point came when the British decided to hold public trials of about 20,000 INA captives. Calcutta was the first centre to rise against this grotesque insult to a 'lost cause'. Subhash was a popular hero among the Bengalis, and this attack upon his political creation came at a moment when Calcutta was reeling under unemployment, inflation and a general economic crisis. The city was now rocked by a series of popular outbreaks which have been compared to the *journées* or 'days of movements' in Revolutionary Paris.

On 21 November 1945, student organizations of many political shades— Communist, Muslim League and Forward Bloc—marched in a body towards Dalhousie Square to protest against the INA trials. To quote a contemporary account by Gautam Chattopadhyay, then a Communist student leader:

Some 50 thousand had jampacked Wellington Square. The tri-colour and students' flags were everywhere. Suddenly from Wellesley Street, we saw a big procession of Muslim students, carrying Muslim League flags, coming towards Wellington Square. These were the students of Islamia College [now Maulana Azad College]. Hundreds of students from the central rally rushed forward, embraced the demonstrators and tied the Muslim League flags together with the tri-colour. At once the whole rally burst into thunderous slogans: Hindu-Muslim Unity *Zindabad*.[11]

When the police stopped the procession from entering Dalhousie Square, the students sat down on Cornwallis Street and remained there the whole night. The Government attempted to disperse the squatters by force. Two students—significantly, one Muslim and one Hindu—died on the spot. The violence spread over the next two days, with Sikh taxi drivers, tramway workers, municipal employees, carters and millhands taking a leading role in putting up street barricades, burning cars and attacking the police. Official observers deplored the violence but were impressed by the way the crowd stood their ground against the police. Three days of turbulence left 33 civilians killed and 200 injured.

Interestingly enough, the established leadership, as on earlier occasions, disapproved of this radicalism and advised restraint. Congress right-wingers such as Vallabhbhai Patel ridiculed the frittering away of energies in encounters with the police; Gandhi began 'friendly' talks with the Bengal Governor, and the Calcutta Session of the Congress Working Committee formally emphasized its faith in non-violent modes of political action.

Such moves could not, however, check popular anger against the insults to national pride. In less than three months, Calcutta saw yet another remarkable spate of popular protest. The sentence of rigorous imprisonment imposed on Abdul Rashid of the INA occasioned a students' strike called jointly by the Muslim League and the CPI. The working class soon entered the scene when a Communist-led general strike brought industrial Calcutta to a halt on 12 February 1946. On the same day, there was an unprecedented rally at Wellington Square addressed by representatives of all the political bodies—Hussain Shahid Suhrawardy (1893–1963) of the Muslim League,

Somnath Lahiri of the CPI and Satish Dasgupta (1880–1979) of the Congress. Clashes between the police and the crowd continued for two consecutive days, leaving at least 84 dead and 300 injured.

The restiveness of the labouring poor spread with great rapidity, as is evident from the strike threats of railway workers and postal and government employees against rising prices and ration cuts. Incidentally, this was the time of the emergence of 'effective countrywide labour organizations': Calcutta, with its rich tradition of labour politics, responded enthusiastically to this trend.

While the police and officials lamented the turbulent times, the Calcutta intelligentsia immortalized them: Sukanta Bhattacharya (1926–47) and Subhash Mukherji (1919–) in their poems, Manik Banerji (1908–57) and Tarashankar Banerji (1898–1971) through their novels and Salil Choudhuri in his music. Calcutta also hosted a number of conferences of the Anti-Fascist Writers' and Artists' Association, a body of progressive cultural workers determined to fight fascism and all forms of reaction.

This spectacular display of the secular anti-imperialist spirit of the Calcutta populace received a crucial setback with the communal hysteria that gripped the city in August 1946. The immediate context of the Great Calcutta Killing from 16 to 19 August was the failure of the Cabinet Mission to bring about a broad agreement on India's 'constitutional issue', and the Muslim League's call for a 'Direct Action' to achieve Pakistan. But there is evidence of a growing 'psychological crystallization' of communal identity at the popular level among both Hindus and Muslims from the 1940s. This resulted from the increasing strength of communal elements in organized politics following the establishment of the League government in Bengal, the growth of Hindu revivalist organizations and their connections with the Bengal Congress, the impact of sustained propaganda for and against Pakistan, a general shift in the balance within Hindu and Muslim leadership from the religious to the political, and the catalytic influence of the Constituent Assembly elections in fostering communal identities rather than leftist or nationalist consciousness.

The Muslim League Government of Bengal declared 16 August a public holiday. The League also sought to organize a general hartal, while the Hindus tried to keep up normal life. Minor confrontations began from the morning, but disturbances started on a large scale in the afternoon, as Muslim processionists returned from a public rally for 'Direct Action Day'. The riot that followed was significantly different from earlier communal outbreaks in the city. It was more organized, directly connected with institutional politics, and hence, in the prevailing climate, more exclusively related to communal politics as well.[12] The League not only utilized its control over the government machinery to mobilize the Muslim community for 'Direct Action Day'; once the riot spread, Mayor Osman and Chief

Minister Suhrawardy, along with his cabinet colleagues, personally intervened for the release of Muslim rioters arrested by the police. On the other hand, the Congress became largely associated with the Hindu crowd.

Certain features of the riot indicate considerable planning before and during each outbreak: attacking shops and houses in a similar manner at a particular time, marking Muslim shops to prevent their being looted by the Muslim crowd, and using Red Cross flags to evade the police and members of the rival community. The crowd no longer consisted overwhelmingly of subordinate social groups, but became a mixture of the upper and lower strata. For the first time, Bengali Hindus and Muslims joined their co-religionists of upcountry origin on a large scale. While the earlier riots were mostly characterized by looting and other forms of violence committed by large crowds, the 1940s also saw the killing of individuals by small groups. The emphasis was now not on economic gain but on revenge and humiliation of the members of the rival community. This rite of violence displayed communal animosity at its peak.

The Great Calcutta Killing, which initiated the Partition Riots of 1946–7, left a profound impact. On the one hand, these clashes presaged an administrative breakdown which made the Viceroy Lord Wavell suggest an early termination of the Raj. At the same time, as I have tried to argue elsewhere, the riots reconciled a large section of subordinate social groups, among both Hindus and Muslims, to the idea of Partition. This was reflected in the changed attitude of nationalist Muslims and the Congress leadership (except Gandhi), whose secular stance gave way to the acceptance of Pakistan as the only real alternative. Muslim and Hindu communal identities had assumed a clear political complexion, nourished by propaganda and hardened by the riots of the 1940s.

The communal carnage did not, however, destroy the potential for anti-imperialist mass struggle across religious lines. Thus on 21 January 1947, barely five months after the riots of August 1946, Hindu and Muslim students joined in 'Hands off Vietnam' demonstrations, demanding an end to the use of Calcutta airport by French aircraft fighting the anti-colonial movement in Indo-China. The tramwaymen waged a successful 85 days strike under Communist leadership. Workers in the port and engineering industries downed their tools on a number of occasions.

Until the last moment, the political pendulum in Bengal continually swung between nationalist and separatist politics; but ultimately mainstream nationalism lost most of its politicized Muslim elements, and a section within it developed a strong Hindu communal identity. Consequently, Calcutta came to suffer from a rather desperate introversion of consciousness, cut off from national events, obsessed by its own uncertainties, unsure whether it would go to Pakistan or not. This sense of pain and alienation was compounded by the influx of refugees and the inability to integrate with the national mainstream after the 'truncated settlement' of 1947.

Placed in this historical context, it is not difficult to appreciate why the political history of modern Calcutta largely constitutes a 'politics of protest'. Hartals, riots, insurrections, demonstrations and rallies have continued to be a recurrent feature in the life of Calcutta. To observers from outside—Indian and foreign alike—this has created a notorious stereotype of the city. But there is a clear historical logic behind Calcutta's political restiveness. Calcuttans have continually upheld the belief that 'when order is injustice disorder is the beginning of justice'. Much of the political life of Calcutta has been motivated by an alternative world view. Enthusiastic Calcuttans draw sustenance from this creative force in the city's political culture. Others, perhaps, have nightmares that the nation might think tomorrow what Calcutta thinks today.

Notes

1. Rajat K. Ray, *Social Conflict and Political Unrest in Bengal 1885–1927*, Delhi, 1984, pp. 21–3.
2. J. McGuire, *The Making of a Colonial Mind: A Quantitative Study of the Bhadralok in Calcutta 1857–1885,* New York, 1983, pp. 120–1.
3. Nirmal K. Basu, *Calcutta 1964: A Social Survey*, Calcutta, 1968.
4. Paul R. Greenough, *Prosperity and Misery in Modern Bengal: The Famine of 1943–44,* New York, 1982.
5. Tarakchandra Das, *Bengal Famine*, Calcutta, 1943.
6. Sumit Sarkar, *Modem India 1885–1947,* Delhi, 1986, p. 218.
7. *Indian Annual Register* of 1922, p. 227.
8. Sumit Sarkar, *Modern India*, op. cit., p. 266.
9. Tanika Sarkar, *Bengal 1928–1934: The Politics of Protest,* Delhi, 1987, p. 25.
10. Ibid., p. 57.
11. Gautam Chattopadhyay, 'Almost Revolution', in *Essays in Honour of Professor S.C. Sarkar*, Barun De et al., eds., Delhi 1976.
12. Suranjan Das, *Communal Riots in Bengal 1905–1947*, Delhi, 1991 and 1993.

CHAPTER 8

NATIONALISM AND POPULAR CONSCIOUSNESS: BENGAL 1942

The Debate

Debates on Indian nationalism have reached a sophisticated level. The nationalist version of a homogeneous and 'unitarian' national movement or early Marxist theory of 'class-betrayal' by Gandhian leadership is now generally considered as too simplistic a paradigm for analysing the development of mass nationalism in late colonial India. Instead, regional subnationalism, factional politics, the imperfect nature of Congress mobilization, autonomous subaltern assertions and peasant nationalism have emerged as competing perspectives in unfolding the complex story of Indian nationalist and freedom struggle against British rule.[1] A 1983 study on the role of popular pressures from below in shaping the nature of national outbursts, particularly enriched our understanding of regional variations in nationalist agitations and radicalization of mainstream nationalism at critical conjunctures.[2]

In recent years the 'disaggregated' view of the Indian nation has taken a new turn with Partha Chatterjee's treatise that emphasizes the essentially fragmented nature of Indian identity in colonial as well as post-colonial India.[3] Chatterjee's intervention is largely a logical corollary to some of the earlier insights on Indian national movement in terms of which the nation viewed from below had extremely divergent meanings and implications depending on regions, localities and perceptions of subordinate social groups.[4] Recognizing the importance of studying the variegated nature of socio-political consciousness of Indians in British India, it would, however, be wrong to deny instances where narrower local or regional or subaltern

*The paper was initially published in *Social Scientist*, vol. 23, nos. 4–6, April–June 1995, pp. 58–68.

identities merged with the broader national persuasion to generate amongst the Indian people interrelated forms of consciousness. The present essay seeks to substantiate the hypothesis of the persistence of an overarching sense of national identity despite the variegated nature of popular[5] consciousness in the light of some evidence on the 1942 Quit India movement in Bengal. It first identifies the forms of popular protest that developed around the August Revolt, and then demonstrates the link between popular protest consciousness and the articulation of nationalist identity.

The Quit India movement, making the penultimate stage of Indian struggle for liberation from the colonial yoke, did certainly unnerve the Raj. This was clearly reflected in the message that a tormented Viceroy sent to his Prime Minister in London on 31 August 1942: 'I am engaged here in meeting by far the most serious rebellion since that of 1857, the gravity and extent of which we have so far concealed from the world for reasons of military security.'[6]

Thanks to strict press censorship, it is difficult to ascertain the actual figure of lives sacrificed for the Quit India movement. But according to an official admission, 1,285 were killed and 3,125 wounded between August and November 1942 alone. As many as fifty-seven and half battalions of army had to be deployed by the Raj to restore order.[7] Analysing the country's 'most massive anti-imperialist struggle' Gyanendra Pandey thus contends: 'Quit India might be fairly summed up as a popular nationalist upsurge that occurred in the name of Gandhi but went substantially beyond any confines that Gandhi may have envisaged for the movement.'[8]

It is, however, generally believed that the 1942 revolt marked a sharp departure from the 1920–2 and 1930–4 outbursts in the pattern of 'radicalization' of mainstream nationalism. While on earlier occasions the 'breaking of Gandhian barrier' was associated with anti-landlord and anti-capitalist outbursts, the Quit India movement is thought to have been comparatively bereft of peasant and labour militancy. Pandey, for instance, remarks, '. . . (although) in its second phase, it (the Quit India Movement) had spread out from the bigger cities and towns into the countryside and assumed the form of a mass peasant uprising . . . (it) led to very few anti-landlord actions.'[9]

Sumit Sarkar also notes:'Unlike in 1919–22 and 1930–34, the radicalisation process in 1942 was on the whole mainly at the level of anti-British militancy alone, with the very extent of anti-foreign sentiments, as in 1857, possibly reducing internal class tensions and social radicalism.'[10]

What is, however, intended here to demonstrate is that the Quit India Movement in Bengal, where the Revolt had one of its best fruitions did encompass a broad spectrum of social protest. The inherent protest consciousness was expressed through popular revolts and agitations that gathered momentum around the August uprising. Such popular outbursts could have occurred independently of the Congress organization. But they gained sustenance from the force of nationalism, a fact usually undermined in the literature on the 'fragmented' nature of Indian political identity and processes during the freedom struggle.

Forms of Popular Protest

The potentialities of popular protest politics developing outside the Congress parameter but becoming a part of the wider Quit India struggle lay within the Congress strategy itself. Unlike the preceding Congress-led mass struggles Gandhi did not impose a rigid plan of action in 1942. Jawaharlal himself confessed:

Neither in public nor in private at the meetings of the Congress Working Committee did he [Gandhi] hint at the nature of action he had in mind, except a one-day general strike. So neither he nor the Congress Working Committee issued any kind of directions, public or private, except that people should be prepared for all developments and should in any event adhere to the policy of peaceful and non-violent action.[11]

The veteran communist theoretician E.M.S. Namboodiripad goes to the extent of suggesting that 'neither Gandhi nor other Congress leaders had any idea as to how to organize and lead the struggle'.[12] It has been argued that in August 1942 the Congress merely stipulated: 'every Indian who desires freedom and strives for it, must be his own guide'. The people were thus allowed a relatively 'free hand' in evolving their own forms of struggle. This was a fillip to an 'open rebellion' in various forms outside the Congress orbit.

It is thus not surprising that Bengal's rural sector witnessed considerable restiveness in the aftermath of 9 August 1942. The communist-led Provincial Kisan Sabha organized agitations for *adhiar* rights, campaigned against hoarders and blackmarketeers and formed broad-based food committees.[13] In Jajigram, Paikar, Murarai, Sainthia, Dubrajpur, Rampurhat, Nanoor, Fatepur, Suri, Ghuskara and Ruppur of Birbhum district, in Habibpur of Malda district and in Munshiganj of Dacca district the peasantry joined in large numbers in no-revenue and no-rent campaigns.[14] Debt-settlement records in Union Board offices were burnt in the districts of Hooghly and Nadia.[15] The *cutcheries* (offices of landlords) of such prosperous zamindari estates as the Midnapur Zamindari Company were raided and their records set ablaze.[16] Thanks to this groundswell of peasant radicalism, the membership of the Bengal Provincial Kisan Sabha rose from a mere 11,000 in 1937 to 1,78,000 in 1944, 1,000 among them being fulltime activists.[17]

The onset of the man-made famine in 1943 provoked another spate of peasant protest. This was seen in a form of food rioting. Large-scale looting of grains from railway wagons, boats and carts were reported from almost all districts of Bengal.[18] The Government of India was so unnerved at wagon-looting cases that it raised special guards for escorting goods trains.[19] Dacoities and raids were also organized to recover the surplus stock of food from wealthy and prosperous families. In Bispur village of Midnapur district between 24 and 31 May 1943 hungry Santhals, Bhaktos and Bagals ransacked ten prosperous households and took away not only stocks of paddy but also paddy seeds.[20] In Narayanpur and Memari of Burdwan a crowd as large as 1,000 marched to the establishments of local merchants and landlords to demand paddy. Such demonstrations turned violent when the police intervened on behalf of merchants and landlords.[21] Official reports themselves testify to the repression unleashed on the so-called 'village looters', and even women members of the families of suspected looters were not spared from maltreatments.[22]

Underlying these collective actions were often manifestations of a strong notion of elementary justice. For example, the villagers in Ukhrid village of Burdwan district seized paddy from a 'leading person', shared it amongst themselves and then submitted to the owner of the stock a list of names specifying the quantity of grain received by each of them.[23] Again, in Mimkhali *hat* of Barisal the villagers looted from a businessman 200 maunds of rice and distributed the quantity equally amongst themselves.[24] In Barisal and Bankura the merchants engaged in exporting rice from the scarcity-hit districts became special targets of crowd fury.[25]

Another aspect of rural insurgency was scattered tribal uprisings. An impressive instance of this comes from Balurghat subdivision of Dinajpur district, inhabited mostly by poor Rajbangshis, Santhals, Oraons and Mundas. The region was struck first by a severe drought and then famine. This natural calamity was the immediate context of a 'people's rebellion' on 13 September 1942 when about 7,000 Rajbangshis, 3,000 Oraons and 1,000 Mundas, carrying their bows and arrows, marched to the town and ransacked post offices, registration offices and civil courts and snapped telegraph wires. The dominant economic motive of this unrest was clearly revealed when the leader of the crowd replied to a police query as to what he wanted: 'I want food for the starving multitude.' A strong popular support for this tribal uprising was borne out when rifle-carrying police parties searching for the ring leaders encountered a stiff resistance from villagers armed with mere bows and arrows.[26] Birbhum and Bankura too experienced tribal unrest where Santhals and Bauris participated in no-rent and no-tax movements and looted *hats* and excise shops.[27] Particular attention may be drawn to an incident of 29 August 1942 when a 4,000 strong Santhal crowd carrying lathies, bows and arrows ransacked the Bolpur Railway Station and uprooted telegraph and telephone wires.

The most sustained tribal insurgency occurred in Sushang and Nalitbari where a dual cry was raised: 'Down with the Imperialist War' and 'Down with Feudal Exploitation'. To undertake an underground movement about 1000 Hajang, Dalu, Koch, Garo and Hadi peasants organized themselves into guerilla groups. Interestingly enough, such formations included women volunteers. A seven-member coordination committee oversaw the activities of three regional committees of Sushang (East), Nalitbari (West) and Haluaghat (Middle). These committees pursued both military and non-military objectives. The former included attacks on symbols of feudal and colonial authority, vigilance against enemy attacks and development of an intelligence network. The latter comprised propaganda warfare, improvement of agricultural production, development of public health and raising the standards of living of the people. At least till January 1945 Sushang-Nalitbari region remained a 'liberated zone'.[28]

In the urban sector, protest politics primarily revolved around labour militancy. The Bengal government itself admitted in its *Fortnightly Political Report for the Second Half of September 1942*: The number of strikes was much larger than normal, and very much larger than is usual at this time of the year.

In Calcutta and its outskirts the boatmen, municipal sweepers, tramwaymen and working hands in jute mills, engineering, aluminium, metal, iron and steel works, pharmaceutical industry and Port Commissioners struck work at periodic intervals between August 1942 and June 1944 for a whole range of economic and work-related demands such as War Bonus, higher wages, better service conditions and reinstatement of fellow workmen.[29] The workers of Bengal Chemical and Pharmaceutical Works in Calcutta struck work, refusing to take part in Military Supply work.[30] Industrial unrest was marked both in Howrah and Hooghly. The Dhakeswari, Chittaranjan, and Luxminarayan Cotton Mills in Dacca Division were on strike in September 1942.[31] Even the labourers of Garbeta and Salbon airbases in Midnapur district observed hartals demanding better working conditions and expressing solidarity with the new stride in freedom movement.[32]

The aftermath of Japanese air raids on Calcutta in December 1942 saw a heightened dose of labour militancy. In Kidderpore Docks out of 60,000 workers 15,000 were on strike; in Howrah and Lillooah railway sheds an estimated 3,000 out of a workforce of 25,000 resorted to strike to press forth their economic demands; labour shortage caused stoppage of production in Mohini Mill and Mahalaxmi Cotton Mill and closure of night shifts in Cossipore Gun and Shell Factory.[33] Strikers often turned violent. For instance, in Guest Keen Williams (Sibpur) a stay-in strike ended with the hurling of nuts, bolts and iron pieces at the managers.[34] The Superintendent of Police himself was not spared when he intervened to restore order. Undoubtedly this spurt of organized labour militancy contributed to a significant increase of trade union membership in Bengal from 175,595 in 1941–2 to 221,635 in 1942–3 and to 289,658 in 1943–4.[35] The period under present consideration also witnessed novelties in working class politics. We have at least two recorded occasions—one in D.V. Kundu Biri Factory at Bankura and another in the biri factory of Lakshman Shaw and Muhammad Ishaque at Birbhum—when the striking labourers could not extract a 'fair deal' from their employers and opted out of their jobs to start cooperative ventures on their own initiatives.[36]

There was yet another aspect of protest politics which needs to be taken note of. This was reflected in clashes between the military and the public. Such confrontations resulted from the military personnel—usually in their drunken states—taking law into their own hands, and the people reacting to such irresponsible acts. On 21 September 1943, when five soldiers unnecessarily assailed some *durwans* (guards) in Rusa Road (south Calcutta) while searching for their missing comrade, intense public consternation was provoked. On 28 August 1943, some soldiers forcibly took away S.K. Alijan and S.K. Islam into barracks and assaulted them for refusing to part with two of the goats they were leading across Gariahat Road. This caused an outcry in the locality. Again, on more than one occasion local residents of the Calcutta Dock area 'punished' drunken soldiers for misbehaving either in eating places or brothels.[37] We also have reports of public distemper incited by the ill-treatment of tribals and young villagers by military personnel under the influence of liquor.[38]

Popular Protest and Nationalist Consciousness

A question still needs to be answered: were the popular protests motivated by the Quit India movement? It is difficult to provide a precise answer. But there are indications to suggest that the protest politics surveyed above drew sustenance from the Quit India movement. The Bengal Government itself realized there is little doubt that the political unrest (following the Quit India movement) was responsible for most of the troubles.[39]

Local Congressmen were involved in most of the peasant insurgencies cited above. While carrying away the looted paddy and burning debt records, the peasants were reported to have raised cries of 'Gandhiji Zindabad' and 'Angrez Sarkar Murdabad'.[40] The Balurghat uprising was undoubtedly stimulated by the news of the Quit India Resolution. In fact, local Congressmen and activists of such nationalist organizations as the Anushilan had lighted the spark of Balurghat rebellion. The tribals in Sushang and Nalitbari raised nationalist slogans and unfurled the national tricolour atop the SDO's office.[41] An impressive labour rally was held in Narayanganj on 17 August 1942 to ventilate economic demands as well as to express solidarity with the nationalist cause.[42] Rumours of nationalist import also motivated protest actions of subordinate groups. For example, during a paddy looting case in Dacca one Nazimala Sardar went round the bazaars (markets) shouting that the Mahatma had paralysed the British administration and hence rice could be looted without any reprisal.[43]

Numerous instances can be cited where strikes had been organized specifically to uphold the nationalist cause. For example, on 11 August 1942, more than 8,000 workers of Belur and Howrah engineering works struck work to mourn the death of the Congress leader Mahadeb Desai.[44] Again, on 3 October 1942, the workers of Bengal Chemical and Pharmaceutical Works downed their tools, demanding the release of imprisoned local Congress leaders.[45] In Dhakeswari and Chittaranjan Cotton Mills the millhands snatched the hats of their Anglo-Indian officers, demanding Gandhi's release.[46] The Bengal Congress Bulletins of 1943 and 1944 also give details of other labour rallies and strikes in support of the Quit India movement. The Indian Federation of Labour, a body sponsored by the Bengal Government, itself realized the danger of this linkage between labour militancy and nationalism when its Joint Secretary remarked on 25 August 1942: 'Bengal is perhaps the most threatened province in the country. . . . The labour politics here has been carried on racial basis. Even today the attitude of these (i.e. European) employers has not undergone much change. So the basis for successful anti-British propaganda is there. If something immediately is not done to remove the burning grievance of these workers . . . a large scale manifestation of discontent . . . is sure to affect the workers in the Industrial Centres.'[47]

And that's what happened.

Political literature connected with the August Revolt also gained in considerable circulation amongst the activists of protest politics. A government report listed the following 'subversive nationalist pamphlets' usually recovered from those charged with organizing urban and rural disorders:

(a) Hindi leaflet *Ingraj ko Pancho Lakh Naya Dushamno Shey* ending with *Har Hindustani ko sukh* or *roti milagi, Inquilab Zindabad*.
(b) Hindi leaflet *Kiya Mahatmaji Hamare Bich Sey uth Jayega?* and ending with *Rail Dak Aor Telephone ka Sammadha . . . ko assambhab bana deo. Isme Mahatmaji Banach Sakta hai.*

(c) A Hindi leaflet entitled 'Bangal key majduro she nibedan' and calling *Hindustan ki is larai me shamil ho jao—karo ao moro.* [48]

Nationalist handbills in Bengali and Hindi of similar nature were also found pasted in central spots of working-class neighbourhood.[49]

There are thus strong indicators to suggest constant interactions between resurgent nationalism generated by the Quit India movement and popular protest developing outside the immediate Congress orbit. Not unnaturally, a Government of India report of 14 November 1942 feared a groundswell of underground sabotage resulting from such conjunctures and advised all provincial governments to maintain 'greater vigilance'.[50] Unfortunately, the kind of linkage between various forms of protest politics and the Quit India movement which contemporary British officials had themselves admitted has largely gone unnoticed in much of Indian historiography.

Muslim leadership unfortunately largely remained unaffected by the Quit India movement. This strengthened the political process that enabled the British to 'Quit' India only after dividing it. But that is a different story. Nevertheless, 'the spirit of 1942 persisted till the end of the Raj'.[51] The movement, followed by the national outcry against INA trials and the RIN Mutiny, drove home the point amongst the rulers and ruled alike that the British days in India are numbered. In many respects the Quit India movement heralded the modern Indian nation about which Pandit Jawaharlal Nehru envisaged: 'The future beckons us. Whither do we go and what shall be our endeavour? To bring freedom and opportunity to the common man, to the peasants and workers of India. To fight and end poverty and ignorance and disease. To build up a prosperous, democratic and progressive nation, and to create social, economic and political institutionss, which will ensure justice and fullness of life to every man and woman.'[52]

Whether the Indian National Congress which had ruled the country uninterruptedly since Independence, except for a brief interlude, has been able to fulfil these cherished goals, I leave it to the readers to draw their own conclusions.

Conclusion

This essay will hopefully prompt the readers to doubt the veracity of the widely held view that the Quit India movement was fundamentally an anti-British militancy, devoid of social radicalism. The Quit India glory has been traditionally appropriated as the Congress glory in the Congress discourse on nationalism. Explaining the Quit India demand to his fellow party members, Gandhiji himself identified the Congress with the emerging Indian nation and had proclaimed: 'The members of the All India Congress Committee are like members of Parliament representing the whole of India. . . . It [the Congress] has claimed ever since its birth to represent the whole nation and on your behalf I have made the claim that you represent not only the registered members of the Congress but the entire nation.'[53]

The following remark of the latest official Congress version of the national movement is equally revealing: 'The Indian revolution [August Revolt] was at its final point and the destiny of the nation hung in the balance. . . . For the Mahatma, it was a day of days in his life, and when he spoke he was pronouncing the death-knell of the British Empire.'[54]

Another aspect of official nationalist exercise was to use the Quit India movement to expose 'the anti-national role of the Communist Party of India (CPI). The CPI did not surely officially join the agitation which, no other than E.M.S. Namboodiripad himself admits, alienated it 'from the people including those who regarded them highly for the part they had played earlier in the anti-imperialist struggles'.[55] But the official Congress discourse appears to be wide off the mark in condemning the Communists for joining 'the other side during the independence struggle'.[56] What the CPI attempted was to attain a complex combination of anti-imperialism and anti-fascism. To quote Namboodiripad again: 'It [the CPI] adopted an independent working class revolutionary attitude facing both the provocations and threats from the rulers and the rising popular sentiments under the leadership of the bourgeoisie. The Communists came out as a party independently organising the people while striving to criticise the British rulers who were fighting the war while suppressing the people and their leaders....'[57]

In fact, the CPI continuously organized campaigns protesting against the British Government's refusal to accept the national demands of the Congress and arresting its leaders en masse. I would like to substantiate this assertion with instances from Bengal. The Superintendant of Police for Jalpaiguri reported how Babu Khagendra Nath Dasgupta, MLA, and a prominent member of the District's Congress Committee, received active cooperation from Student Federation members in 'connection with the recent Congress programme'.[58] The involvement of rickshawpullers and carters in the Quit India movement in Jalpaiguri was largely possible due to the support from local Communist activists.[59] The District Officer of Birbhum, Nadia and Pabna also reported how the local CPI units initiated processions, demonstrations and meetings demanding unconditional release of Congress leaders, criticizing the oppressive policies of the Raj, and urging 'unity for independence'.[60] In Calcutta the CPI organized a well attended meeting in the University Institute Hall, chaired by Muzaffar Ahmed himself, to demand independence for the country and immediate unconditional release of Gandhi.[61] In the Malda town the first open demonstration in support of the Quit India demand was organized by communist activists by picketing government-aided schools and shops selling English products.[62] The District Officer of Faridpur noted with apprehension: 'I am afraid the CPI are gradually joining up (the nationalists)'.[63] What the Party, however, erred was a failure to maintain the thin distinction between anti-fascism and anti-imperialism. Consequently, certain strategic mistakes were committed in organizing mass struggles and on some occasions identifying too much with the British government. We learn from Namboodiripad's own admission that the Party indulged in considerable 'self-criticism' for such failures at the second Party Congress held in Calcutta in 1948.[64]

What has unfortunately been lost in such traditional projections on the 1942 upsurge is the world of popular social consciousness, that amalgam of perceptions, values, experiential patterns and goals. Viewed from below the Quit India movement—as the present submission on Bengal seeks to do—marked a basic continuity in the long chain of nationalist assertions. In tune with the anti-Rowlatt agitation, the Non-Cooperation movement and the Civil Disobedience outburst the Quit India movement also occasioned an expression of an 'ideology of protest' outside the parameter of mainstream nationalism but not necessarily divorced from it. The affirmation of 'protest identity' along class lines might not have been as pervasive as *on* previous occasions when Gandhian nationalism became radicalized, much against the wishes of the mentor himself. But it would be ahistorical to either undermine or ignore the radical potentials within the August Revolt—the realization of which, as demonstrated in the case of Bengal, occurred within an overarching nationalist identity. A detailed study on the Quit India movement in Midnapur district of Bengal has shown how 'the national movement had by 1930 become a part of the popular culture' in that region.[65] Popular struggles in the heyday of nationalism cannot thus be viewed in disjunction of or autonomous from the freedom movement. Even Antonio Gramsci—writing on Italian history—who had drawn our attention to the 'fragmented and episodic' nature of the history of subaltern social groups did acknowledge 'provisional tendencies' of 'unification in the historical activity of those groups'.[66] Studies on African and other Third World nationalisms have also emphasized such symbiotic relationship between mainstream nationalism and popular protest politics, and of 'peasant political ideology' powerfully contributing to the programme of national rural guerilla war.[67] A proper deciphering of Indian nationalism—especially the disentangling of the complexities of popular social consciousness motivating national outbursts—requires the adoption of a similar analytical framework.

Notes

1. For a critique of the historiography, of Indian nationalism, see Tapan Raychaudhuri, 'Indian Nationalism as Animal Polities', *Historical Journal,* vol. 22, no. 3, 1986; Howard Spodek, 'Pluralist Politics in British India: The Cambridge Cluster of Historian of Modern India'; Bhaskar Chakrabarty, 'From Sub-Nation To Subaltern: Experiments in the Writing of Indian History', in *Dissent und Consensus: Social Protest in Pre- Industriat Societies,* Basudeb Chattopadhyay et al., eds., Calcutta, 1989.

2. Sumit Sarkar, *'Popular' Movements and 'Middle Class' Leadership in Late Colonial India: Perspectives and Problems of a 'History from Below',* Calcutta, 1983.

3. Partha Chatterjee, *The Nation and its Fragments: Colonial and Postcolonial Histories,* Delhi, 1994.

4. See the contributions in Ranajit Guha, ed., *Subaltern Studies* volumes.

5. The term 'popular' is used in this work in the same way that Sumit Sarkar used it to denote a broad spectrum of subordinate social groups like tribals, peasants, artisans and labouring groups in a situation where 'precise class analysis is . . . difficult'. See Sumit Saikar, 'Popular Movements and Middle Class', op. cit., p. 2.

6. T. Wickenden, *Quit India Movement: British Secret Report,* P.N. Chopra, ed., Faridabad, 1976, see the Introduction.

7. File-642/42 Part, West Bengal State Archive (hereafter WBSA), Home, New Delhi, to all provincial governments No.3/34/42–Poll(l) 14 November 1942.

8. Gyanendra Pandey, ed., *The Indian Nation in 1942,* Calcutta, 1988, p. 5.

9. Ibid.

10. Sumit Saikar, *'Popular' Movements and 'Middle Class' Leadership,* op. cit., p. 49. Sarkar also asserts: 'The Calcutta industrial belt was also largely quiet, . . . Communist opposition to the movement probably played a considerable role in restraining the workers.' See his *Modern India 1885–1947,* Delhi, 1986 edn., pp. 396–7.

11. Cited in E.M.S. Namboodiripad, *A History of India's Freedom Struggle,* Trivandrum, 1986, pp. 753–4.

12. Ibid., p. 753.

13. Ranajit Das Gupta, *Economy, Society and Politics in Bengal: Jalpaiguri 1869–1947,* Delhi, 1992.

14. *District Officers' Chronicle of Events of Disturbances consequent upon the AICC Resolution of 8 August 1942 and Arrest of Congress Leaders,* WBSA, pp. 4–13, 114–15.

15. Ibid., pp. 34–6, 91.

16. Ibid., p. 91.

17. Sunil Sen, 'Peasant Uprisings in Bengal 1885–1947', in *Challenge: A Saga of India's Struggle for Freedom,* N.R. Ray et al., eds., Delhi, 1984.

18. Files-477/43, Col. 2 and 413/43, WBSA. Also see the Bengal Congress Bulletins and District Officers' Chronicle, op. cit.

19. File-477/43, WBSA.

20. File-396/43, WBSA, SP Midnapore to DIG Burdwan Range, 3 June 1943 and DM Midnapur to Commissioner, Burdwan Division, No. I300C, 2 June 1943.
21. File-413/43, WBSA. SP Midnapur to DM Midnapur, 12 June 1943.
22. File-413/43, WBSA.
23. File-413/43 SP Midnapur to DM Midnapur, 12 June 1943.
24. *Bengal Congress Bulletin* (Calcutta), 22 January 1943, no. 5
25. Ibid.
26. For an account of the Balurghat turmoil see Biren De Sarkar, 'The People's Revolution: Balurghat 1942', in *Challenge,* op. cit.
27. File-642/42, WBSA Home Department, India, to All Provincial Governments, No. 3/34/42–Poll(I) of 14 November 1942; District Officers' Chronicle, op. cit., pp. 4–17.
28. For details of this insurgency see Pramatha Gupta, *Tribal People in Liberation Struggle,* Calcutta, 1983.
29. See File-6–S-15/44, Commerce and Labour (Commerce Branch) B March 1943, Progs. 293–338, WBSA; File-Home (Conf) 253/43, WBSA.
30. File-Home (Conf) 253/43, WBSA.
31. Ibid.
32. Intelligence Branch Records, Bengal Police (hereafter IB Records).
33. Ibid.
34. Dist. Officers' Chronicles, op. cit., pp. 37–41.
35. Panchanan Saha, *History of the Working Class Movement in Bengal,* Delhi, 1978, p. 179.
36. Commerce and Labour Department (Commerce Branch) B March 1943 293–338, WBSA.
37. See File-609/43, WBSA.
38. See File-460/43 and 617/43, WBSA.
39. *Fortnightly Political Report of Bengal for the second half of September 1942,* WBSA.
40. IB Records.
41. Biren De Sarkar, *The People's Revolution,* op. cit.
42. IB Records.
43. File-Sml/43, WBSA, T.H. Ellis, Registrar. High Court of Judicature, Bengal, to the Chief Secretary, Government of Bengal, No. 776R of 1 February 1943.
44. Commerce and Labour Department (Commerce Branch) B March 1943 293–338, WBSA.
45. Ibid.
46. Home (Poll) 7L-1/42 B October 1942 267–68, WBSA.
47. Ibid.
48. IB Records.
49. District Officers' Chronicle, op. cit., pp. 37–41.
50. File-642/42, WBSA, Home, New Delhi, to all provincial governments No. 3/34/42–Poll (I) 14 November 1942.
51. M.N. Das, 'Introduction' in B.N. Pande, ed., *A Centenary History of the Indian National Congress (1885–1985),* vol. III, Delhi, 1935, p. 55.

52. Ibid., p. 109.

53. *Collected Works of Mahatma Gandhi,* vol. 76, p. 378.

54. See M.N. Das, Introduction', op. cit., p. 50.

55. E.M.S. Namboodiripad, *A History of India's Freedom Struggle,* op. cit., p. 769.

56. Ibid.

57. Ibid., pp. 773–4.

58. File-W-776/42, WBSA SP Jalpaiguri to Add. Secy., Government of Bengal. No. 3420/33–42 of 2 September 1942.

59. Ibid.

60. See District Officers' Chronicle, op. cit., pp. 18–23, 87–9, 111–13.

61. Ibid., p. 87.

62. Ibid., p. 114.

63. Ibid., p. 147.

64. E.M.S. Namboodiripad, *A History of India's Freedttm Struggle,* op. cit.

65. Hiteshranjan Sanyal, 'The Quit India Movement in Medinipur District', in *The Indian Nation,* Gyanendra Pandey, ed., op. cit.

66. Q. Hoare and G.N. Smith, eds. and trans, *Selections from the Prison Notebooks of Antonio Gramsci,* New York, 1973, pp. 54-5.

67. Terence Ranger, *Peasant Consciousness and Guerilla War in Zimbabwe,* London, 1985.

CHAPTER 9

The Indian National Congress and The Dynamics of Nation-Building: Aspects of Continuity and Change

Introduction

Nation-building in India is largely linked with the history of the Indian National Congress. Not that the story of Indian politics over the past hundred years can be reduced to the Congress experience. But it either 'became a point of reference' or directly influenced 'many of the continuities and changes in India's intellectual, social and political life' as pointed out in Masselos' *Struggle and Ruling: The Indian National Congress 1885–1985*. Originally representing a movement for freedom, the Congress was transformed into a party with a rigid vertical and hierarchical organization. In the post-Independence period, the party experienced at least two major splits, had itself renamed as the Congress(I) in 1978, and became the principal instrument for the establishment of what has come to be called 'one-party democracy' in the country. In delineating the contours of such changes, standard scholarly works have recognized 15 August 1947 as a dividing line when a 'Great Congress' started to give way to a 'Dirty Congress', operating the administrative machinery left behind by the departing colonial rulers, and thereby losing its credibility as a fighter for freedom.

This essay questions this simplistic formulation, in favour of portraying the dialectics of the Congress in the context of ideology and state power.

*The first version of this paper was published in T.V. Sathyamurthy, ed., *State and Nation in the Context of Social Change*, vol. I, Delhi, 1994, pp. 274–97.

It is argued that those features of the post-1947 Congress, which are recognized as having generated 'negative' or 'regressive' elements in Indian democracy, were already latent at the time of the freedom movement. The Non-Cooperation movement begins this survey because it marked the first major all-India nationalist affront to British colonialism. The analysis ends with the death of Jawaharlal Nehru in January 1964 which brought to a close the first phase of nation-building in India.

The Indian National Congress: Aspects of its Historical Legacy

The Dialectics of Congress Nationalism: The Politics of Controlled Mass Politics and Marginalization of Radicalism

The predominant feature of mainstream Congress nationalism was its disapproval of class politics. Gandhi's immediate objective was to forge national unity against British colonialism, cutting across class lines. Contemporary leftist critics such as Saumyendranath Tagore, however, sought to expose the myth of Gandhi's multi-class front:

The idea of national bloc is an illusion, and indeed a very dangerous one. . . . The Indian bourgeoisie is not so fast asleep nor so stupid as not to see that a revolution here, while destroying British domination, would also inevitably destroy their own domination. It would rather share the profits with the British imperialists than have no profits at all. . . . Two different classes, two different attitudes towards British imperialism—that is the sole reality.[1]

Significantly, at all major critical junctures during the freedom movement, the Congress High Command inevitably intervened to curb 'mass turbulence'. This is explained either in the context of the Gandhian attempt to present the Congress as a broad national platform cutting across all social groups or as a deliberate class strategy to ensure that the freedom struggle did not threaten the economic interests of small landlords and rich peasants in the countryside, and of the nascent Indian bourgeoisie in towns.

In the wake of the Non-Cooperation movement of 1920–1, agrarian riots rocked such parts of the United Provinces as Rae Bareli, Pratapgarh, Fyzabad and Sultanpur. But established local nationalist leaders tended to distance themselves from the uprising, surprising even British officials.[2] Not surprisingly, when the peasant leader Baba Ramchandra was arrested on 10 February 1921, all-India Congress leaders such as Motilal Nehru and Gauri Shankar Misra remarked: 'We must not be unhappy over this and must not even try to get him released.'[3]

Recent researches have also argued that the Bihar Provincial Congress sought to ensure the stability of the small landlord/rich peasant alliance by organizationally insulating itself from anti-planter agitations between 1917 to 1923, not involving itself with the Swami Vidyanand-led 'peasant outbursts against the Darbhanga Raj, and disclaiming any connection with attempts to fuse peasant anger with nationalist fervour during the Non-Cooperation movement.[4]

Such aspects of popular militancy in Bengal in the 1920s as the labour unrest in Calcutta jute mills, the peasant protest against indigo cultivation, the anti-Union Board, and anti-Chaukidari tax agitations, the peasant resistance to Settlement operations and the jail-breaks did not also invoke enthusiastic response from the Congress High Command.[5] When the Bengal communists made their presence felt during the late '20s the mainstream Congress leadership opted to close ranks against the 'new menace'. As has been remarked, 'Gandhi's insistence on non-violent revolution on the one hand, and deprecation of communism on the other, lightened the government's task, but it cost Gandhi his claim to mass leadership [in Bengal].'[6]

Other parts of India experienced crossing the Gandhian limits. The princely states of Ajmer, Mewar and Udaipur witnessed peasant protest against feudal exactions. Madras—long considered to be the backyard of Indian politics—was rocked by a spate of labour turbulence in British-owned textile mills which brought into prominence Singaravelu Chettiar, the first communist of south India. In the Andhra region, nationalism linked itself with poor peasant discontent through the 'forest satyagrahas' of 1921–2, while the millenarian Moplah uprisings in Malabar shook the local socio-political order. The relatively isolated district of Assam was itself struck by sporadic strikes and violence in the tea gardens of Darang and Sibsagar districts; but they did not evoke much interest or excitement amongst the provincial Congress leaders.[7]

Such radical potentialities within the Non-Cooperation movement alarmed both Gandhi and the British, even if for different reasons. Gandhi was disillusioned because of the failure to keep the movement within his ideological parameters; the British were threatened by the spread of disaffection within society at large. At this juncture when at Chauri Chaura an angry crowd burnt alive 22 policemen Gandhi withdrew the Non-Cooperation movement on the ground that it had degenerated into violence. This 'retreat' caused deep anguish amongst the contemporary Left, who suspected that Gandhi's action was primarily dictated by a need to protect the feudal classes who appeared to have been threatened by the dynamism of the Non-Cooperation movement. Interestingly, the Congress Working Committee's Bardoli Resolution of 12 February 1921, which ratified the discontinuation of the Non-Cooperation movement, reiterated that '[the] withholding of rent payments to the *zamindars* is contrary to the Congress resolutions [and that the] Congress movement in no way intended to attack their (zamindars') legal rights.'[8]

During the Civil Disobedience movement, too, the Congress High Command sought to separate political from social issues pressing brakes on any radical action likely to involve a direct conflict between the exploiters and the exploited in Indian society.[9]

At the height of peasant unrest in Agra, Rae Bareli, Baroda, and Bilaoti, following the economic depression of 1930–1, the Congress leadership of the United Provinces advocated 'an amicable settlement . . . and a maintenance of truce'.[10] Gandhi assuaged the UP Zamindars' Association in 1931: 'We do not want that the tenants should stand against *zamindars* . . . we assure *zamindars* that their rights would be given due consideration in a *Swaraj* constitution.'[11]

In another message to the Uttar Pradesh *kisans* on 24 May 1931, Gandhi was more explicit. '[L]et me warn you against listening to the advice if it has reached you that you have no need to pay the *zamindars* or *taluqdars* any rent at all.'[12]

When local leaders like Kalika Prasad preached 'no-rent' and promised lower rents under Swaraj, they were restrained by the Congress High Command. In working class politics also, the High Command inevitably forced the adoption of compromise postures with Indian mercantile and industrial groups.

In Bihar—despite popular enthusiasm—the Civil Disobedience movement hardly assumed the form of a no-rent campaign, largely because the Congress leadership's distinct conservative landlord orientation.[13] The Bihar Congress leadership disapproved of Swami Sahajanand's Kisan Sabha agitations between 1936 and 1939 and Rajendra Prasad indicated that Congress was ready to compensate the foreign cloth dealers for their 'heavy loss' due to the Civil Disobedience movement.[14] Similarly, Bengal witnessed considerable popular militancy, which so alarmed the High Command that the Provincial Congress Committee was directed not to 'alienate the tradesmen and professionals'.[15] Much of the peasant and workers' politics which developed in Bengal between 1928 and 1934 accordingly remained outside the parameters of Congress nationalism.[16] In Gujarat, as Hardiman demonstrates, whenever the Patidar movement threatened the social structure, it was checked either by mobilizing the richer peasants or by withdrawing the agitation.[17] During the same period, other parts of the country were also affected by what the Congress national leadership referred to as 'less manageable forms of agitation'.

The emergence of revolutionary alternatives from within the Civil Disobedience movement threatened the existing indigenous social order which, as Sarkar shows, impelled the Indian Business interests to pressurize Gandhi to terminate the Movement and conclude the Peace Pact with Viceroy Irwin.[18] Khaitan, in his presidential address before the Calcutta

Indian Chamber of Commerce, had asserted: '[I]t may not be amiss to suggest to Mahatma Gandhi and the Congress that the time has come when they should explore the possibilities of an honourable settlement. . . . We all want peace.'[19]

The withdrawal of the Civil Disobedience movement re-emphasized the conservative face of mainstream Congress leadership. In 1927, Gandhi had represented the working class impressively during a prolonged strike in the Tata Iron & Steel Works. But when, in 1935, the Ahmedabad Mill Owners' Association ordered a 25 per cent cut in wages, Gandhi advised the workers to 'accept that'.[20] In an open letter to the Ahmedabad millhands Gandhi remarked,

I hope you will welcome the settlement which has been reached on the question of your wages and cheerfully accept the reduction. . . . I have not the least doubt that it will be in your interests to do so and thereby your prestige will be enhanced . . . the millowners have invested their capital, your capital is labour. Either would be worthless without the other. . . . If you have imbibed this truth, you will recognize that the settlement safeguards the interests of both the parties.[21]

By 1934 the 'leftist' Jawaharlal Nehru had accepted the authority of the conservative sections of the Congress High Command, and Tej Bahadur Sapru noted with satisfaction the change in a man who a few days ago . . . was going strong and preaching his new philosophy of socialism everywhere[22] in the midst of crowded audiences.

Conservative centralism, which had emerged as the dominant feature of the Congress in the course of the 'movement phase' of the '20s and '30s was strengthened further in the post-1936 period, once the Congress formed provincial ministries under the Government of India Act 1935. The Quit India movement of August 1942 outstripped the traditional constraints imposed by the central Congress leadership; the August Revolution, however, was Gandhian in name but not in form.

The 1935 Act and After: Consolidation of the Right within the Congress

The Congress election machinery set up to contest the 1936 legislative assembly elections had a distinct conservative leverage. Candidates were mostly selected from local businessmen, contractors, and landlords, who could not only take care of their own campaigns but could also replenish the party's exchequer.[23] Defections from non-Congress parties were also encouraged in provinces where the party's organization was not yet strong.[24] This process 'increased the strength of the conservatives',[25] and it was this section inside the party which clinched political power when the Congress formed ministries initially in the six provinces of Madras, Bombay, Central Provinces, Orissa, Bihar, United Provinces, and later in the North-West Frontier Provinces and Assam.

The rightist orientation of Congress ministers was reflected in similarities between their style of functioning and that of the preceding British officers. Several members of the Indian Civil Service noted with relief that 'fire-eating agitators' had turned into 'responsible ministers'. Symington, for instance, observed this metamorphosis in Bombay:

It was a momentous occasion when, in the month of April, we came under the rule of the party which had been agitating against the British Raj for more than twenty years. But, if anyone at the time expected dramatic and revolutionary changes, he was in for an anticlimax. Our new Government had enough sense and experience to realise that nine-tenths of its work would lie in the field of day-to-day administration, and that spectacular reform must be a fringe activity.[26]

Masterman, then a Secretary in the Madras secretariat, had a roughly similar story to tell when he proudly noted: 'He [Rajaji] told me once that he had much greater confidence in the judgement of his British secretaries than in his Indian colleagues.'[27]

This element of continuity between the Congress ministries and their British predecessors could be best felt in their respective reactions to various strands of popular protest. By December 1937 the Congress governments were faced with a dilemma. While the Kisan Sabhas—enthused by the formation of 'popular regimes'—pressed for fundamental agrarian reforms, the landlords urged the Congress to contain the 'radical elements'.[28] The Congress was predisposed more favourably to the latter than the former. In Bihar the 'credibility' of the Tenancy Act was considerably undermined when the Congress submitted to landlord pressures at every stage of the legislation,[29] which prompted Sinha to remark appreciatively: 'the Government in Bihar . . . were very reasonable and some concessions were secured by Zamindars in Bihar which no other Government would have allowed.'[30]

In this context, Rajendra Prasad's advice to the Bihar peasants is worth quoting: 'The Kisans should maintain those relations with their landlords which were in existence. They should not create any friction with the landlords.'[31]

Sardar Vallabhbhai Patel went a step further when he warned in April 1938: 'We do not want a Lenin here. . . . Those who preach class hatred are enemies of the country.'[32]

The Bihar government imitated the Raj in undertaking a vilification crusade against popular Kisan Sabha activists, and Congressmen in such 'trouble-prone' districts as Saran were instructed to shun all association with them. In the United Provinces too, there was, throughout the '30s, 'a steady movement towards Congress by landlord elements'.[33] The Madras government of Rajagopalachari likewise did not hesitate to prosecute such prominent Socialist leaders as Yusuf Meherally and S.S. Batliwala.[34] K.M. Munshi, the Bombay Home Minister, followed the British practice of using the Criminal Investigation Department against communists and other leftist political agitators.[35]

The Ministry also period coincided with an upswing in labour militancy: a 158 per cent rise in strikes and lockouts; a 131 per cent increase in the number of strikers; and a 230 per cent upward swing in the curve of working days lost.[36] The Congress government, however, sought to tackle this situation not by supporting labour against capital but 'by a system of government-sponsored arbitration', a strategy which found its best reflection in the Bombay government's Industrial Disputes Act of November 1938. Strikes or demonstrations in Bombay were met with police action.[37] The Madras government pursued a 'policy of internal settlement', even if it meant accommodating employers' interests. A case-study of the labour dispute in the Tata Iron & Steel Company demonstrates how the Bihar ministry's policy of 'compromise and restraint' remained silent on the 'company misdeeds' but emphasized 'maintenance of discipline in the works'. The Uttar Pradesh government employed section 144 of the Criminal Procedure Code—the very law introduced by the Raj for counteracting nationalist agitations—to imprison Kanpur labour leaders. A new organization—the Hindusthan Mazdoor Sabha—was established in 1938 to counteract non-Congress and Leftist influence on the trade union movement. These moves were intended to assure the indigenous capitalist protection 'from an assertive labour force'.

Inside the Congress High Command, Jawaharlal Nehru privately expressed his unhappiness at the way the Congress governments dealt with popular protest. On 28 April 1938 he wrote to Gandhi: 'I feel strongly that the Congress ministries are . . . adapting themselves far too much to the old order and trying to justify it . . . we are losing the high position that we have built up . . . in the hearts of the people. We are sinking to the level of ordinary politicians who have no principles to stand by and whose work is governed by a day to day opportunism.'[38]

On another occasion Nehru noted: 'The Congress has now attracted into its fold thousands who are not eager for achieving *Swaraj* or to join the fight, but are merely seeking personal gains . . . Congress has lost the . . . opportunity of action, of fighting imperialism directly and thus of deriving more strength.'[39]

Such confessions, however, made little institutional impact on the party, since Nehru and his group refused to make public their critique of the Congress governments under the pretext that 'We cannot agitate against ourselves'.[40] Furthermore, Nehru did not dispute the All India Congress Committee resolution of September 1938, which warned those who 'have been found in the name of civil liberty to advocate murder, arson, looting and class war by violent means'.[41] This was presumably in order to provide organizational sanction for the use of state force by Congress governments against protest politics. In fact, by 1938 the Right inside the Congress noted with some satisfaction: 'Jawaharlalji has been veering around to our view and the differences which used to be so marked between his viewpoint and ours on many points is less prominent today.'[42]

Vallabhbhai Patel was more candid when he wrote to Gandhi: 'He [Nehru] has done wonderful work, and has been burning the candle at both ends. We found not the slightest difficulty in cooperating with him and adjusting ourselves to his views. . . .'[43]

The stage was being set for Nehru to become the epitome of centrist leadership of the post-1947 Indian National Congress.

The Congress Government in Independent India: Continuity or Change?

Despite certain obvious outward changes in forms of governance, or use of new political hyperboles, the Indian government under Jawaharlal Nehru represented, in many respects, a continuation of British attitudes, both in form and substance. Alavi has shown that, as in other postcolonial regimes, the Indian state was 'over-developed'.[44] The British Raj had reared a repressive state apparatus which exceeded the needs of an 'underdeveloped and poor post-colonial state'. Incidentally, the Congress government, after 1947, tended not to develop an alternative state structure', but to maintain the police and paramilitary organizations inherited from the British.[45] As Bettelheim contends, the administrative system in independent India was renewed without being remodelled, thus retaining many of the colonial system's imperfections'.[46]

The Indian people were, thus, 'confronted with the same civil servants, the same policemen who treat them with the same scorn and brutality as under British rule'. The Gandhian Nirmal Kumar Bose himself admitted in the late 1950s:

. . . by virtue of the circumstances of peaceful transfer of power, the Congress inherited an administrative structure which it tried to use for a new purpose. Its idea became not to disrupt the *status quo,* but to build up its 'socialistic pattern' of economy on the foundation of the existing order without a violent disturbance. In this prosaic task of reformation, the Congress party . . . had tried to convert every problem of national reconstruction into an administrative problem. . . . The identification of the Congress with the *status quo,* even if the ultimate intention may be of using it as a spring-board for reform . . . has made the organization unpopular. . . . The loss of ethical quality in the contemporary endeavours of the Congress in the reorganization of its party machinery, or in the matter of running an old administrative machinery without sufficient proof of desire or capability of reforming the latter, has created a kind of frustration, and even of cynicism amongst those who had made the attainment of political freedom synonymous with the advent of social revolution or moral regneration.[47]

The Congress relationship with police and military signified a shift from ostensible antagonism until 1947 to increasing 'interdependence' in the post-colonial period.[48] Between 1949 and 1950 the Congress government in Delhi used about 12,000 armed police personnel to curb the Telangana peasant uprising; in the first decade of Independence, as many as 800 recorded deaths resulted directly from police actions; the police expenditure of the Indian government increased from Rs. 9 million in 1951–2 to Rs. 800 million in 1970–1; the army assisted the civil authorities to restore order on 476 occasions between 1961 and 1970, and on 350 occasions between 1980 and 1983.[49]

Despite Jawaharlal's socialist commitment he had to reconcile himself with the strength of the Right within the Congress while evolving his government's economic policy. The Industrial Policy Resolution of 1956 thus made him opt for a 'socialistic' and not a 'socialist' pattern of society. Though the basic dictum of Five Year Plan model was a mixed economy, throughout the Nehruvian period the private sector maintained a commanding presence, prompting many to argue, what was actually resulted was 'a move towards state capitalism'. Table 9.1 aptly demonstrates the importance of the private sector during Nehru's stewardship of the country.

It has been estimated that about nine-tenths of the total domestic product came from the private sector at the close of the Third Five Year Plan period, while the public sector's share increased by only 4 per cent in fifteen years.[50] In terms of the relative contribution to the National Income, the picture was similar: the private sector's contribution ranged between 90 per cent in 1950–1 and 85 per cent in 1960–1, while the public sector's ratio increased from 7.4 per cent in 1950–1 to only 10.7 per cent in 1960–1.

TABLE 9.1: Importance of the Private Sector during Nehru's Stewardship

	First Five Year Plan	Second Five Year Plan
(Crores of rupees at current prices; 1 crore = 10 million)		
Public	55	938
Private	283	850

Source: A. Chaudhuri, Private Economic Power in India: A Study in Genesis and Concentration, Delhi, 1975, p. 160.

The few top business houses with a strong communal and regional character—20 according to the Mahalanobis estimate[51] and 75 according to the Monopolies Inquiry Commission Report of 1965—retained a controlling voice in the economy; the public sector failed to meet its designated goals of self-sufficiency and balanced economic development.[52] Besides, the foreign capital transactions throughout this period had been considerable: the volume of direct foreign investment rose from Rs. 2,176 million in 1948 to Rs. 6,185 million in 1964, and the share of foreign companies in gross profits of the Indian corporate sector increased from 29.8 per cent in 1959–60 to 33.3 per cent in 1962–3.[53]

Indeed, the political economy that developed in India in the aftermath of independence received the tacit approval of leading indigenous industrialists. As early as 1944, Birla, Tata, Shroff, and Mathai had formulated the Bombay Plan, which was similar to the 1951 draft outline of the First Five Year Plan. The Indian bourgeoisie rapidly carved out its own niche within the Congress. Not surprisingly, subsidies for the party's organizational work were forthcoming from all major business houses. In 1957–8 alone, the Tata Electric Company had contributed Rs. 3,00,000 to the Congress party's coffer. During the 1962 poll—the last to be held under Nehru's premiership—officially the three highest declared donations to the Congress were from the Tata and Birla groups (Rs. 1 million each) and a cement company (Rs. 5,00,000).[54] Financial connections between the Congress and Indian industrialists were such that the latter did not seem to have been apprehensive of Nehru's attachment to socialism, and in 1956, Birla is on record as having expressed his agreement with Congress' socialistic ideals.[55] Six years later and two years before Nehru's death, Kilachand, the spokesperson of the Indian bourgeoisie, announced more confidently: 'The business community is in complete agreement with the socialistic objectives of the government and there are no two opinions on that score. There is no fundamental or ideological difference between the business community and the government.'[56]

The element of continuity between the British Raj and Nehru's government outlined above was sustained by the strength of a conservative lobby within the Congress party, which had maintained its prominence throughout the nationalist struggle. A particular method of decision-making within the Congress—the reliance on consensus—helped the Right to continue its stranglehold on the party. With a 3 : 1 ratio in favour of the Patel-led conservatives in the Congress Working Committee from the mid-'50s onwards, the modus operandi of consensus proved to be propitious for the maintenance of the status quo. What followed was a 'sort of democratic centralism' where the right wing could make its weight felt, while the 'left' minority had to be satisfied with concessions. Thus, while Nehru adopted an anti-capitalist and anti-landlord stance in his public pronouncements, he had to refrain from incorporating such sentiments in the party's election manifesto and restricted himself to such vague assurances as the lowering of land rents.[57]

Many scholars feel that a shift of power within the Congress from urban and intellectual groups to a new rural/urban mix of medium-sized landowning dominant castes, cultivating owners and superior tenantry, small town middle and upper middle-classes of larger cities—especially the new industrial and commercial classes—buttressed this conservative weight.[58] Besides, a systematic marginalization of socialist dissent also contributed to the hegemony of the Right within the Congress High Command. The manner in which the Socialists under Acharya Narendra Dev were forced to secede from the parent body in 1948 is a case in point. When the Socialists, following their resignations from the Congress, surrendered their seats in the Uttar Pradesh legislature, and sought re-election, the Congress High Command mobilized its new 'electoral machinery' to defeat all thirteen Socialist candidates, and prove the 'political wilderness' of the opposition.[59] Placed in such a predicament, compromise with the Right for the sake of consensus and political stability remained a persistent trait in Nehru's political life as the first Prime Minister of independent India.

The Party and Government: From an Uneasy Relationship to Governmental Supremacy

Another aspect of the post-independence Congress politics affecting the process of nation-building was the way in which the relationship between the party and government was resolved. A party-government contradiction can be traced back to 1946 when Nehru—on being appointed the leader of the Interim Government—had to surrender the Congress presidency. Acharya J.B. Kripalani, the new Congress President, demanded that all important pronouncements by Congress members of the Interim Government be subjected to prior ratification by the Congress President and the Working Committee—perhaps because of his close links with the Congress central office. On the other hand, Nehru, acutely conscious of the 'coordinating and leadership' roles of a Prime Minister in a cabinet government, favoured a limited role for the party. The Nehru-Kripalani differences reached a crisis when the latter publicly disapproved of the government's alleged 'timidity' towards Pakistan, advocated an economic blockade of Kashmir, and demanded revocation of 'standstill agreements' with the Nizam of Hyderabad.[60] Such overt reprobation of government policy presaged Kripalani's resignation from the Congress presidency in

November 1947. In a moving speech before the All India Congress Committee (AICC) delegates, he thus recapitulated the ideological content of his stand against the government's supremacy over the party:

If there is no free and full co-operation between the Government and the Congress organization, the result is misunderstanding and confusion, such as is prevalent today in the ranks of the Congress and in the minds of the people. Nor can the Congress serve as a living and effective link between the Government and the people unless the leadership in the Government and in the Congress work in closest harmony. It is the party which is in constant touch with the people in villages and in towns and reflects changes in their will and temper. It is the party from which the Government of the day derives its power. Any action which weakens the organization of the party or lowers its prestige in the eyes of the people must sooner or later undermine the position of the Government. . . .[61]

Judged by hindsight, the exit of Kripalani constituted a foretaste of the future. Rajendra Prasad, his interim successor, rendered an indispensable service to Nehru by neutralizing the Party's challenge to its parliamentary wing. Pattabhi Sitaramayya, the next President, accepted the restricted role of the Party in his presidential address before the Jaipur session of the Congress as follows:'A Government must govern and is therefore concerned with the problems of the day, and with the passions of the hour. Its work is concrete, its solutions must be immediate. . . . The Congress is really the Philosopher while the Government is the Politician. . . . That is why the Government of the day requires the aid of unencumbered thinking.'[62]

The bid to retain the supremacy of the organizational wing of the Party was revived in August 1950 when Purushottam Das Tandon won the presidential election, despite Nehru's covert opposition. This was the time when India was confronted with political turbulence caused by communal violence in East Pakistan and an influx of Hindu refugees into West Bengal; factors which strengthened Hindu conservative forces inside the Congress. Driven by a fear that the new party President might infringe upon governmental prerogatives, Nehru resigned from the Working Committee on the pretext that Tandon had alienated nationalist Muslims such as Kidwai. The consequential crisis that followed was preordained: Tandon's forced resignation and his replacement by Nehru in September 1951. This episode more or less ended the party/Government struggle and confirmed the primacy of the Prime Minister in the Indian polity.

Viewed from a historical perspective, this trend of replacing a potentially recalcitrant president by a more 'manageable' one (evidenced initially after the Tripuri Congress and replicated in Kripalani's resignation in 1947 and Tandon's exit in 1951) foreshadowed the growth of the cult of the Nehru family, which provided an apparent stability to the Indian polity in post-

Independence India. Each of the Congress presidents after 1954—Dhebar (1954–9), Indira Gandhi (1959–60), Reddy (1960–2), and Sanjivayya (1962–4)—belonged to the 'secondary generation' of Congressmen, who were not yet distinguished enough to question the Prime Minister. The new line of Congress Presidents readily accepted the subordinate position. Dhebar thus noted that:

It is a mistake to consider that there is a dual leadership in the country. India, for the last forty years, has been accustomed to think in terms of a single leadership and by the grace of God, we have been endowed with men who had borne the brunt out of consideration or service to the country singularly well. There is only one leader in India today and that is Pandit Jawaharlal Nehru. Whether he carries the mantle of Congress Presidentship on his shoulders or not, ultimately, the whole country looks to him for support and guidance.[63]

It is true that towards the end of Nehru's career in August 1963, an attempt was made to enhance the party's influence over the government through what came to be known as 'the Kamaraj Plan'. The idea was to revert government ministers to party positions after a certain tenure. Nehru sympathized with the theory but many doubt if he put the required weight behind its implementation. Instead, his right-wing critics like Morarji Desai alleged that the Kamaraj Plan came handy to Jawaharlal to clear all possible contenders 'from the path of his daughter, Indira Gandhi'.[64] In fact, the Kamaraj Plan did create a new dispossessed group within the Congress who had been deprived of their ministerial positions. This increased intra-party factional squabbles and the spirit of the Kamaraj Plan was hardly realized.

During this period of party/government contradictions, a dichotomy between theory and practice was manifested in Nehru's political disclosure, which left a deep impact on the country's emerging political system. Nehru had agreed in principle 'with our friends and comrades . . . who have objected to the high offices of Prime Minister and Congress President being held by one and the same person'. But when the Congress Presidency was virtually thrust on him, once in 1951 and again in 1953, he accepted it on grounds of having 'no alternative'. In his Presidential address before the 58th session of the Congress, Nehru thus rightly placed the onus on his party colleagues and the emergent political situation: 'I am here at your bidding . . . And yet, I feel a little unhappy once again—as Congress President . . . I tried hard that this should not occur and pleaded with my comrades . . . to make some other choice, but their insistence and the circumstances were against me in this matter. I felt that for me to go on saying "No" in spite of the advice of so many of my valued colleagues, would not be proper.'[65]

Again, when Indira Gandhi was 'unanimously' elected as Congress President in 1959. Nehru reportedly expressed 'surprise' at the idea, remarking: 'I gave a good deal of thought to this matter and I came to the conclusion that I should firmly keep apart from this business and not try to influence it in any way except rather generally and broadly to say that it had disadvantages . . . it is not a good thing for my daughter to come in as Congress President when I am Prime Minister.'[66]

Yet he never vetoed the proposal, either because he realized administrative expediency during a period of political transition required a convergence between the offices of Prime Minister and of Congress President, or because he felt compatibility between the two high offices was required to counter a perceived threat to his political authority. Whatever might have been the case, many critics feel, seeds of the future 'dynastic democracy' had been allowed to sprout.

Nevertheless, the government's authority over the Party was not total. For example, during the last days as a party president, even the Nehru loyalist Dhebar had expressed uneasiness at the increasing 'bossism' of 'governmental leaders in party matters'.[67] He even publicly referred to Nehru's occasional intolerance for 'party criticism'. It needs, however, to be stressed that this cleavage between the organizational and governmental wings of the Congress was common to most parties assuming power following decolonization with no experience of a telescoping of political and social revolutions. Sukarno of Indonesia, Nasser of Egypt, Kenyatta of Kenya—all sought centralization of authority or personal dictatorships, causing erosion of the efficacy of their respective political parties.

Victory of Political Centralism

The political system that developed under Nehru had a particular duality. On the one hand, the country experienced a broad spectrum of political formations. On the other hand, the establishment of Congress hegemony resulted in a one-party political order. The Congress party won impressive majorities in each parliamentary election and maintained organizational strength outside legislatures; the opposition groups, except the communists and Jana Sangh (now the Bharatiya Janata Party—BJP) were mostly formed by rebels from the Congress itself, many of whom either rejoined the parent body or became champions of local interests. The opposition groups failed to present a united national front against Nehru, thus enabling the Congress to win 60–80 per cent of parliamentary seats without winning 50 per cent of the votes cast. The Congress dominance came to coexist with 'competition but without a trace of alternation'.[68]

Social scientists have long grappled with the problematic of the Congress ability to establish its hegemony over the political space of post-independent

India. Some have argued that social complexities and ambiguities prevented the growth of sufficient class polarizations and other contradictions that could 'fracture' an all-embracing alliance of interests represented in the Congress.[69] Others connect the Congress success with its reliance on the spirit of conciliation, a traditionally revered value in Indian society.[70] Many ascribe the Congress to its 'loose' institutional structure that presented 'a functional equivalent of the leadership conflict, policy struggles and alternatives in power provided in most two or multi-party systems'.[71] Still others seek to explain the Congress hegemony by positing it as a 'highly desirable political franchise' in a 'developing electoral market'.[72] But perhaps the most plausible clue to the strength of the Congress lay in its management skill: its ability to co-opt discontented social groups through the maintenance of democratic rites and a display of concern for minorities and backward communities.[73]

Nevertheless, between 1952 and 1964 Nehru imposed President's Rule (a constitutional term for Central Rule) on federal units at least five times, either to dislodge non-Congress Chief Ministers (PEPSU 1953; Kerala 1959) or to offset the collapse of merger moves between the Congress and non-Congress groups (Andhra Pradesh 1954; Kerala 1956; Orissa 1961). Indeed, Nehru's 1953 election slogan 'The Congress is the country and the country is the Congress' was imparted as embodying the national political spirit. In fact, political, administrative, and financial centralization under Congress guidance became the hallmark of the Indian polity. In the words of a leading commentator: 'The most important state leaders were attracted to the Centre, and the Centre had enough prestige to bring local party leaders and legislators into line.'[74]

State governors were inevitably 'hand-picked' by the Centre; the Planning Commission which formulated the Five Year Plans, the Finance Commission which allocated financial resources for the States, the University Grants Commission which oversaw the higher education, the All-India Radio which ran the broadcasting network—all these were, and are still, controlled by the Central government. Such a centrist process, reminiscent of the Viceregal style, has been called 'the dominance of gubernatorial politics'.[75] This centrist posture in Indian federalism caused 'distortions in the functioning of the constitution and concentration of all powers ... leading to inequalities in economic advance.[76] Big business, urban professionals and bureaucracy—civil and military—provided the main social force behind this centralized political structure.[77] Such unitary features bred 'corrosive tensions', causing outbursts often taking the forms of sectarian violence and political anomie, which undermine the very basis of national unity that centralization is supposed to achieve.[78]

In a multi-ethnic state, with uneven economic and centralized polity, any ethnic or linguistic or regional dissension tended to acquire an anti-Delhi character.[79] This has happened during many of the ethnic-based protest movements in India.

Conclusion: Retrospect and Prospect

It was feared that the 'Most Dangerous Decades' of the post-Independence period would end with India splitting 'into a number of totalitarian small nationalities'.[80] Such concerns mirrored British colonial assessments: 'there is not and never was an India, or even any country of India . . . no Indian nation, no people of India . . .'.[81] The pattern of post-independent Indian politics has, however, belied such pessimistic commentaries. India has survived as one nation, won acclaim as the world's largest democracy, experienced economic growth far outstripping many other Third World countries and created a niche in world polity. To a large extent, this success must be attributed to the Congress. But, equally, the Congress cannot escape the responsibility bears a heavy responsibility for certain negative facets of Indian federalism: the centrist atrophy of our polity, uneven political and economic growth, and a widening gap between rich and poor.

This essay re-examines the historical origins of this Congress *problematique*. The question of how to rid the country of its ills demands a separate analysis involving a necessary re-structuring of socio-economic order, a reordering of Centre-State relations and the enrichment of a common Indian nationhood based on a reconciliation of socio-cultural diversity with essential features of an overarching national unity. The fact remains that if the process for pluralism and principles of equity and justice within our federal policy is not strengthened, the cost in terms of national unity and integrity will be heavy indeed.

Notes

1. Cited in G. Bandyopadhyay, *Constraints in Bengal Politics 1921–41: Gandhian Leadership*, Calcutta, 1984, p. 182.
2. P.D. Reeves, 'The Politics of Order: Anti Non-Cooperation in the United Provinces 1921', *Journal of Asian Studies*, vol. 25, no. 2, May 1966, pp. 261–74; W.F. Crawley, 'Kisan Sabhas and Agrarian Revolt in the United Provinces', *Modern Asian Studies*, vol. 5, no. 2, 1971, pp. 95–109.
3. S. Sarkar, *Modern India 1885–1947*, Delhi, 1983, p. 223.
4. S. Henningham, *Peasant Movements in Colonial India: North Bihar 1917–42*, Canberra, 1982.
5. S. Sarkar, *Modern India*, op. cit.
6. G. Bandyopadhyay, *Constraints in Bengal Politics*, op. cit.
7. A. Guha, *Planter Raj to Swaraj: Freedom Movement and Electoral Politics in Assam 1926–1947*, Delhi, 1977.

8. R.P. Dutt, *India Today*, Lahore, 1979, p. 290.
9. G. Pandey, *The Ascendancy of the Congress in Uttar Pradesh 1926–34: A Study in Imperfect Mobilization*, Delhi, 1978, p. 208.
10. Ibid., p. 198.
11. G. Bandyopadhyay, *Constraints in Bengal Politics*, op. cit.
12. S. Sarkar, *Modern India*, op. cit., p. 315.
13. S. Henningham, *Peasant Movements*, op. cit.
14. G. Bandyopadhyay, *Constraints in Bengal Politics*, op. cit., p. 201.
15. T. Sarkar, *Bengal 1928–34: The Politics of Protest*, Delhi, 1987, p. 97.
16. S. Das, 'Themes of Political Protest' in *Economic and Political Weekly*, vol. 23, no. 44, 29 October 1988, pp. 2269–72.
17. D. Hardiman, *Peasant Nationalists of Gujarat: Kheda District 1917–1939*, Delhi, 1981.
18. S. Sarkar, 'The Logic of Gandhian Nationalism: Civil Disobedience and the Gandhi-Irwin Pact 1930–1' in *The Indian Historical Review*, vol. 3, no. 1, 1976, pp. 114–46.
19. Cited in G. Bandyopadhyay, *Constraints in Bengal Politics*, op. cit., p. 200; Also see S. Sarkar, 'The Logic of Gandhian Nationalism', op. cit.
20. G. Bandyopadhyay, *Constraints in Bengal Politics*, op. cit., p. 206.
21. Ibid.
22. Cited in ibid., p. 205.
23. B.R. Tomlinson, *The Indian National Congress and the Raj 1929–1942*, London, 1976.
24. C. Baker, 'The Congress at the 1937 Elections in Madras', *Modern Asian Studies*, vol.10, no. 4, 1976, pp. 557–89.
25. O.P. Gautam, *The Indian National Congress: An Analytical Biography*, Delhi, 1985, p. 104.
26. R.C. Hunt and J. Harrison, *The District Officer in India 1930–1947*, London, 1980, pp. 196–7.
27. Ibid., p. 198.
28. G. McDonald, 'Unity on Trial: Congress in Bihar 1929–39', in *Congress and the Raj: Facets of the Indian Struggle*, D.A. Low, ed., London, 1977.
29. V. Damodaran, 'Office acceptance and some aspects of Congress ministry in Bihar 1937–1939', M.Phil. thesis, Jawaharlal Nehru University, New Delhi, 1984; V. Damodaran, *Broken Promises, Popular Protest, Indian Nationalism and the Congress Party in Bihar 1935–1946*, Delhi, 1992.
30. A.N. Das, *Agrarian Unrest and Socio-Economic Change in Bihar 1900–1980*, Delhi, 1983, p. 158.
31. Ibid., p. 146.
32. G. Pandey, 'Congress and the Nation', in *Congress and Indian Nationalists: the Pre-independence Phase*, R. Sission and S. Wolpert, eds., Berkeley, 1988, p. 129.
33. P. Reeves, 'Adjusting to Congress Dominance: The UP Landlords 1937–1947', in *Congress and Indian Nationalists*, R. Sisson and S. Wolpert, eds., op. cit.
34. B. Chandra, M. Mukherjee, A. Mukherjee, K.N. Panikkar and S. Mahajan, *India's Struggle For Independence*, Delhi, 1990.
35. Ibid.

36. V.B. Karnik, *Strikes in India*, Bombay, 1967.

37. G. Kudaisya, 'Office Acceptance and the Congress 1937–39: Promises and Perceptions', M.Phil. thesis, Jawaharlal Nehru University, 1984; B. Chandra et al., *India's Struggle*.

38. J. Nehru, *A Bunch of Old Letters*, Delhi, 1988, pp. 283–4.

39. Cited in S. Gopal, ed., *Jawaharlal Nehru: Selected Works*, vol. 8 (first series), Delhi, 1976, p. 393.

40. B. Chandra et al., *India's Struggle,* p. 337.

41. Ibid.

42. R. Prasad, Manuscript, I/RP/PSF(I)/1937, National Archives of India, New Delhi.

43. All India Congress Committee (AICC) Papers, 1936, Nehru Memorial Library and Museum, New Delhi, File-G-85(I) of 1936.

44. H. Alavi, 'The State in Post-colonial Societies: Pakistan and Bangladesh', *New Left Review*, vol. 74, July/August 1972, pp. 59–81.

45. M. Shepperdson and C. Simmons, eds., *The Indian National Congress and the Political Economy of India 1885–1947*, Aldershot, 1988, p. 15.

46. C. Bettelheim, *India Independent* (tr. W.A. Caswell), London, 1968, p.116.

47. N.K. Bose, 'Social and Cultural Life in Calcutta', *Geographical Review of India*, vol. 20, December 1958, pp. 27–8.

48. D. Arnold, *Police Power and Colonial Rule: Madras 1859–1947*, New Delhi, 1986; D. Arnold, 'The Congress and the Police', in *The Indian National Congress*, M. Shepperdson and C. Simmons, eds., op. cit.

49. M. Shepperdson and C. Simmons, eds., *The Indian National Congress*, op. cit., p. 16.

50. A. Chaudhuri, *Private Economic Power in India: A Study in Genesis and Concentration*, Delhi, 1975, p. 161.

51. *Government of India, Report of the [Mahalanobis] Committee on the Distribution of Income and Levels of Living*, New Delhi, 1964.

52. A.K. Bagchi, 'Public Sector Industry and Quest for Self-reliance in India', *Economic and Political Weekly*, vols. 14–16, 17 April 1982, pp. 615–28.

53. N.K. Chandra, 'Role of Foreign Capital in India', *Social Scientist*, vol. 5, no. 9, April 1977, pp. 3–20; G.K. Shirokov, *Industrialisation of India*, Moscow, 1973.

54. G. Rosen, *Democracy and Economic Change in India*, Berkeley, 1967, p. 85.

55. C. Bettelheim, *India Independent*, op. cit., p. 131.

56. A. Chaudhuri, *Private Economic Power in India*, op. cit., p. 157.

57. R. Som, *Differences within Consensus: the Left and Right in the Congress 1929–1939*, London, 1995.

58. G. Rosen, *Democracy and Economic Change in India*, op. cit.; P. Brass and F. Robinson, eds., *The Indian National Congress and Indian Society 1885–1985: Ideology, Social Structure and Political Dominance*, Delhi, 1989; M. Weiner, 'Political Leadership in West Bengal: The Implications of its Changing Pattern for Economic Planning', *The Economic Planning*, vols. 28–30, 11 July 1959, pp. 925–32; A.C. Mayer, 'Rural Leaders and the Indian General Election', *Asian Survey*, vol.1, no. 8, August 1961; F.G. Bailey, *Politics and Social Change: Orissa in*

1959, Berkeley and Los Angeles, 1963; A. Beteille, 'Politics and Social Structure in Tamilnadu', *The Economic Weekly,* vols. 28–30, 15 July 1963, pp. 1161–7; Also see the essays in A. Beteille, *Democracy and Its Institutions,* New Delhi, 2012.

59. P. Brass and F. Robinson, *The Indian National Congress,* op. cit.

60. G. Rosen, *Democracy and Economic Change in India,* op. cit.

61. *All India Congress Bulletin,* no. 6, 1947, Delhi, AICC office, pp. 11–12.

62. B.P. Sitaramayya, *Presidential Address, The Indian National Congress Fifty-fifth Session,* Delhi, 1948, pp. 48–50.

63. Cited in S.A. Kochanek, *The Congress Party of India: The Dynamics of One-Party Democracy,* Princeton, 1968, p. 61.

64. K. Nayar, *Between the Lines,* Bombay, 1969.

65. J. Nehru, *Presidential Address, The Indian National Congress Fifty-eighth Session,* Delhi, 1953, p. 1.

66. *The Times of India,* Delhi, 8 February 1959.

67. S.A. Kochanek, *The Congress Party of India,* op. cit., p. 65.

68. W.H. Morris-Jones, 'Dominance and Dissent: Their Interrelations in the Indian Party System' in his *Politics Mainly Indian,* Madras, 1978, pp. 213–32.

69. Ibid.

70. M. Weiner, 'Traditional Role Performance and the Development of Modern Political Parties: The Indian Case' in *Journal of Politics,* no. 26, no. 4, November 1964, pp. 830–49.

71. P. Brass and F. Robinson, eds., *The Indian National Congress and Indian Society,* op. cit., p. 3.

72. R. Sission, 'Dominant Party or Marketing Franchise: The Congress Party in Early Independent India', paper presented at a seminar on *India: The First Ten Years 1947–57,* University of Oxford, 1990 (mimeo).

73. R. Kothari, 'The Congress "System" in India', *Asian Survey,* no. 13, December 1964, pp. 161–73.

74. G. Rosen, *Democracy and Economic Change in India,* op. cit., p. 70.

75. P.B. Mayer, 'Development and Deviance: The Congress as the Raj', in *Struggling and Ruling: The Indian National Congress 1885–1985,* J. Masselos, ed., Delhi, 1987, pp. 182–97.

76. B.T. Ranadive, 'National Problems and the Role of the Working Class' in *National Problems and the Working Class in India,* Calcutta, 1989, p. 16.

77. P. Bardhan, 'Dominant Proprietary Classes and India's Democracy', in *An Analysis of Changing State-Society Relations,* A. Kohli, ed., Princeton, 1988.

78. Ibid., p. 224.

79. B. De and S. Das, 'Ethnic Revivalism—Problems in the Indian Union', in *Ethnicity, Caste and People: Proceedings of the Indo-Soviet Seminars held in Calcutta and Leningrad 1990,* K.S. Singh, ed., New Delhi, 1992.

80. S.S. Harrison, *India: The Most Dangerous Decades,* Princeton, 1960.

81. J. Strachey, *India: Its Administration and Progress,* London, 1903, p. 4.

CHAPTER 10

THE 'GOONDAS': TOWARDS A RECONSTRUCTION OF THE CALCUTTA UNDERWORLD THROUGH POLICE RECORDS

To A SOCIAL scientist crime is essentially a social problem. It represents a form of social deviance; it provides us with an entry point for comprehending the changing relations between the citizen and state, especially in the realm of regulating social behaviour. Research on the history of British and American crime has shown that at particular historical junctures, crime becomes politics—it can be a prologue to conscious and articulate resistance by the dispossessed.[1] According to some historians, in England poaching and smuggling illustrated hostility to the emergence of class society; infringements on enclosures of land represented protests against the violation of traditional rights of commoners to use pastures, commons and forests, and food rioting expressed popular anger caused by the erosion of a moral economy based of collective bargaining.

For India, too, studies of crime and deviance should provide unofficial commentary on the social past. However, such insights might not always shed light on historical reconstructions of popular struggles, for the subjects of crime could be conformists rather than challengers of the establishment. But as G.M. Jones reminds us, a historian on the left should 'not . . . confine attention to the history of labour movements, oppressed classed or parties of the left, but rather . . . to reconstruct historical totalities'.[2]

*This essay is based on a collaborative research project undertaken with Professor Jayanta K. Ray. The work was sponsored by the Department of History, University of Calcutta. Thanks are due to Jashim Mukherjee who worked as our research assistant and rendered valuable assistance in the compilation of the data. The article was published in *Economic and Political Weekly,* vol. xxix, no. 44, 29 October 1994, pp. 2877–83.

It is in this context that I intend to analyse some hitherto unutilized Bengal Police files on goondas—traditionally viewed as the 'casual residuum' of Calcutta society—who generated, and continues to provoke, fear and anxiety, especially among the propertied classes. Historical reconstructions based on such police papers covering the period between 1926 and 1971 are bound to be partial.[3] They require to be corroborated and supplemented by other official and non-official sources of information. We have particularly to search for confirmatory evidence in vernacular literature, or what Chevalier calls 'qualitative evidence'[4] which has been so effectively used to recapture the details of the criminal world in London and Paris.

The Goonda File: Its Structure

Lawless social groups certainly existed in India before the coming of the British. However, what happened under colonialism was their classification into neat legal categories such as goondas, thugs, dacoits, criminal tribes, etc. This social engineering was related to the new colonial perception of crime. While the traditional indigenous understanding of crime was 'based on sin and paternalistic beliefs about authority', the colonial state 'separated the criminal from the rest of the society'[5] who was not only to be punished, but was to be reformed and controlled through the police and prison. Following Foucault's paradigm, it may be contended that this colonial exercise was part of a new strategy for the exercise of power.[6]

The Bengal government's Goonda Act of 1926 made it mandatory for the police to maintain under the broad term 'goonda' the files on convicted or suspected deviants of a broad spectrum, ranging from thieves, gamblers, pickpocketers, smugglers, toughs and cocaine dealers to political activists. The ostensible purpose of the act was to ensure forced exclusion from Calcutta of the criminals labelled as goondas. Each file conforms to the structure laid down by the act. It usually contains a cover note introducing the convict and reasons recommending his deportation. A goonda file also contains the heads of charges against the accused and a history sheet of the suspect. Often representations and depositions of local residents against the 'goonda' used as evidence for classifying an accused as a 'danger to ordinary peace loving citizens'—are appended to a file. Even the language used in the files bears an imprint of similarity.

In official discourse the goonda came to be more described than defined. He or she was seen as a social category who was to be controlled and subjected to state power rather than to be understood. A particular vocabulary accordingly was invoked to homogenize the act of labelling a criminal. To quote a perceptive comment: 'Accordingly, *goondas* are presented as socially unplaced and the ultimate effect is to create an image of the man, and of a group of men, as brought up outside the sphere of normal society—to peripheralise them.'[7]

In the process of constructing this image of a goonda as 'invisible and peripheral', he or she was defined as 'someone not only expendable and undesirable, but also outside the worthy citizen-community which it was the British police force's job to protect'.[8] Significantly, the same police perception still survives in independent India.

Before I start examining goonda files, it will be pertinent to draw parallels between the way officials in England and India respectively used the terms hooligan and goonda. The term hooligan registered an 'abrupt entry' into English vocabulary during what is known as the 'hot summer of 1898', to describe the rowdy youth.[9] But as with goonda and goondaism the official and media discourses turned hooligan and hooliganism to be terms of 'more general notoriety' so that they became 'controlling words' for any unexplained crime. The hooligan, like the goonda, 'embarked on a remarkable career, appearing in name, if not in person, before numerous governmental and semi-official bodies of enquiry'[10] as the main subject of what has been called 'respectable fears'.

Deciphering The Goonda World

Reconstruction of goonda files dispels some popular myths of the goonda world in Calcutta, For instance, the notion of a well-structured homogeneous Calcutta goonda community does not appear to be correct. One is struck by a considerable heterogeneity in the social background of convicts, the factors, behind their criminalization, their links with institutional politics and in the type of crime committed.

Interestingly, the 50–odd files made available to us hardly refer to 'Muslim goondas'. But this could have hardly been a historical reality. In an earlier work[11] I have indicated the links between Muslim League politicians and the Calcutta Muslim underworld which particularly came to the fore during the Great Calcutta Killing of August 1946. A possible reason for the conspicuous absence of files on Muslim goondas was their destruction during the Muslim League ministry in Bengal Presidency.[12]

Within a particular 'gang', however, loyalties did cut across religious lines. We even have two Anglo-Indians—Eric Mitchell and Charles Neville Chambers—and a Chinese with a foreign passport among the prominent goondas.[13] There is also the instance of a female 'goonda' leader, Nirmala Dasi (alias Shanti). She spent her childhood in Midnapore amidst extreme financial distress due to the untimely death of her father. At the age of 16 she was deceived by a man, who brought her to Calcutta on the pretext of arranging a decent marriage, but instead was dumped in a prostitute's den.

Henceforth Nirmala earned her living by soliciting and other criminal activities in and around Masjidbari Street.[14]

A Social Victim?

The history sheet of a goonda file can be a useful index to understand why and how someone became a goonda. I am aware that any explanation of 'criminal' deviance is likely to be subjective. The deviant himself as well as his primary group—his gang, family and circle of friends—may with all seriousness believe that either he or she was not committing a 'crime'; or that he was justified in violating the established social rules. As Gersham Sykes warns us:

The definition of 'criminal' activity as wrong . . . is not an all-or-none affair; it is a matter of degree, subject to the influence, of rationalisations, personality disturbances, subcultural traditions, the exigencies of the situation, and so on. Committing violent acts and taking the property of another may be viewed as only 'quasi-criminal' by many people, under certain circumstances; and for some offences against public safety and morals, this may even be more true.[15]

It is, however, ahistorical to categorize any individual or social group as abnormal or biologically prone to violence. As early as 1842, Karl Marx drew our attention to 'how civil law or liberal legislations infringe upon the customary rights of the poor based on . . . hybrid, indeterminate forms of property' without creating an alternative framework.[16] He elucidates this thesis with the pertinent example of the dissolution of monasteries. To quote Marx:

The monasteries were abolished, their property was secularised, and it was right to do so. But the accidental support which the poor found in the monasteries was not replaced by any other private source of income. When the property of the monasteries was converted into private property and the monasteries received some compensation, the poor who lived by the monasteries were not compensated. On the contrary, a new restriction was imposed on them, while they were deprived of an ancient right.[17]

Similarly, the colonial transformation of India and the subsequent spate of modernization in independent India resulted in an erosion of customary space in indigenous society upon which the 'deviants' traditionally relied upon for survival. This left the 'social outcasts' in cities like Calcutta with the option of taking to crime as a viable means of livelihood. The goonda files illustrate how such material factors as economic distress, neighbourhood, broken home or marriage, and geographical mobility, led people astray. This will demonstrate that the Calcutta underworld need no longer be cast aside as 'lamentable victims' but recognized as a force in itself.

Gamini Salgado has established links, between London's social structure and the rise of an 'Elizabethan Underworld' thus:

London then, was a place of vivid contrasts. There was the contrast between the largest and most crowded city in Europe and the little havens of rural peace within and around it. . . . For one thing London offered far greater opportunities for beggary and fraud than the rest of England, and the chances of apprehension were smaller, for the London underworld appears to have had its own security system and intelligence network which were probably more than a match for the rudimentary and quasi-amateur police force which was all the city could boast.[18]

Jones also demonstrates how the emergence of an 'Outcast London' was shaped by such features of London as 'the substitution for primary contacts of secondary ones, the weakening of bonds of kinship, the decline of the social significance of the family, the undermining of the traditional basis of social solidarity and the erosion of traditional methods of social control'.[19] Peter Linebaugh develops this argument to assert: '. . . first that the forms of exploitation pertaining to capitalist relations caused or modified the forms of criminal activity, and, second, that the converse was true; namely, that the forms of crime caused major changes in capitalism.'[20]

As the second city of the British empire, Calcutta too imbibed much of the characteristics of London which contributed to the creation of its underworld. On the one hand, the city had by the turn of the twentieth century emerged as the nucleus of a variety of economic activities. On the other hand, Calcutta had clean racial and class divides: the 'white locality' was juxtaposed with the 'native area', and the stately mansions of prosperous Bengalis and Marwaris stood against unhealthy slums. Besides, seven-tenths of the metropolitan population were migrants from the upcountry.[21] They earned their livelihoods as labourers, carters and coolies, constituting a permanent volatile social group.[22] These aspects of Calcutta's social map contributed in varying degrees to the creation of the city's goonda world. Within the Calcutta metropolis itself can be deciphered a zone comprising its northern and central parts (especially Upper Circular Road, Amherst Street, Narkeldanga, Beliaghata, Bowbazar, Rambagan and Muchipara) where the goondas were particularly active.[23] We need to develop for Calcutta a conceptual framework for analysing the geography of 'crime' and see if such spatial factors as environment can have a bearing on the types of 'crime' committed by the goondas.[24] After all, in many areas crime can be a daily reality where the deviants are locked along with their victims in a spatial setting characterized by social tension, low self-esteem, fear, and opportunity for misbehaviour.[25]

Let me now cite instances where the neighbourhood conditions drove some towards criminality. The families of Phoolchand Kahar and Ranjit Debnath had migrated to Calcutta in search of livelihood, but had to be content with settling in slums which made them easy prey for 'local anti-socials'.[26] Similarly, Subodh Chandra De, born in a lower middle class family in Dhaka, had moved to a Beliaghata slum following the 1947 Partition. He was placed in an unknown terrain and failed to gain honourable employment, which gradually pushed him to the underworld.[27] Paltu Das lost his parents in infancy and was reared by his elder sister who was a prostitute. Paltu thus gained early contacts with local 'lawless groups' and degenerated into an alcoholic and a member of 'harlots'.[28] Sheikh Shahjahan's father was a poor coolie who could not provide his son with a proper living. This helped the 'bad characters' of the locality to introduce Shahjahan to gambling in his childhood. Shahjahan ultimately became the leader of a notorious 'goonda gang'.[29] Some of those registered as goondas also reportedly inherited the 'criminal background' of their own families. Thus, Amit Maity's father was a 'notorious hooligan[30] and Dilip Singh's father was a gambler of ill repute.[31] Besides, Calcutta witnessed the last significant wave of Hindu migration following the 1950 communal disturbances in East Pakistan, and many of those refugees who were frustrated in their search for an honest living became easy recruits for the Calcutta underworld.[32]

Economic insolvency resulting from family proverty, a failure of family business, or a loss of employment was another major determinant of initiation into the Calcutta underworld. Brajendra Sarkar (alias Shambhu) and Chitta Pal had to discontinue their studies for lack of finance, which, encouraged them to be associates of 'local hoodlums'.[33] Rabindranath Das, Rahul Amin, Adhir Pramanik (alias Bhaia), Indu Bhusan Goswami, Austo Ghorai and Ranajit Goala lost their fathers at an early age, which placed them in acute economic distress. This made them search for 'ready money' by selling illicit liquor, by acting as agents of gambling dens and brothels, or by committing violence on persons.[34]

Nuru lost his mother at the age of 14 when his father Mahammad Shah remarried. But Nuru's stepmother subjected him to 'economic torture' and this drove him to join a 'goonda gang' to earn a living.[35] Krishnabahadur Nepali—born in a poor family in Darjeeling in 1926—was reared first by a Chinese man and then by a port vendor. But he always suffered from emotional instability, to escape from which he 'struck up bad companionship',[36] Babulal Khatik and Lakshmi Narayan Porel of north Calcutta forged links with local 'criminals' and eventually established their own 'gangs' when they found the maintenance of their family shops unprofitable.[37] Basanta K. Saha (alias Bhenda) joined the 'criminal' world after he lost his job in the US Air Base at Rishra for being implicated in a smuggling case.[38] Bhulu Das lost his father in childhood, and lack of any access to meaningful employment impelled him to turn 'a vicious outlaw'.[39]

Correlation between an economic crisis and initiation to goondaism need not necessarily imply that the Calcutta underworld was essentially an outgrowth of 'iniquities and class arrangements determined by supra-local structures'. Unlike the London outcasts or the Tyburn victims, the goondas were not necessarily 'the labouring poor'. Not all those categorized as goondas came from marginalized social groups. We have convicts from landlord, educated and professional middle class families. Lal Mia was the son of a petty landlord of Mymensingh in East Bengal who had trading interests in rice, jute and sugarcane.[40] Amarendra Mazumdar studied till the Second Year in Government Arts College; Salil Mazumdar and Animesh Gupta were Intermediate students in Vidyasagar College; Subrata Chakrabarti passed the Higher Secondary examination in 1960 and obtained a diploma in Mechanical and Electrical Engineering from the Calcutta Technical School in 1967.[41] Satyapriya Bhattacharya of Beliaghata belonged to the family of a lawyer who had been employed in the Bengal Credit Bank and the Government Rationing Department.[42] Chittaranjan Guha and Dwaraka Nathan were both sons of physicians; Khalil Ahmed Querishi's father was a quack doctor in central Calcutta;[43] Pradyut Guha's brother was the managing director of a factory.[44]

Interestingly, the history sheets demonstrate that some leaders of the underworld had previous military connections. Anil Bose had joined the Royal Indian Navy but lost his job in 1946 for participating in the Bombay Naval Mutiny.[45] Prakash Das worked as an electrician in the US Military Camp in Dhakuria (south Calcutta) during the Second World War but was imprisoned for allegedly sexually harassing a nurse,[46] Ram Singh Gill worked as a jamadar in the Indian Army in the 1940s.[47] Tapan Bose and Utpal Kumar Pandey had served in the Indian Navy during the 1960s.[48] We also have at least two examples—and that too from the not too distant past—of Calcutta police officers being convicted for having 'criminal' connections.[49] One of them even came from a respectable family whose father had been a librarian of the National Library and his elder brother a security officer in the Calcutta Electric Corporation.

We have a number of examples to show that the traumatic event of the 1946 Great Calcutta Killing drove many into the underworld.[50] The name which finds constant mention in this context is Gopal Mukherji (alias Gopal Patha) of Malanga in central Calcutta, who raised the Bharat Jatiya Bahini to protect Hindus during the riot.[51] The Bahini, to quote a police report, was a 'private army' trained in the use of explosives and firearms.[52] Its activists were mostly like Krishna[53] who had to leave behind their establishments in Muslim majority areas in search of safety. Others, like Dinabandhu Datta (alias Andrew, alias Indu) or Santosh Kumar Pal or Bhanu

Bose, belonged to middle class families but had joined the Bahini to retaliate the humiliation suffered by their community at Muslim hands.[54] Sometimes known musclemen such as Basanta of Beadon Street were recruited by Gopal Mukherji to repulse what he called 'Muslim marauders'. There were also examples of people such as Lakshminarayan Porel (alias Lakha) who associated themselves with the Bahini to acquire an expertise in the manufacture of unlicensed firearms.

The Bahini received liberal financial help from prosperous Hindu persons during the communal fury. But once the rioting subsided, this support was withdrawn and the very figures who had been hailed as saviours from Muslim brutalities were now looked down upon with social contempt.[55] This probably induced Gopal Mukherjee and his followers to take recourse to organized 'crime' as a means of livelihood. Their involvement ranged from armed dacoities like the Sonarpur Dacoity case and Guinea Mansion Dacoity case to armed hold ups, house burglaries, smuggling, petty snatching, and theft.[56] Some of Gopal's followers remained 'energetic participants' in subsequent communal clashes in Calcutta and retained a deep communal antipathy towards the Muslims.[57] A section of Gopal's Bahini developed a close association with the Congress Party. But others like Ram Chatterjee became involved with Left politics and at one time served as a minister in the Left Front government.[58] Interestingly enough, we have only one example of a Muslim—Lal Mia—who was initiated into the 'criminal' world during the days of the 1946 riots.[59]

Many of the registered Hindu goondas shared general revivalist stereotypes. One of them proudly recalled how he had set fire to Muslim huts during a communal clash in 1961 and gave vent to his anti-Muslim feelings thus: Muslim males maltreat their females. They contract more than one marriage, mainly because they want to increase Muslim population as much so as to place Hindus at a disadvantage.[60]

We also have instances of non-Bengali convicts generating tensions between the city's Bengali and non-Bengali inhabitants. For instance, Bairam Munia and Bala Shaw, originally hailing from Bihar, had their 'goondaism characterized by extreme communalism . . . towards Bengalis', and utilized any opportunity like the communal turmoil of 28 May 1967 to organize violent attacks on Bengali localities in northern and central parts of the metropolis.[61] On the other hand, Subodh Chandra De of Narkeldanga gained a particular notoriety in terrorising non-Bengalis, while Ramjam Ali of Canal West Road excelled in persecuting Bengali Hindus with the help of 'non-Bengali ruffians'.[62]

Often an adverse or unanticipated happening in one's personal life goaded one to join the goonda life. Ranjit Kumar Bose (alias Runu) was a prominent football player for Kalighat Sporting Club. But the Club's defeat by the Dalhousie Club in 1944 was widely attributed to his betrayal for a bribe of Rs. 3,000. This suspicion caused his expulsion from the Club and an ignominious end to his sporting career. Runu then became a frustrated person, readily developing connections with bad characters and degenerating into a 'tough and alcoholic'.[63]

Goondaism: Forms of Expression

The goonda files throw light on the modus operandi of the goondas. The activities of the Calcutta underworld recorded in police files cover a wide range—snatching, extortion, theft, murder, robbery, dacoities, wagon-breaking, smuggling, gambling and blackmarketeering. The goondas usually operated in organized groups, often in the name of clubs such as Bharatiya Jatiya Bahini, Frontier Batch and Bullet Sangha.[64] Local gymnasia and physical training centres provided them with operation bases.[65] Firearms and missiles of all sorts were freely used.

Some convicts specialized in particular crafts. Ram Singh Gill was adept at raiding taxis and automobiles on highways.[66] Sheikh Ismail and Rabindranath Dhar excelled in rail dacoities.[67] Babulal Kalwar employed a number of massage-boys in the Maidan who were trained to extort money after performing a massage.[68] Milan acted as an agent of landlords to dislodge tenants.[69] Charles Neville Chambers (alias CN) developed an expertise in photographing young girls and then raping them.[70] A close link can be detected too between brothels and goondas. Many of those listed as goondas began their careers as pimps, some even as procurers for American soldiers, stationed in Calcutta during the Second World War.[71] Such toughs often clashed with each other for control over prostitutes; the prostitutes themselves were subjected to various forms of extortion by goondas over the share of the spoils.[72]

It was not unnatural for a goonda to amass an impressive fortune. Hemanta Kumar Mandal owned a lorry and a limousine. A police raid on his house once yielded Rs. 65,485 in cash and the discovery of his rich bank account containing about Rs. 2 lakh, 1,535 gm of gold, and bank drafts and cash certificates to the tune of Rs. 55,000.[73]

The Calcutta police in the aftermath of independence introduced a new category of goonda files specifically concerned with what came to be dubbed 'political goondas'—a term used to segregate the 'law-breakers' who had political connections. But such a classification appears to be a misnomer. The files of the so-called 'political goondas' belong to the period of Congress ministries in West Bengal. A careful reading of their History Sheets reveals that the convicts were essentially Left activists belonging either to the CPI(M), CPI, RCPI, or CPI(ML)[74] whose characterization as 'goondas' enabled the police to treat them not as political prisoners but as ordinary criminals. On many occasions the police did not even bother to insert details of convictions against the Left activists arrested for 'goondaism'.[75] But many of the accused having leftist sympathies were arrested during such political struggles as the 1949 agitation demanding a fair deal for East Bengal refugees, the 1953 anti-tram fare rise movement, or the 1959 protest against inflation. Their convictions under the Goonda Act did not strictly conform to the spirit of that piece of legislation.[76] Some amongst those who were categorized as 'political goondas' such as Dhora Mahato and Punit Goala, and implicated with smuggling or other anti-social business, were actually noted trade unionists.[77] Significantly enough, the entries in the files of some 'political goondas' having Naxalite affiliations suddenly stop after their arrests.[78] Perhaps this indicates their deaths in police custody—a recurrent event in those tumultuous days of the 1970s. We interviewed some political activists, once listed as goondas in police files but now leading settled lives with self-employed jobs. They admit to having used firearms and bombs against their political rivals but would distinguish their acts from ordinary criminal violence. Looking back to the past they now appear to realize how political leaders had utilized their muscle power for narrow interests. Consequently, they nurse a deep disillusionment with those who wield power in society.[79]

Goonda and State:
Contours of a Symbolic Relationship

While the police remained busy in bringing 'disruptive political activists' within the 'criminal' fold, some of the listed goondas could forge links with the administration. One Dilip Singh secured his release from the high court because of a deliberate faulty use of a punctuation mark in a crucial passage of the police detention order.[80] The link between the state and some goondas become particularly self-evident when the police record admits withdrawal of their cases 'in public interest'[81] or when someone like Prithwish Kumar Bose—once dubbed by the local thana as a 'notorious criminal'—has his history sheet discontinued after a particular year.[82] It is also doubtful how Nang Wai (China Tony), holding a foreign passport, continued to defy a government order for his repatriation without the police acting as an accomplice.[83] Sometimes senior police officials confidentially described a character as 'a dangerous criminal',[84] or 'a menace',[85] or a 'pest to the people of the locality',[86] or a 'desperate criminal (having) insatiable greed for easy money',[87] or a 'danger to law and order',[88] or a 'notorious dacoit',[89] or as one 'who carried on his anti-social operations with unabated fury'.[90] Yet, the criminal could not be convicted before the law-court for lack of sufficient evidence. Phoolchand Kahar or Ranjit

Kumar Hazra thus continued to commit crimes by paying insignificant fines and suffering small bouts of imprisonments.[91]

According to the police, a dearth of evidence against a criminal was caused by a general refusal by local residents to act as witnesses for fear of retaliation by the followers of goondas. But this was not always true. The police files themselves contain references to witnesses recognizing a culprit during an identification parade[92] or a crowd seizing the goonda and handing him over to the thana.[93] We also have an example where the police had to act due to popular pressure. This happened in Gouriban when the local people, dismayed by the police silence at Hemanta Mandal's misdeeds, organized a resistance movement under the aegis of a Shanti (Peace) Committee and forced Hemanta's arrest.[94]

Popular and Police Perceptions of a Goonda

At this juncture I would like to introduce some complexity into this apparently simplistic presentation. Let me draw your attention back to Gopal Mukherjee (Gopal Patna) and juxtapose the police perception of him with a popular attitude towards him. He was, and is still, viewed by many of his neighbours as the grandson of the great revolutionary Anukul Mukherjee, as one who had protected Hindu women during the 1946 Calcutta carnage, as one who is a patron of philanthropic activities, as one who assists in the organization of national celebrations such as Netaji's birthday. What is true of Gopal Mukherjee might also be true of great many goondas. Like any other member of the society, a goonda also possesses multiple identities, one form gaining precedence over others at particular historical junctures. A goonda may generally indulge in 'lawless acts' out of self-interest, but on some other occasions he can be a 'protector' for his neighbours against outside interference.[95]

To resolve this problematic of reconciling the two antithetical perceptions, the official and the popular, we need to evolve an appropriate methodology. In western historiography of crime, such dichotomies between official and popular perceptions on 'criminals' have been to a large extent resolved by a judicious use of broadsheets, pamphlets and anonymous letters or handouts whose linguistic form, content and dictum indicate that they had emanated from the lower social order.[96] Peter Linebaugh has recently utilized the biographies of men and women hanged at Tyburn to establish the relationship between crime and civil society in eighteenth-century London.[97] Unfortunately, largely because of the low literacy level, it is difficult to lay our hands on such popular literature in India. In such circumstances, oral history, despite its inherent dichotomies, can be of great help. But I have found a great degree of reluctance on the part of convicts to recount their past deeds. How to understand the popular perceptions of the goondas will remain a challenge for historians working on the Calcutta underworld.

CONCLUSION

The set of police files on goondas examined above—which today would fashionably perhaps be called texts—could have been presented in a different light. For example, the post-modernists—believing in the dictum 'history is never present to us in anything but a discursive form'—would have surely undertaken an exercise of deconstruction.[98] The 'deconstructive strategy', as Derida puts it, involves an overturning of 'hierarchies' and 'release of dissonances' within any speech or writing, and hence a 'disorganisation of an inherited order of thought'.[99] Undoubtedly the 'deconstruction methodology' can yield interesting results. But those who view history as a study of changing social structures are faced with an analytical problem when postmodernists argue that reality is defined purely as language and consequently past dissolves into literature. An extreme postmodernist position would extend the argument on the autonomy of discourse to the point of making it a historical factor in its own right. This, as one critic points out, blocks off explanations of change over time based on more complex interactions of material conditions, culture, ideology and power. . . . If there is nothing outside the text, then history as we have known it collapses altogether, and the fact and fiction become indistinguishable from one another.[100]

To quote a pertinent comment by Gabrielle M. Spiegel:

Our most fundamental task as historians . . . is to solicit those fragmented inner narratives to emerge from their silences. In the final analysis, what is the past but a once material existence, now silenced, extant only a sign and as sign drawing to itself chains of conflicting interpretations that hover over its absent presence and compete for possession of the relics, seeking to discribe traces of significance upon the bodies of the dead?[101]

We thus need to identify the overarching coherence evident in the polity, economy and the social system. The documents on crime require to be examined in this context.

Methodologically, therefore, the goonda files have immense potential to open new dimensions in our understanding of a particular aspect of crime and criminality in twentieth-century Calcutta. The goondas need no longer be looked either as criminals per se to be 'cast, forgotten, on the dust heap of time', or in the context of law which in modern times has become central to ruling class ideology, substituting in many ways the role that religion used to play earlier. The hitherto untapped police files give us an entry point for understanding the goondas as social entities who not only challenged the established legal structure but often their own class too.

Karl Marx had aptly noted, 'The "criminal" produces not only crimes, but also "criminal" law, and with this the professor who gives lectures on "criminal' law.'[102]

A historian of crime need not be an expert on criminal law. But his study of criminal behaviour must go beyond the investigation of isolated acts. Society, crime and criminals are interrelated, and any worthwhile research on criminality depends on the adoption of an appropriate contextual framework, as is the case with the histories of nationalism, imperialism or other facets of social life. Historical scholarship on crime in India is still in its infancy.[103] The more we can utilize such unexplored sources as the goonda files, the richer will be our historical understanding of the Calcutta underworld, which certainly demands detailed research as a relevant theme for reconstructing the social history of the metropolis.

Notes

1. See D. Hay et al., eds., *Albion's Fatal Tree: Crime and Society in Eighteenth-Century England,* London, 1975; E.P. Thompson, *Whigs and Hunters: The Origin of the Black Act,* London, 1975; E.P. Thompson, 'The Moral Economy of the English Crowd in the Eighteenth Century', *Past and Present,* vol. 50, 1971; G. Rude, *The Crowd in History,* New York, 1964; E. Hobsbawm, *Bandits,* Harmondsworth, 1969; E. Hobsbawm, *Primitive Rebels,* Manchester, 1959; D. Underdown, *Revel, Riot and Rebellion: Popular Politics and Culture in England 1603–1660,* Oxford, 1985; L. Chevalier, *Labouring Classes and Dangerous Classes in Paris during the First Half of the Nineteenth Century,* London, 1971; David Downes and Paul Rock, *Understanding Deviance: A Guide to the Sociology of Crime and Rule-Breaking,* Oxford, 1982.
2. Gareth S. Jones, *Outcast London: A Study in The Relationship between Classes in Victorian Society,* London, 1984, p. xiv. Also see Gareth S. Jones, 'History: The Poverty of Empiricism (A Critique of the English Historiographic Tradition)', in *New Left Review,* 1967.
3. These Files are well available in Lal Bazar, the Calcutta Police headquarters. We are extremely grateful to S.I. S. Ahmed, IPS, formerly deputy commissioner (DD). Calcutta Police, and Nihar Roy of the Central Record Office, Lal Bazar, for granting access to the files.
4. Louis Chevalier, *Labouring Classes and Dangerous Classes,* op cit.
5. A similar transition in the official perception of crime, was seen in England itself in the nineteenth century. See Randall Eugene McGowen, *Rethinking Crime: Changing Attitudes Towards Law-Breakers in Eighteenth and Nineteenth Century England,* Ph.D. thesis, University of Illinois at Urbana-Champaign, 1979. But at the same time the 'goonda behaviour' is not ascriptive where the participants were solely victims of a labelling process.

6. See Michael Foucault, *Discipline and Punish: The Birth of the Prison*, 1975. He detects an 'astonishing coincidence between the new prison and other contemporary institutions like hospital, factory and barrack' and argues that our 'own societies are maintained not merely by army, police or a centralized state apparatus, but precisely by the. diffused power at work in (such) caceral institutions'.

7. Dilip Basu, 'Notes on Criminal Biographies: Calcutta 1931', unpublished paper, November 1987.

8. Ibid.

9. For an analytical study on 'Hooligan', see, Geoffrey Pearson, *Hooligan: A History of Respectable Fears*, London, 1983.

10. Ibid.

11. Suranjan Das, *Communal Riots in Bengal 1905–1947*, Delhi, 1991.

12. This hypothesis is supported by some retired Indian civilian and police officers.

13. Central Record Office. Lalbazar, Calcutta (hereafter CRO) HS-R 39399:61, 37342:58, 36587:57.

14. CRO, HS 229317:52.

15. Gersham M Sykes, *Crime and Society*, Random House, New York, 1967, 2nd edn., p 78.

16. Karl Marx, 'Debates on the Law on Thefts of Wood', in *Collected Works*, Karl Marx and Frederick Engels, vol. I, New York, 1975, pp. 232–3.

17. Ibid.

18. Gamini Salagado, *The Elizabethan Underworld*, London, 1977, p. 20.

19. Gareth S Jones, *Outcast London*, op. cit., p 13.

20. Peter Linebaugh, *The London Hanged: Crime and Civil Society in the Eighteenth Century*, Harmondsworth, 1991 and 1993.

21. By upcountry is meant Bihar, Uttar Pradesh and Madhya Pradesh.

22. Suranjan Das, *Communal Riots*, op. cit. See Chapter One.

23. In Police perceptions this area continues to be particularly prone to 'lawlessness'.

24. See David Herbert, *The Geography of Urban 'Crime'*, London, 1982 and James M. Byrne and Robert J. Sampson. *The Social Ecology of 'Crime'*, New York. 1986 for a geographical approach to the understanding of 'crime'.

25. See Susan Smith, *Crime and Society*, Cambridge, 1986, for this analytical framework in the English case.

26. CRO HS-R 19848 of 1947; CROHS-T 41896–1968.

27. CRO HS-G 42493–1967.

28. CRO HS-T 39989–1962.

29. CRO HS-G 42614–1967.

30. CRO HS-G 2147–1967.

31. CRO HS-G 42656–1968.

32. CRO HS-G 38935–1960.

33. CRO HS-R 25071–1950; CRO HS-G 42223–1966.

34. CRO HS-R 24957–1950; CRO HS-R 28303–1952; CRO HS-G 39369–1961; CRO HS-R 43300–1969; CRO HS-R 43193–1969; CRO HS-G 42445–1967.

35. CRO HS-G 42443–1967.

36. CRO HS-R 21299 of 1949.

37. CRO HS 18392–1946; CRO HS-G 23849 of 1950.

38. CRO HS-R 19951 of 1947.

39. CRO HS-FR 22972–22978 of 1950.

40. CRO HS-R 30459:53.

41. CRO HS-R 20215–48. 29878:53, 37204:58; CRO D 43726:71.

42. CRO HS 23652:50.

43. CRO HS 25108:50, 32255:54; CRO HS-D 38420:60.

44. CRO HS-1928 and interview with Pradyut Guha, March 1989.

45. CRO HS-R 25058:50.

46. CRO HS-R 24017:58.

47. CRO HS-R 28176:52.

48. CRO HS-D 43806:71; CRO HS-G 43134:69.

49. CRO HS-R 43807:71. 44354:75.

50. For details of this killing see Suranjan Das, *Communal Riots,* op cit.

51. CRO HS: K 235865–1950, R 195862–1947, R 23193–1950, 18888–1946.

52. CRO HS 18888–1946.

53. CRO HS-R 21299–1946.

54. CRO HS-R: 19862–1947, 23193–1950, 18888–1946, 29878–1953.

55. CRO HS-R 21299–1949.

56. CROHS: 18888–1946, 25108–1950: CRO D 24665–1950; CRO HS-R 25317–1951, 25071.

57. CRO HS-R 25071–1950.

58. CRO HS-R 29511 of 1953.

59. CRO HS-R 30459–1953.

60. Interview with Kanai Datta of Jadavpur, 28 March 1989.

61. CRO HS-G 4267:1967, 42464:67.

62. CRO HS-G 42493:67, 42449:67.

63. CRO HS-R 34522:55.

64. CRO HS-PD 24052:1950.

65. CRO HS-R 33400:55; CRO HS 32255:54.

66. CRO HS-R 28176:52.

67. CRO HS-R 29326:52; CRO HS-G 42 of 984–1968.

68. Ibid.

69. CRO HS-R 37516:59

70. CRO HS-R 37342:58.

71. FR 18374:46; CRO-HS-PD 24052:50: CRO HS-R 28303:52, 37541:59.

72. CRO HS-G 39143:61; CRO HS 38019:59.

73. CRO HS-R 42716:68.

74. CRO HS-R 30893:53, 36988:58, 26981:50, 24017:50, 24016:50, 43072:69; CRO HS-D 43396:70; 43722:71; 43911:72.

75. CRO HS-R 44159:73.

76. CRO HS-R 30893:53, 31723:54, 28751:50, 24101:50.

77. CRO HS R 36777:57, CRO HS-M 23420:50..

78. For instance sec CRO HS-D 43396:70.

79. For instance, the interview with Ranjit Ghatak (alias Bapi) of Ganguly Bagan. 23 March 1989.
80. CRO HS-G 4265:68.
81. CRO HS 36777:57.
82. CRO HS-PD 24052:50.
83. CRO HS-R 36587:57.
84. CRO HS 18888:46; CRO HS-R 27575:51, 27574:51.
85. CRO HS-R 34522:55.
86. CRO HS-R 30907:53.
87. CRO HS-R 33400:50.
88. CRO HS-G 42984:68.
89. CRO HS-M 23420: CRO HS 25108:58.
90. CRO HS-R 18392:46.
91. CRO HS-R 19848:47, 43176:69.
92. CRO HS-R 29329:52.
93. CRO HS 42647:68.
94. CRO HS-R 42716:68.
95. Some scholars have called this a 'cross-cultural problem' in Crime Studies which has to be borne in mind by any student or historian working on such subjects as 'goondas'.
96. E.J. Hobsbawm and G. Rude, *Capital Swing Corresponding*, Harmondsworth: 1973; D Hay et al., eds., *Albion's Fatal Tree*, op. cit.
97. Peter Linebaugh, *The London Hanged*, op. cit.
98. For a review of the current debate on 'History and Post-Modernism' see *Past and Present, no.* 135, May 1992.
99. J. Derida, *Positions* (translated and annotated by Alan Bass), Chicago, 1981.
100. See the contribution by Lawrence Stone in *Past and Present*, op. cit.
101. See the contribution of Gabrielle M. Spiegel in *Past and Present*.
102. Quoted in Paul Philips, *Marx and Engels on Law and Laws*, Oxford, 1980, p. 161.
103. For some of the best examples of historical writings on 'crime' in India, see A.A. Yang, ed., *Crime and Criminality in British India*, Tuscon, 1985; Basudeb Chattopadhya, *Crime and Control in Early Colonial Bengal 1770–1860*, Calcutta, 2000; Arun P. Mukherjee, *Crime and Public Disorder in Colonial Bengal 1861–1912*, Calcutta, 1995; Radhika Singha, *A Despotism of Law: Crime and Justice in Early Colonial India*, Delhi, 1998. Also see her 'Provincial Circumstances: The Thugee Campaign of the 1830s and Legal Innovation', in *Modern Asian Studies,* vol. 27, no.1, 1993.

CHAPTER 11

BEHIND THE BLACKENED FACES: THE NINETEENTH-CENTURY BENGALI DACOITS

DURING THE TIME I am writing about, decoity in almost all districts of Bengal was endemic, even though during the first part of the Englush rule, the practice of committing decoities after serving prior notice, as did Raghunath, Baidyanath or Biswanath, had declines to some extent. However, dacoities committed with cruelty and inhuman actions were still common in Bengal. . . . What had been earned or saved in a lifetime could be looted in one night, but wealth or belongings were not the only casualty, lives of the householder were also at stake.[1]

That was how a daroga (local police official) Girish Chandra Bose recounted nineteenth century dacoities in Bengal in his reminiscences. Dacoity, a legal term used by colonial administration to categorize a system of robbery in India 'by gangs, and (is) derived from daka parna, meaning "plunder"',[2] was most rampant in Bengal between 1841 and 1857, especially in the districts of 24 Parganas, Barasat, Howrah, Hooghly, Burdwan, Nadia, Murshidabad, Jessore and Midnapore. The dacoity curve in the nineteenth-century Bengal—reaching its peak in 1851 with 524 recorded cases—dwindled to 92 by 1856.[3]

Dacoity in colonial Bengal has certainly attracted the attention of contemporary observers and professional analysts. For, as G.R. Elton aptly remarked: 'Crime and the criminal eternally fascinate; they rather than politics supply the journalist's daily bread, nor is this particularly modern order of preference'.[4] We already have interesting insights on the social and political context of dacoity in colonial Bengal.[5] Many scholarly exercises have, however, tended to view dacoity in colonial Bengal as an element of popular protest or as a social aberration.[6] In popular vernacular literature

---

*This essay was published in *Economic and Political Weekly*, vol. XLII, no. 35, 1 September 2007, pp. 3573–9.

dacoits have also been categorized into 'noble' or 'ignoble'.[7] The present essay, however, stresses the need to examine dacoity in nineteenth-century Bengal in the backdrop of rural Bengal's exploitative social structure, the motivations behind joining dacoit groups, the social profile of those accused of committing dacoity, the typology and ritual of dacoity, the organizational structure of dacoit gangs and the nexus between the dacoits and the police. Dacoity certainly constituted a particular form of deviance, usually associated with violence. But the nature of dacoity varied from time to time and from place to place. The specificities of dacoity, as I propose to suggest, were related to historical conjunctures of time, space and society.[8] The present essay seeks to recapture aspects of the world of mid-nineteenth century Bengal dacoits through a reading of hitherto relatively unused official reports on dacoities and confessions of some of the accused. The current exercise intends to highlight the importance of a new database for reconstructing an interesting facet of the social history of colonial Bengal.

Why a Dacoit Became a Dacoit?

Some colonial observers nursed a stereotypical image of dacoity as arising out of hot blood, ungovernable temper, and the natural inclination of the villager, who is generally miles away from any police, to take the law into his own hands and to fight out his quarrel on the spot. There is nothing like this in the agricultural districts in England.[9]

But there were other perceptive colonial officials who realized that men were driven to commit dacoity by specific historical circumstances. None other than J.R. Ward, the commissioner for the suppression of dacoity, posed the question: 'Is a man dacoit before or after he has committed dacoity'?[10] After all, an overwhelming number of accused were first generation dacoits. An analysis of the confessions of the accused throws interesting light on why one turned a dacoit.

The neighbourhood influence, or what has been called 'the social ecology of a criminal area'[11] drove many to join dacoity. Local or family acquaintance had a considerable role to play in this context. Sunath Haree confessed: 'It so happened that Gosain Dass Haree Surdar and myself were residents of the same place, . . .[His] nephew is married to my sister, and the Surdar himself is my son-in-law. One day as we sat drinking [he] . . . through persuasions got me to consent to join him in a dacoity.'[12]

Faquir Dutt recounted how two head dacoits of his village, who regularly purchased 'treacle' from his sugar cane ground, told him how they had 'got a great deal of property' and persuaded him to join them.[13] The following instance of Sonatun Mondal represented another process of induction into a dacoity. Once on his way to Santipoor, he fell in the hands of 'lathials' (specialists in wielding the lathi), who felt that the youth was 'khoob jawan' (young and strong), and took him to their master. For the next four years Sonatun committed several dacoities as a member of the group.[14]

Interestingly, many of the accused were employed as lathials in the indigo plantations.[15] The sons of non-Indian indigo factory owners were charged with complicity with dacoit gangs.[16] Probably the indigo crisis of the period had made their employment in plantations uncertain which drove them to opt for alternative occupations and turn to dacoity. The sirdars (chief of the group) would identify local 'barkandazes' (matchlockmen, footmen under direct order of 'sadar *cutchery*'—official establishments) who had lost their jobs, or neighbours, who were unable to maintain their family by their lawful occupations, to lure them to join their groups for ready money.[17] In Murshidabad those who once served as the nawab's sepoys (soldiers), but now rendered unemployed, joined dacoit gangs.[18] Peasants, driven to distress by failure of crops, were also induced by local sirdars to become their partners. There are examples of unsuccessful practitioners of indigenous medicine being drawn into local dacoit groups.[19]

Prospects of instant gains often attracted many to dacoity. One accused had a neighbour who used to bring to him ornaments, vessels and clothes for valuation. When he learnt that these acquisitions were the result of dacoities he, too, got enticed to join the profession.[20] Similarly, Dhamu Mundal had 'dealings in silk' with his neighbour Prosad Ghoraut without knowing that he was a dacoit, but once he learnt Ghoraut's identity he also got lured into committing dacoities.[21] Again, there were instances of men like Babooram Bagdi of Burdwan who confessed: 'I kept a mistress in those days, and she spent more than I could earn. I took to dacoity to enable me to support her.'[22]

To silence any local persons who knew about a dacoit group, its sirdars would often force them to join him.[23] The sirdars maintained close touch with their neighbours who had knowledge about the local notables and gradually allured them to be their associates.[24] They also kept a watch on local youths adept at use of lathies (sticks), and used their local connections to recruit them in their groups.[25] The masters of households, themselves dacoits, often made their servants join their gangs.[26] The burkandaz Ubdool Faqueer, for instance, was induced to join a group by his employer, Mundle Mahajan.[27]

Organization of Dacoities

Dacoities were essentially a rural phenomenon. Based on colonial records one can identify three major forms of dacoities.[28] First, there were dacoities 'committed by the immediate neighbours of the party robbed'. Second, dacoities were committed by 'bands of upcountrymen passing up and down the Ganges and Jamuna in boats'. Besides, dacoities were related to clash of interests between local notables, cutting across religious lines. Ubdool Faqueer deposed how the Hindu 'mahajans' (moneylenders) Ufzal Mundle and Choonee Mundle of Pasooree Police Station in Rajshahi district employed such well known Muslim dacoits of the locality as Shaik Guddaie, Shaik Jahan Buksh and Shaik Owjul to raid the establishment of their coreligionist Ubdool Kareem Khan.[29] At the same time a leading Muslim would organize dacoity in the establishment of another influential Muslim of the same locality because of personal rivalry.[30] On some occasions the mahajans themselves participated in dacoities that they organized in the establishments of their rivals.[31] Zamindars [landlords] like Ishan Baboo also organized dacoities to 'teach lessons' to his rival zamindar Keshub Baboo.[32] We have reference to an influential rich shikaree Muslim in Barasat district, who maintained in his estate a group of dacoits and himself received 'a ten-anna share of the proceeds' from their ventures.[33] The zamindar of Nakaseepara appointed the 'notorious sirdars' Golakata Hursha (nicknamed from having received a severe wound in the neck during a river dacoity) 'to watch over the female apartments, thus officially (frustrating) . . . all attempts at arresting him'.[34] Interestingly, Ward referred to a zamindar who publicly condemned the 'insufficiency of chowkeedaree and police systems', but himself protected one accused of being a dacoit by appointing him as a 'gomashta' (officials in the zamindar's establishment).[35] Sreemanto Ghosh, a convict, thus sarcastically commented, 'Were the zamindars transported, dacoity and theft would stop'.[36] There are references of dacoit sirdars becoming mahajans after acquiring 'considerable wealth'.[37]

The dacoits were usually known in their locality as dacoits, a fact rather proudly admitted by a number of the accused.[38] We hardly have any reference to clashes between the dacoits and their villagers. Instead, they developed local networks with villagers, who mostly helped them carry out their operations. There were local informers—mostly 'husbandmen and patwaree men'[39]—who informed the sirdars about potential targets and received rewards upon the completion of raids.[40] Servants of local notables would also act as informers of sirdars.[41] Villagers, working as informers, kept a close watch on local businessmen and if they changed bank notes of considerable value or kept a large stock of merchandise in their houses, they would promptly inform the sirdars.[42] A sirdar and members of his group usually refrained from keeping the stolen goods in their possession preferring to deposit them with their 'receivers'.[43] Local mahajans, gomasthas and amlas (officials in the establishment of the landlords) of zamindars, small landowners, shopkeepers, distillers, dyers, coppersmiths, carpenters, goldsmiths, and merchants, irrespective of caste and creed, acted as receivers of such plunder.[44] Normally, after a raid the spoils were carried to the receiver or mahajan (moneylender) who bargained for a low price for it, and yet, kept a large share of the sale proceeds as his share.[45] Many of the receivers would carry on this business with local dacoit groups behind the facade of running a normal business, like grocery shops. Often the local informers were receivers of booty too.[46] Some of them were considerably wealthy.[47] One Ram Mokerjee was once a beggar, but made a fortune by becoming a receiver of dacoits.[48] Women also acted as receiver of looted property.[49]

A receiver or a particular mahajan with whom a dacoit group had a regular business often provided his clients with monthly subsistence or loans in times of difficulties. Take, for instance, the following deposition, 'Kamal Adhikari gives subsistence to me . . . and we always sell the plundered property to him, and when he pays us for it he subtracts what he had given us for maintenance. . . . He has about 30 bighas of land'.[50] Many of the accused, however, alleged that they were cheated by the receivers who would give them 'Rs. 6 for an article worth 10'.[51] Aviram Doss thus complained, '1 am an ignorant man, and know nothing about accounts. I conclude the mahajan has his own accounts. If we gave him any property worth Rs. 100, we only got Rs. 50'.[52] Often a dacoit would hide a part of his booty from his traditional receiver or thangeeedar (local village official) and sell it to some other person for a better price.[53]

The sirdars of dacoit groups also developed a cash nexus with the local police, which made them immune from arrests or prosecutions in courts. They would regularly advance money to darogas and chowkidars (subordinate police officials who acted as watchmen) to ensure their connivance at 'our (dacoits') non-apprehension'.[54] Sirdars even provided advance notices of their operations to the local police.[55] At the same time chowkidars themselves would provide the sirdars with information about prospective victims in lieu of a share in the booty.[56] Even after an arrest the police would be bribed to write a report in favour of the arrested so that 'he was not looked after again'.[57] The police even ensured that no witnesses were present in court hearings.[58] We also have instances where in the event of a dispute between a daroga and sirdars about the quantum of bribe, the matter was settled by paying a higher amount to the nazir (subordinate official in the establishment of the landlord).[59] Sreemonto Ghosh, an accused, admitted: 'We were all safe. If we got arrested, we paid to the Police, and if we were challenged, for twenty or twenty-five rupees, we could always get witnesses to say we were with them on the night in question. The Judge always believed them . . . .'[60]

The local police usually had full knowledge of the links between the dacoits and the receivers.[61] One of the accused submitted: '. . . the *darogah*, *mohurer* and *burkandazas* (an armed retainer who mainly used musket as a weapon) apprehend them (dacoits) and on receiving a remuneration . . . release them again. . . . All the *chowkidars* of the village are in the confederacy of the sardars. . . .'[62]

A convict was not overstressing when he commented: 'I cannot say how many times I have been arrested and put on trial, but I have been only four times sentenced to any form of imprisonment.'[63]

Some darogahs in 24 Parganas, Hooghly and Barasat districts reportedly 'entered into agreements with some sirdars not to molest them provided their *thannah* jurisdictions were not disturbed'.[64] Many of the accused remarked that in localities where there was no complicity between the police and sirdars dacoities were absent.

A perusal of the confessions of the accused reveals instances of chowkidars, jamadars and barkandazs themselves participating in dacoities.[65] Ubdool Faqueer testified how a chowkidar accompanied them in a dacoity, disguising himself 'by rubbing blacking on his face, and afterwards washed it off and went to his duty'.[66] We have the example of Yaroo chowkeedar who 'went to commit dacoity. And receiving his share . . .(and) returned and equipped himself for duty as chowkeedar'.[67] A chowkidar even acted as a head dacoit.[68] Often a jamadar played the role of a mediator to decide the division of the spoils amongst the group. Not unnaturally, in a number of instances police jamadars were convicted for complicity with dacoits.[69]

Colonial officials like Ward themselves acknowledged the complicity of local police with dacoit groups. In his report to the commissioner of circuit, Burdwan division he admitted how 'distressed' he was 'to see how little the Police exert themselves, and how indifferent the deputy magistrate continues to be. If there is one crime, in which the Police must not only be urged into activity, but be helped in their difficulties, it is in that of dacoity'.[70]

T.E. Ravenshaw, the commissioner for the suppression of dacoity, himself testified to cases where dacoities 'had been planned and carried out with the full knowledge and assistance' of police jamadars.[71] The complicity between the police and sirdars becomes evident from cases where the accused after being released from bouts of imprisonment would rejoin dacoit groups without any impunity.[72] A question may pertinently be raised: if the police–dacoit nexus was so persistent how do we explain the considerable success attained in the suppression of dacoity by 1856? The answer perhaps lies in the adoption of a new mechanism by the colonial government to meet the challenge of dacoity. Drawing lessons from Sleeman's operations against 'thugees' (highway robbers belonging to a particular religious community who were particularly active in upper India), the Bengal government also appointed the dacoity commission in Bengal that proved quite effective. Besides, the local police, especially the darogahs, remained careful not to extend protection to the dacoits at the cost of their jobs. Once the government tightened its machinery—largely following the Sleeman model—the local police–dacoit link considerably weakened.

Social Profile of Dacoits

Writing about dacoits of Bengal, the colonial official C.H. Keighly wrote of 'great difference between gangs of hereditary dacoits or thugs in other parts of India and the dacoits of Bengal'.[73] While the former belonged to particular castes and operated in small groups, the latter comprised 'every class and caste of the rural population of those districts in which the crime is rife'.[74] Ward noted how in the dacoit groups were included, 'every class of society, from the petty Jungle Rajah, . . . to the lowest class, the *khodma*, the *khaurah*, the *keechuck* . . .'.[75]

Those accused in dacoity cases were overwhelmingly from the subordinate social groups of both Hindu and Muslim communities, and most of them could neither read nor write. But zamindars, gomasthas and other officials of *cutcheries* were also connected with dacoit groups, although they did not directly participate in the raids. Amongst the Hindus the following are particular by mentioned: bagdis, kayets, koibuts, telees, manjees, sadgopes, santals, brahmins, chamars, kaivartas, chandals, hajams, lohars, sonarpunth, dhobees, harees, domes, bustums, gosais, rajputs, tantis, napits, telis, koormees, majhis, and goalas. Railway coolies, Oriyas and upcountrymen were also prominent amongst the accused.[76] Many of those charged with dacoity were lathials or employees in the service of zamindars which made it difficult for the local police to arrest them. Ward thus noted 'the impunity' with which landholders in Bengal defied the local authorities to protect 'proclaimed criminals'.[77] Gomasthas of leading zamindars were also convicted for being involved in dacoities.[78] The 'goalas' (milkmen)—who were adept at using lathies and were employed as lathials by zamindars and indigo planters—were particularly active. Some goala sirdars like Gore Goala in Krishnanagar or Satcowree Ghosh of Kalna or Sonatun Mundul of Santipur-Nadia area gained notoriety for their physical prowess and had become household names.[79] In Hooghly we have reference to Kenaram Goala, who was always well-armed and roamed about 'unmolested'. A reward was announced for his apprehension, but none dared to help the police.[80] In Howrah and Hooghly districts there were the prominent Rajapoor and Hurripaul gangs. There were instances of people from humble social background amassing economic fortune by turning dacoits.[81] Amongst the Muslims we have particular mention of sarkiwalas.[82] The average age of dacoits was between 30 and 45 years,[83] although there were some instances of men above 50 being convicted for committing dacoities.[84]

A reading of the confessions indicates the existence of a strong hierarchical order within a daocoit gang. Each group had a sirdar and between 50 and 80 subordinates.[85] Usually the sirdar and his associates belonged to the same locality, religion and caste. But there were instances of groups with mixed religions and castes where bagdis, brahmins, manjis, chamars, mandals and Muslims worked or served under a Muslim sirdars.[86] The composition of the group of Ram Coomar Chung of Hooghly—as reported by Ward—was an apt example of such a mixed grouping, 'There were three Gwalas . . . two Chundals . . . a Kyburt . . . two Booyan Coolies, who worked on the Railway, . . . a Mussulman . . . a Dhawa . . . a few Bagdees and Harees.'[87]

A sense of symbiotic relationship bound the sirdars and his followers. Members tended to serve the same sirdars;[88] the sirdars provided loans to members of his group, which they repaid by instalments from their share of the booty.[89] Cases of desertion from a group or intra-group clashes were virtually unheard of.[90] When a member of the group either died or was apprehended by the police, the sirdars looked for replacements. Even when four or five sirdars joined hands for an operation, members of different groups remained accountable only to his own sirdars.[91] The division of the booty also followed a rule. A sirdar's entitlement was always higher than what was paid to other members of the group in accordance with the work performed by them during the raid. But there were cases when members of a group displayed open discontent at the quantum of their share. One accused reported, 'I received ten rupees as my portion and know nothing of what was shared to others. The ornaments were all retained in the custody of the sardars . . .'.[92]

Again, after the raid on the establishment of Joynaroin Karmakar, a leading blacksmith of Char Burredee in Pabna district, the booty was handed over to the receiver and informer Nobo Sircar. But when subsequently the members of the group who conducted the dacoity went to reclaim their share Nobo Sircar '. . .came with a party of men, and pointing to the boat said "this boat contains feraries (fugitives)" whereon we jumped out and showed them our heels, but the boat was secured and taken'.[93] The situation turned so serious that the sirdars had to assuage a member of the group by forsaking his own share. Sometimes the sirdars paid the members of his group monthly salary, in which case they were not granted access to the booty at all.[94] One such member of a group complained, 'I got nothing. I was told: "You are my servant and have regular wages". You get no share in this (plunder).'[95] Often the sirdars kept members of his group for some days in a place adjacent to the house proposed to be raided to get them acquainted with the locality.[96]

Rites of Dacoities

Robbers in India are remarkable for the dexterity with which they accomplish their schemes of plunder. In this field they were almost certainly not behind any other nation in the world. They have been known to enter a bungalow and remove everything worth taking, leaving the party to whom it belonged and his wife upon the cane-work of the bedstead on which they slept, with no other covering except their nightclothes, and this without waking either of them.[97]

This claim certainly betrayed a colonial preoccupation to portray Indian practices in terms of oriental uniqueness. Surely, robberies in England and Europe were not bereft of organized patterns. Nevertheless, an analysis of the depositions of the accused reveals not only traits of considerable planning behind each dacoity but also well-defined rites of dacoities. Each sirdars had an informer who kept him informed about prospective targets and received a share from the booty.[98] Interestingly, we have reference to one woman informer.[99] When a sirdar was informed of any establishment worth raiding, he personally made enquiries, and once convinced, he contacted his headmen to mobilize the required number of men along with necessary weapons and implements.[100] The headmen were also told of the 'khorakee' (daily allowance) that was to be paid to each of his men.[101] The dacoities were usually committed during midnight. Before setting off for the dacoity, members of the group assembled to perform 'kalipuja' (offering prayers to the goddess Kali), dressed as 'pykes' (guards of houses of notables), coloured their faces black, red or white to disguise their identity, let their hair down over their faces, tied clothes over their heads, armed themselves with lathies, swords, shields, muskets, pistols, 'kodaleees' (shovels), 'saungs' (instruments), 'mashals' (torches), bows and arrows and then at a propitious moment selected by the sirdars proceeded in an orderly manner to the establishment that was to be pillaged. The performance of the kalipuja involved an elaborate ritual. The dacoits would sit in a line; a 'bhar' (a small earthen pot) of oil or liquor, torches and all weapons would be put on a cloth or a clear space; the sirdars would then dip his finger into the oil or liquor as the case may be, and touch the forehead of each member of the group with a shout of 'kali', making them promise never to confess. Upon the completion of this process the sirdars would break the bhar of oil or liquor and then all would rush to the establishment which had been chosen as the target. On one occasion the sirdars even dressed himself as a female.[102] The accused Sadhu Charan Deb narrated his own experience during the pre-raid preparation:

I started off . . . and arrived . . . where the other dacoits were assembled; it was then about three hours after sunset—we stayed there for about an hour and ate and drank and smoked our hookas; after 9 o'clock we left the house . . . taking swords and shields . . . axes . . . sticks and . . . torches, we then proceeded in a southern direction till we came to a tank . . . it was then about 11 o' clock—we performed our devotions to kali, and smearing our faces we again started; at midnight we reached the house (that was to be raided).[103]

To 'test the mettle of his men' a sirdars would often apply a burning chillum to the thigh of each, and only those who could 'go through the trial without wincing' were admitted into the group.[104] In cases of river dacoities there were, however, no regular kalipuja.

The sirdar normally stood as a sentry during the raid, encouraging and giving directions to the group. While the new members of the group were made to hold torches or 'act as coolies in taking away the property', the experienced ones broke open boxes, chests and plundered all they could. With cries of 'Kali, jai Kali' the group would break the door of the establishment with axes, seek to execute the operation systematically and retire in an orderly manner.[105] During a raid the dacoits used nicknames to call each other. Each group used particular words to imply specific items: a 'koorool' with which doors were broken was called 'kopa' or 'boidee', a torch was called 'phool', oil was called 'ross', a gun was called 'bheel', 'kodalee' was called 'kopah', a lathie was called 'koda' and a dacoit was called 'rungermanush'. Once the operation was completed the men in the group who carried the plunder proceeded first, whilst others followed and those who had acted as sentries—the strongest in the group—guarded the rear. Boats were sometimes used to transport the spoils. If someone in the group was severely wounded he was killed and his body thrown into a river or a pond. The average size of a dacoit group ranged between 10 and 50.[106]

Although houses and establishments of local notables like zamindars, mahajans, rich peasants and businessmen were the usual targets of the dacoits, there are also instances of ordinary villagers becoming their victims. Sreenath Haree thus remembered instances where the booty could be only one bundle of new cloth worth Rs. 30, two brass utensils, two 'lotas' (tumblers) and two dishes.[107] When the house of a village blacksmith Gunga Ram Isur was raided the booty was only Rs. 50 in cash and some ordinary clothes and utensils.[108] Another accused narrated how during a dacoity in the house of an ordinary Muslim in Hooghly his share of the plunder was dnly a copper 'handee' (utensil), which so frustrated him that he threw it into a pond.[109] Houses of 'local women of bad character', who had amassed a fortune, were also ransacked.[110] Dacoities were usually organized in the area 'only so far as can be compassed in one day's journey'[111] from the village where the sirdars resided. But when two or three sirdars became partners a dacoity was committed far away from the place to which the group belonged.[112] Such raids—usually on big establishments—bore evidence of efficient organization. The confession of Babooram Bagdi before the dacoity commissioner testified to the dacoity committed in the house of the Raja of Tamluk by a group consisting of men from Calcutta, Chandannagore and Burdwan.[113] We have reference to Calcutta groups committing dacoities in 24–Pargunnahs, Howrah, Baraset, Hooghly, and

Burdwan.[114] Since in such cases the people of the locality where dacoities were committed did not know the dacoit groups, it was difficult for the police to produce witness, and hence prosecutions against the accused usually fell through. The Calcutta group of dacoits had a pre-eminence of hackney drivers.[115]

Usually, the villagers did not resist the dacoits, but if there was any such intervention the dacoits avoided confrontations and left the spot.[116] There is hardly any recorded instance of a household member losing his or her life in the hands of the dacoits. If resisted, the dacoits would tie them up or keep them locked in a room while they ransacked the house. There were, however, some exceptions, as in the case cited by Sreenath Haree when some household members on account of their resistance were killed and buried.[117] Women as a rule were not subjected to any physical assault. An accused thus stated that they looked upon a woman as a kali who could be made to take off her ornaments but was never to be touched. Those who injured women were categorized as 'not good dacoits'. During a raid all kinds of things were taken away—clothes, utensils, cash and jewellery.

We learn from the depositions that the dacoits, especially their sirdars, believed in 'favourable and unfavourable' omens.[118] For instance, if during the performance of the kalipuja the sirdars broke the bhar with one blow it was believed to be a good sign for the proposed raid. But if the bhar was broken with two or three blows then it was suspected that either the raid would be unsuccessful or the group would be 'discovered' or something ominous would happen. In fact, in the Belpookur and Deopara cases the bhars could not be broken with one blow, and the raids not only failed, but many in the groups were captured. Again, if while proceeding for a dacoity the group saw on the right hand a young girl or a woman with a 'kalshi' (earthen pot) filled with water, or if a jackal passed from the right to the left, it was considered an auspicious sign. But if a lizard's sound was heard, or a bull bellowed, or anyone in the group sneezed, before a raid was embarked upon, it was believed to be inauspicious. Besides, while Tuesday, Wednesday and Friday were considered as 'good days', Thursday and Saturday were believed to be 'unlucky days'.

Conclusion

The foregoing analysis has hopefully demonstrated how some little used documents concerning a particular type of 'crime' in colonial, rural Bengal may be used for addressing such issues as crime as a social phenomenon, the social profile of those committing the crime, typology of the crime, the rites of violence associated with the perpetration of that crime, and the contemporary attitudes to that crime. Karl Marx had perceptively remarked,

'Crime, i.e. the struggle of the single individual against the dominant conditions, is as little the product of simple caprice as the law itself. It is rather conditioned in the same way as the latter. The same "visionaries" who see in law the rule of an independent and general will, see in crime a simple breaking of the law.'[119]

Dacoity in colonial Bengal was certainly a form of social deviance. But, as the present submission has shown, the dacoits did not belong to identifiable ethnic categories whose traditional profession was dacoity. None other than the governor-general Warren Hastings himself acknowledged this as early as 1770s.[120] On the other hand, as has been indicated above, the spurt in the incidence of dacoity during the period under present consideration was casually related to the disruptive effects of colonial rule in rural Bengal. At the same time the rise in dacoities provided the colonial administration with a pretext for strengthening its instruments of control. Studies have shown how widespread fear following 'the garrotting panic' in nineteenth-century London presaged 'a considerable extension of police powers, and, indeed, effectively silenced any lingering opposition within the middle class to the whole idea of an English police force'.[121] It has also been demonstrated how the ruling authority in England labelled recalcitrant social groups as 'outcastes' or 'dangerous' as a strategy of cooption.[122] Studies need to be undertaken if such processes were at work in colonial Bengal in the context of 'the dacoity fear'. But that demands a separate enquiry.

Notes

1. Girish Chandra Bose, *Sekaler Darogar Kahini* (in Bengali), Calcutta reprint, 1983. English translation mine.
2. S.M. Edwards, *Crime in India: A Brief Review of the More Important Offences Included in the Annual Criminal Returns with Chapters on Prostitution and Miscellaneous Matters,* London, 1924, p. 40.
3. See Appendix C in the Report by J.R. Ward, Commissioner for the Suppression of Dacoity of 31 January 1856, p. xvi, *Selections from the Records of the Government of Bengal, No. XXVI, Reports on the Suppression of Dacoity in Bengal for 1855–56,* Calcutta Gazette Office, Calcutta, 1857 (hereafter *RSD 1855–6*); *Selections from the Records of the Bengal Government, No. XXXI, Reports Relating To the Suppression of Dacoity in Bengal for 1856–57 and 1857–58,* General Printing Department, Calcutta, 1859 (hereafter *RSD 1856–7 and 1857–8*) Appendix K. The spellings of Indian names used in this article are as found in the two documents.
4. See The Introduction in J.S. Cockburn, ed., *Crime in England 1550–1800,* London, p. 1.
5. For example Basudeb Chattopadhyay, *Crime and Control in Early Colonial Bengal 1770–1860,* Calcutta, 2000; Arun P. Mukherjee, *Crime and Public Disorder in Colonial Bengal 1861–1912,* Calcutta, 1995. David Arnold has effectively

demonstrated a correlation between dacoity and food prices at the all-India level. See his *Famine: Social Crisis and Historical Change*, Oxford, 1988. Also see Anand A.Yang, ed., *Crime and Criminality in British India,* Arizona, 1985 for an honest effort to sample research interests of some historians interested in the social history of crime.

6. See for example Ranjit Sen, *Social Banditry in Bengal: A Study in Primary Resistance 1757–1793,* Calcutta, 1988; Ranjan Chakrabarti, *Authority and Violence in Colonial Bengal 1800–1860,* Calcutta, 1997.

7. A similar categorization has also been made for west European bandits. See Florike Egmond, 'The Noble and the Ignoble Bandit: Changing Literary Representations of West European Robbers', in *Ethnologia Europea,* XVII, pp. 139–56.

8. Historical reconstructions of crime in England along these lines have already yielded fruits. See the section on Problems, sources and methods in J.A. Sharpe, ed., *Crime in Seventeenth-Century England: A County Study*, London and Paris, 1983.

9. Sir Cecil Walsh, *Indian Village Crimes with an Introduction on Police Investigation and Confession*, London, 1929, pp. 10–11.

10. J.R. Ward, Commissioner for the Suppression of Dacoity, to A.R.Young, Offg Secy, to the Government of Bengal. Fort William, 5 March 1857, para 20, p. 13, *RSD 1855–6.*

11. Terence Morris/Foreword by Hermann Mannheim, *The Criminal Area: A Study in Social Ecology,* London, 1966.

12. This and other confessions of those accused for dacoities were made before W. Riddell, Assistant General Superintendent. They were incorporated in a printed volume, a copy of which is available in the Library of the History Department of Calcutta University. Also see Serial Nos. 8, 12, 14, 27 of the digitized versions of *Selections from The Records of The Government of Bengal* (hereafter *Selections*). The particular confession of Sunath Haree was on 17 January 1845, see *Selections*, p. 47.

13. Ibid., pp. 65–6.

14. Ward to The Commissioner of Circuit, Burdwan Division, no. 31, 31 January 1856, para 20, p. 14, *RSD 1855–6.*

15. *RSD 1856–7 and 1857–8,* see Additional Session Judge's remarks on the trial of Obhorshee Bagdi, p. xxxv; T.E. Ravenshaw, Commissioner for the Suppression of Dacoity to the Secy, Government of Bengal, Fort William, no. 40, 21 February 1859, p. 15; See confession of *Mahajan Sirdars,* Appendix F, p. xli.

16. *RSD 1856–7 and 1857–8* Ravenshaw to Commissioner of Circuit, no. 44, 4 February 1859; Dy. Magistrate for Suppression of Dacoity to Commissioner for Suppression of Dacoity, no. 29, 29 January 1859.

17. *Selections*, pp. 79, 81, 101, 123, 132, 157, 166.

18. Ravenshaw to Commissioner of Circuit, Burdwan Division, no. 44, 4 February 1859, para 44, *RSD 1856–7 and 1857–8.*

19. *Selections*, p. 101, confession of Gooroochuran Pan.

20. *Selections*, p. 74, confession of Kanai Lohar.

21. Ibid., p. 167, confession of Dhanu Mundul.

22. Ravenshaw to Commissioner of Cicuit, Burdwan Division, no. 384, 4 October 1858, p. xiii.
23. *Selections*, p. 150, confession of Kalachand Khan.
24. Ibid., pp. 102–3, 114.
25. Ibid., pp. 1–27.
26. Ibid., pp. 50, 59.
27. Ibid., p. 1, confession of Ubdool Faqueer on 25 November 1843.
28. See H.L. Dampier, Offg Jt Magistrate to Commissioner for the Supppression of Dacoity, Hooghly, no. 31, 19 January 1857, Appendix I, *RSD 1855–6*.
29. Ibid., p. 3.
30. Ward to Young, no. 35, 5 March 1857, para 43, p. 23.
31. *Selections*, p. 5.
32. Ibid., pp. 18–19.
33. Ward to The Commissioner of Circuit, Burdwan Divison, no. 31, 31 January 1856, para 7.
34. Ibid.
35. Ward to Young, no. 35 of 5 March 1857, para 26, p. 17.
36. Appendix A, paragraph 38 of Ward's note of 4 February 1857, p. iii.
37. *Selections*, pp. 18–19.
38. Ibid., p. 9, confession of Gooroochura; confession of Khaibul Doss, p. 116; Purshed Shenna thus confessed: 'everybody knows they commit dacoity', p. 20.
39. Ibid., pp. 112, 124.
40. Ibid., p. 123.
41. Ravenshaw to Commissioner of Circuit, Burdwan Division, no. 384, 4 October 1858, pp. xxii, xxiv, *RSD 1856–7 and 1857–8*.
42. See Appendix F, *RSD 1856–7 and 1857–8*, pp. xliv-xlvi.
43. *Selections*, p. 87, confession of Sham Doss.
44. *Selections*, pp. 1–27, 31, 58, 63, 67, 72, 83, 108, 109, 119, 124, 136, 160–2, 165.
45. Ibid., pp. 22, 112, confession of Dholab Ghose.
46. Appendix F, *RSD 1856–7 and 1857–8*.
47. *Selections*, p. 100.
48. Ibid., p. 35.
49. J.R. Ward, Commissioner for the Suppression of Dacoity to the Junior Secy, to the Government of Bengal, Fort William, no. 18, 12 January 1857, *RSD*.
50. *Selections*, p. 84. Also see pp. 33, 52, 84.
51. Ibid., pp. 47–8.
52. Ibid., p. 90.
53. Ibid., see the confession of Sreenath Haree, p. 35.
54. Ibid., p. 49; there were instances of yearly monetary contracts between sirdars and local police station, see p. 116.
55. *Selections*, p. 90; Ward to the Commissioner of Circuit, Burdwan Division, no. 31, 31 January 1856, para 23, p. 16.
56. *Selections*, p. 164, see the confession of Sadhu Charan Deb.
57. Ibid., pp. 1–27.
58. *Sekaler Darogar Kahini*, pp. 28–9.

59. *Selections*, p. 77.

60. Appendix A, paragraph 38 of Ward's note of 4 February 1857, p. 39.

61. *Selections*, p. 116, see the confession of Khaibul Doss.

62. Ibid., p. 18; also see p. 59, the confession of Madhusudan Doss.

63. Ibid., p. 88.

64. Ward to the Commissioner of Circuit, Burdwan Division, no. 31, 31 January 1856, para 24, p. 17.

65. *Darogas* of the time also admitted this fact. See *Sekaler Darogar Kahini,* p. 18.

66. *Selections*, confession of Ubdool Faqueer on 25 November 1843 before W. Riddell, p. 11.

67. Ibid., p. 12.

68. Ibid., pp. 166–8.

69. See letter no. 32 of 19 February 1856 from Offg. Commissioner of Circuit, Burdwan Division, cited in *RSD 1855–6*.

70. J.R. Ward, Commissioner for the Suppression of Dacoity to A.R. Young, Offg Secy, to the Government of Bengal, Fort William, no. 35, 5 March 1857, para 17, p. 12.

71. Ravenshaw to Commissioner of Circuit, Burdwan Division, no. 44, 4 February 1859, para 23, *RSD 1856–7 and 1857–8*.

72. Ward to the Commissioner of Circuit, Burdwan Division, no. 31, 31 January 1856, para 29, p. 14.

73. C.H. Keighly, Assistant General Supdt to J.R. Ward, Commissioner for the Suppression of Dacoities, Hooghly, no. 14, 10 January 1856, *RSD 1855–6*.

74. Ibid.

75. Ward to Young no. 35, 5 March 1857, para 55, p. 29.

76. *Selections*, confession of Kanai Lohar, p. 76; Ward to Young, no. 35, 5 March 1857, para 29, p. 19.

77. Ward to Young, para 26.

78. Ibid., para 42, p. 23.

79. See *Sekaler Darogar Kahini*, op. cit., pp. 9–10.

80. C.H. Keighly, Offg Dacoity Commissioner to the Commissioner of Circuit, Burdwan Division, no. 43, 12 February 1858, pp. 4–5.

81. *Selections*, p. 75, confession of Kanai Lohar.

82. Ibid.

83. Ibid., p. 21, confession of Purshad Shenna.

84. Ward to Young no. 35, 5 March 1857, para 35, p. 21.

85. *Selections*, p. 171.

86. Ibid., pp. 9, 11–14, 16, 26. 29, 42, 47, 67–8, 71, 73, 75, 82, 84, 86–7, 89, 94–6, 100, 104–5, 121, 125, 127, 134, 136, 140, 144, 151, 155, 158, 162, 165, 170, 172, particularly see the confession of Ubdool Faqueer.

87. Ward to Young no. 35, 5 March 1857, para 29, p. 19.

88. *Selections*, p. 59, confession by Modhusudun Doss.

89. Ibid., pp. 60, 123.

90. Ibid., p. 49.

91. Ibid., p. 115, see the confession of Dholab Ghose.

92. Ibid., p. 26, confession of Purshad Shenna on 22 December 1843.

93. Appendix F, p. lviii, *RSD 1856–7 and 1857–8*.

94. Ibid., pp. 2, 6.
95. Ibid., p. 53, confession of Modhusudun Doss.
96. Ibid., pp. 3–4.
97. Jam H. Carey, 'Robbery and Dacoity in British India During 1600–1858', *Folklore,* no. 6, vol. 13, 1972.
98. *Selections*, pp. 32, 36–7, 40, 42.
99. See the deposition of Sheikh Molan Ooddeen, p. 124.
100. *Selections*, p. 121.
101. Ibid. Usually after a raid the sirdars earned almost the double of what he spent for *khorakee* for the members of the group.
102. Ibid., p. 124.
103. Ibid., p. 161.
104. Ward to Young, no. 35, 5 March 1857, para 46, p. 25.
105. *Selections*, p. 49.
106. *Selections*, p. 91; *RSD 1856–7 and 1857–8*, Appendix F, pp. Iii, Ivi.
107. *Selections*, pp. 36–7.
108. *Selections*, pp. 43–4.
109. Ravenshaw to the Commissioner of Circuit, Burdwan Division, no. 384, 4 October 1858, p. xxv, *RSD 1856–7 and 1857–8*.
110. *Selections*, pp. 54–5.
111. Ibid., p. 60.
112. Ibid.
113. Ravenshaw to the Commissioner of Circuit, Burdwan Division, no. 384, 4 October 1858, pp. xvii–xviii.
114. Ward to the Commissioner of Circuit, Burdwan Division, no. 31, 31 January 1856, para 6.
115. J.R. Ward, Commissioner for the Suppression of Dacoity to the Commissioner of Circuit, Burdwan Division, no. 71, 14 February 1857, para 4, p. 5, *RSD 1855–6*.
116. *Selections*, p. 12; Ravenshaw to the Commissioner of Circuit, Burdwan Division, no. 384, 4 October 1858, p. xxiv, *RSD 1856–7 and 1857–8*.
117. *Selections*, see the deposition of Sreenath Haree, p. 46.
118. This is clear from perusal of *RSD 1855–6*, *RSD 1856–7 and 1857–8* and confessions of the accused in *Selections*.
119. Quoted in Norman Alan Bowers, 'Crime, Punishment and the Mode of Production: An Exploratory Foray', University of Missouri—Columbia Ph.D. thesis, 1975, p. 417.
120. See Basudeb Chattopadhyay, *Crime and Control in Early Colonial Bengal 1770–1860*.
121. See Jennifer Davis, 'The London Garotting Panic of 1862: A Moral Panic and the Creation of a Criminal Class in mid-Victorian England', in *Crime and the Law: The Social History of Crime in Western Europe since 1500,* V.A.C. Gatrell, Bruce Lenman and Geoffrey Parker, eds., London, 1980.
122. Ibid. As Foucault noted that 'the prison manufactured delinquents but delinquents turned out to be useful'. See J.J. Brochier, 'Prison Talk: An Interview with Michel Foucault' in *Radical Philosophy,* 16, Spring 1977, p. 10.

INDEX